"Scott Rubin is the most effective middle school pastor I have ever known. He has built a team of adult volunteers who would take bullets for junior high students. The students themselves love our middle school ministry, and parents rave about how Christ is working in their adolescents' lives. I read this book in two sittings and learned more about middle school ministry than I have learned in the previous decade. Way to go Scott and Mark!"

—Bill Hybels, senior pastor, Willow Creek Community Church; president of board, Willow Creek Association

"It's not often I find a book that's both fun to read and a great go-to resource—this is it! Marko and Scott address the vital issues within middle school ministry, and they do it with honesty, insight, and humor.

"Thank you for waving the flag of middle school ministry with boldness and pride. As a pastor committed for life to this age group, I was affirmed, encouraged, inspired, and rejuvenated. If senior high youth workers have the guts to read this book, we may even have some new converts on our hands.

"Between saying 'Amen!' out loud and thinking, *I need to teach my volunteers this whole section*, I felt understood and motivated as a leader of middle school youth workers. Marko and Scott's experience in the trenches is invaluable—especially all the documented small group discussions."

—Heather Flies, junior high pastor, Wooddale Church, Eden Prarie, Minnesota

"From the moment I heard Scott and Mark were writing a book together, I couldn't wait to see the final product. After all, when two of the sharpest minds in young teen ministry combine forces to create a resource for the rest of us, you know it's going to be a good read. In fact, *Middle School Ministry* is more than just a good read; I believe it will become a classic—if not *the* classic—book on middle school ministry for years to come. Thanks, guys, for putting your years of experience in writing; you've provided the youth ministry world with a wonderful gift."

—Kurt Johnston, junior high pastor, Saddleback Church, Lake Forest, California

"Middle school years are incredibly formative. Mark and Scott know and love people going through early adolescence and are wise guides and experienced thinkers to help anyone with a heart for those in this season of life. If you work with or care for middle schoolers—don't miss this book."

—John Ortberg, pastor, Menlo Park (California) Presbyterian Church; author, *The Life You've Always Wanted*

"THE middle school text book written by people who ACTUALLY work with middle school students, get it, and can teach it!"

—Johnny Scott, director, CIY Believe

"I wish this book had been written 20 years ago when I was starting to work with middle schoolers. I hope every leader who works with middle school kids reads and applies its insights. I'm recommending it to our church's middle school pastor."

—Kara Powell, executive director, Fuller Youth Institute

"Middle school ministry has changed quite a bit in recent years, and this book does a wonderful job bringing us all up to date. Marko and Scott's love for middle schoolers and their many years of experience gives this book credibility and passion like no other. I give it five stars!"

—Wayne Rice, cofounder, Youth Specialties

MIDDLE SCHOOL MINISTRY

a comprehensive guide
to working with early adolescents

Mark Oestreicher
& Scott Rubin

 ZONDERVAN®

ZONDERVAN.com/
AUTHORTRACKER
follow your favorite authors

 youth
specialties

YOUTH SPECIALTIES

Middle School Ministry: A Comprehensive Guide to Working with Early Adolescents
Copyright 2009 by Mark Oestreicher and Scott Rubin

Youth Specialties resources, 1890 Cordell Ct. Ste. 105, El Cajon, CA 92020 are published by Zondervan, 5300 Patterson Ave. SE, Grand Rapids, MI 49530.

Library of Congress Cataloging-in-Publication Data

Rubin, Scott.
  Middle school ministry : a comprehensive guide to working with early
adolescents / Scott Rubin and Mark Oestreicher.
     p. cm.
  Includes bibliographical references.
  ISBN 978-0-310-28494-9 (soft cover)
  1. Church work with preteens. 2. Church work with teenagers. 3. Middle
school students—Religious life. I. Oestreicher, Mark. II. Title.
  BV1475.9.R83 2009
  259'.23—dc22   2009021661

Cover design by SharpSeven Design
Interior design by Mark Novelli, IMAGO MEDIA

Printed in the United States of America

09 10 11 12 13 14 • 20 19 18 17 16 15 14 13 12 11 10 9 8 7 6 5 4 3 2

For Wayne Rice,
the godfather of middle school ministry.

Were it not for Wayne's trailblazing insistence
that young teen ministry is a legitimate calling—
as well as years of speaking and writing about
young teen ministry—we wouldn't be where
we are today.

Acknowledgments

From Marko and Scott: We'd like to thank Kurt Johnston, who fleshed out the basic ideas for this book—including the first Table of Contents—with Marko years ago, and graciously handed over the project to the two of us when it didn't fit in his schedule. We also want to thank the ever-patient publishing staff of Youth Specialties who've seen this project through years of noodling and dreaming (and, eventually, writing): Jay Howver, Roni Meek, Dave Urbanski, Laura Gross, and David Conn. We'd also like to thank our friends and peers from the "Junior High Pastors Summit," a group of middle school ministry veterans who share our passion for early adolescence, and whose conversations have sharpened and refined much of our thinking. In particular this includes (in no particular order) Christina Robertson, April Diaz, Alan Ramsey, Alan Mercer, Sean Meade, Nate Severson, Kurt Johnston, Jason Raitz, Johnny Scott, Andy Jack, Jeff Buell, Phil Shinners, Heather Flies, Corrie Boyle, Ken Elben, Brooklyn Lindsay, Nate Rice, Kurt Brandemihl, Ken Rawson, Mark Janzen, Eric Venable, Jim Candy, Alex Roller, Cristin Hamman, Steve Friesen, Judy Gregory, Curt Gibson, and John Wilson.

From Marko: I'd like to thank the middle school ministry at Journey Community Church, in La Mesa, California, for continuing to give me a place to actively engage in the lives of middle school kids. Thanks also to Cosmo's Coffee Café for the comfy writing couch and free wifi (the perfect writing spot). And to my wonderful family, Jeannie, Liesl, and Max—you guys are the best.

From Scott: I'd like to thank Bill Hybels and Willow Creek Community Church for being people that believe in middle schoolers and in me; Scott Pederson for being Willow's amazing founder of middle school ministry; the Elevate team (Wes, Courtney, Jason, Brandon, Chris, Leah, Melissa, Jill, Robin, Matt, Aaron) for being all that "team" is to me; every middle school ministry volunteer everywhere (especially Kenton, Nick, Pam, and pilot Paul); Gloria, who prayed; John Ortberg, who coached me; and Young Life that helped me realize Jesus loves me. Thanks to Mom and Pop who loved me through my own middle school years and to the Buddies—Tanner, Dawson, and Brock. And to my partner Lynette, who I love.

Contents

Introduction

The middle school years (11 to 14 years old) are one of the most misunderstood and underappreciated developmental periods of human life. They're misunderstood by adults in general, to be sure; and they're misunderstood by churches more often than not.

In the church, ministry with early adolescents has usually been an add-on ministry—seen as either an extension of the children's ministry or as preparation for high school ministry (what some consider "real youth ministry").

Culturally, there's been a *massive* shift in the last 20 years. As the age of puberty drops and youth culture becomes the dominant culture in our world, young teenagers are no longer living the waning years of an innocent childhood.[1] Decisions that used to be the stuff of high school—decisions that have enormous implications for the rest of life—are now played out daily in the lives of 12- and 13-year-olds. This has dramatically changed the nature of both middle school ministry *and* high school ministry.

Our contention (and we realize we're biased by our calling and our love for middle schoolers) is that high school ministry *used to be* the make-or-break space for critical formation. These days, we see high school ministry as being "corrective" in nature, while middle school ministry is now the make-or-break space (or "preventive" in nature).

There's a complicated and messy intersection of realities playing out in the world of young teens. It's the second massive period of change in the lifespan of a human being[2], combined with two other factors:

- A culture that obsesses about everything "youth"—teenagers (including young teens) are marketed to more than ever and have a greater influence on adults than they ever have (an influence we've granted them).

- A culture flooded with information—anything and everything is readily available at the click of a mouse (and often thrust upon them even without mouse-clicking).

It's unprecedented, really, how—in a shockingly short span of years—the middle school years have become such an epicenter for lifelong implications. Normally this kind of human developmental change takes place over centuries.

Who We Are (A Bit of Our Own Stories)

We're writing this book from our lives and experiences, as well as our study. We write from our passion, and we hope this book has a conversational tone to it. We aren't academics, and this isn't intended to be a true academic book.[3] We're practitioners of middle school ministry: Two guys who feel a calling to this age group.

Really, we're two guys who just love middle schoolers. They energize us. We find young teens to be life giving. We believe they're fun and insightful and capable of so much more reflection and world shaping than most people give them credit for. Every word in this book pours out of that perspective, that affection.

So we thought it might be helpful for you to know just a tiny bit of our own stories...

MARKO

I grew up in youth group, in a large church in the Detroit area. My own experience in middle school (and high school) plays a huge role in my shaping and calling.

By the time I was a senior in high school, I had a sense that I should be a youth pastor, and I went to college pursuing that call. My youth internship and volunteer work were mostly with middle school kids (merely by default, since I was so close in age to the high schoolers). And when my new wife, Jeannie, and I started volunteering in the youth ministry where I'd eventually get my first paid role in middle school ministry, the church had more need in the middle school than high school area, so we ended up there.

I began as a "junior high pastor" part time, but I quickly fell in love with it. As I worked with this age group more, I began reading and discovering many of the realities expounded on in this book. All that, plus a personality that just seems more akin to young teens than older teens, began to draw me into a sense of lifelong calling to young teen ministry.

I worked in a few more churches as a full-time junior high pastor. And along the way, my thinking about middle school ministry was stretched and challenged and deepened. I made lots of stupid mistakes, learned how easy middle schoolers are to manipulate, and saw countless misconceptions played out and then smashed.

Ten years ago, I started working at Youth Specialties, training, resourcing, and encouraging youth workers. But I could not, and would not, move away from my calling to middle schoolers, and I've been a volunteer middle school youth worker ever since. (These days I'm leading a 6th-grade boys' small group on a weekly basis.)

What began as a generalized calling to youth ministry, about 28 years ago, is now a calling I hope and pray will play out in my life for many more years to come.

SCOTT

My journey into the land of middle school ministry is pretty different from Marko's. Our family always attended church when I was a kid, but I don't believe I was in any danger of being a sincere Jesus follower. I didn't really understand the life-changing power of Jesus until right around my seventeenth birthday, when I went to a Young Life camp.

I worked at some high school camps during the summers while I was getting a degree in business from Michigan State University, and after a brief detour through Australia, I moved to Chicago to work at a consulting firm, unaware that student ministry would ever be a part of my vocational life. But I did know that I wanted to help teenagers know the power of Jesus. So I started volunteering at my church as a leader in the high school ministry.

A couple of years later, I was invited onto the staff of my church, in the small groups department for adults. I really believed my days of student ministry were done. But one day my phone rang. The voice on the other end (my boss) told me about the need our church had for a middle school pastor. I remember pausing for about five seconds, and then I said, "I can't think of anyone to recommend for that job." Boy, did I feel like a dork when he said he wasn't asking for a recommendation.

At first I gave the "Christian answer" to his question. (I bet you know it.) "I'll pray about it," I said. Well, to make a long story longer, the next weekend I decided to stand in the back of the room where the middle school ministry met "just to look." I remember my heart beating faster as I looked at those middle school faces—and the leaders around them. For me, it was the beginning of something pretty cool.

In the years since then, my love for middle schoolers has only grown. These days I'm also leading a weekly small group of 6th-grade boys, and my wife and I lead a middle school student leadership group in our basement. I hope I get to do this stuff for a long, long time!

Why We Wrote This Book

We love middle schoolers; that's no secret. And we love adults who work with middle schoolers. We find hanging out with others who share our passion and calling to middle school ministry extremely energizing. It's like our ultimate sweet spot.

But that's not enough reason to write a book.

The reality is, as guys who are regularly asked for reading suggestions on middle school ministry, our list of recommendations was short. My (Marko) little book for volunteer youth workers, *Help! I'm a Junior High Youth Worker!*, is a good primer, but it's barely more than a magazine article in scope. There are a few other books on the practical stuff of middle school ministry, but they don't have the developmental stuff that's so critical. And the godfather of young teen ministry, Wayne Rice, wrote a book called *Junior High Ministry* back in the Dark Ages. The third edition is still in print, and it's still a very helpful book. But we felt there was a need for something more up to date.

So we set out to write, as our book's subtitle says, something fairly comprehensive. We hope the length of this book isn't overwhelming for you. Please feel free to take it in bits and pieces. You might even view it as two or three books.

So we suggest that you:

- Read the first chapter now, to inspire you.

- Then read the first section on developmental stuff, for a deeper understanding of what's going on in the lives of young teens.

- Finally, consider the second section, which is about more practical stuff, a second book (although it's thoroughly informed by the sections that precede it).

That way, after you finish this book, you can say you read *two* books.

A Few Words about Terminology

We've chosen to title this book *Middle School Ministry* because, as we peruse the American scene, *middle school* seems to represent the dominant terminology and framing. But don't get hung up by that terminology if your church or schools still refer to *junior high ministry* or some other term. Canada seems to almost exclusively use "junior high ministry"; and in the United Kingdom, neither of those terms makes much sense, and young teens are usually just referred to as "11 to 14s."

We considered using all these terms (*middle school, junior high, 11 to 14s*), but have chosen to use only *middle school* so as not to imply we're differentiating between the three terms.

We'll also use *young teen, early adolescence* (or *early adolescents*), and, occasionally, *teens* (which we've found middle schoolers like to be called, but high schoolers hate).

Much of the media has started using the word *tween*, and we believe this term is often more confusing.[4] The word was originally used to describe the group we'd call "preteens" (10- and 11-year-olds, or 5th and 6th graders). But now it's often used (wrongly, we believe) in place of *young teen*. Since there's overlap between a preteen concept of 5th and 6th graders and a middle school notion of 6th through 8th graders, the terms and concepts get even more confusing. We'll mostly steer clear of the word *tweens* and use *preteens* when we're writing about the kids just prior to middle school.

A Few Words about the "Why I Do This" Essays

Early on, when we were working on the shaping of this book, we knew we wanted to include a bunch of other voices. We wanted you to hear from other people in addition to us who are passionate about working with middle schoolers; people who understand the beauty and importance of ministry with young teens.

We asked a wide variety of youth workers—paid and volunteer, young and not so young, evangelical, mainline, and Catholic—to write short essays. We hope these personal statements help you:

- See the variety of reasons people are called to middle school ministry.

- Hear more reasons than we might have included (from our own experiences) about why middle school ministry is so critical and so completely cool.

- See your own story among them—that one or more of these essays will reflect something of your own calling to middle schoolers.

You'll find these essays scattered throughout the book under the title "Why I Do This." They were written in response to one of two questions: *Why do you work with middle schoolers?* or *What do you love about middle schoolers?*

Our Hopes for You

We hope you'll be inspired by what you read on these pages.

We hope your understanding of middle schoolers will dramatically increase and that this will lead to a strengthening of your calling.

We hope your thinking will be pushed and prodded, that you'll see middle schoolers in a new light and rethink some of your assumptions and ministry approaches.

We hope you'll experience multiple "Aha!" moments, where what you're reading suddenly makes sense of previously confounding behaviors and other realities you've experienced with middle schoolers.

We hope you'll formulate your own ideas about the practical stuff of middle school ministry, new ways of approaching teaching and relationship building and small group discussion, even possibilities for reframing the structure of your ministry.

We hope you'll develop a language that will be useful for talking about young teens with other ministry leaders, parents, and your church leadership.

We hope you'll sense God's great affection for you, and God's enjoyment of your willingness to come alongside these middle schoolers whom God so deeply loves.

And we hope you'll be deeply encouraged—that you'll have a renewed sense of confidence that the ministry you're doing with middle schoolers really does matter and really is making a difference (even when it doesn't feel like it).

We're honored to come alongside you in this journey.

Your partners in middle school ministry,

Marko and Scott

CHAPTER 1

Middle School Ministry? Isn't It Just Baby-Sitting?

Derek was, well, a challenging kid to have in our middle school group. He was a natural leader, charismatic, good looking. And he was disruptive. Not disruptive in an "Oh, he just needs to take his medication" way, or even in a "He has all the squirrelly characteristics of a young teen boy, turned to 11 on the dial" way. Derek was intentionally disruptive. His timid mom couldn't control him, and she had no idea what to do with him.

Smart and scheming, Derek would (at best) regularly manipulate entire hordes of boys and girls in our group into behaviors that would create havoc and (at worst) get everyone except Derek in trouble with their parents. If there were a group of kids hiding somewhere in a stairwell, Derek was usually the kid who got them there. If students were caught smoking or drinking, then Derek was likely the provider. If a whole section of kids were sitting with their arms crossed and "I dare you to teach me something" expressions firmly fixed on their faces, then they were almost assuredly imitating Derek.

I (Marko) chatted on the phone and met many times with both Derek and his mom. I took Derek out for sodas and meals and showed him grace and love. I tried to help his mom with her challenging role of setting boundaries for him.

While there were certainly many factors involved, the struggle, as it pertained to Derek's disruption in our group, came down to two particularly vivid facts: He didn't want to be there, and his mom used attendance at our group as a punishment. She revealed this to me once, with only the tiniest bit of embarrassment. When she grounded him, he simply ignored it. When she took away other privileges, he either overrode her or manipulated her into reversing her decision. The only thing she'd found that "worked" was telling Derek he had to come to our church middle school group. And since he was in trouble almost nonstop, we saw Derek fairly regularly.

I asked Derek's mom about this approach and, more specifically, if she thought it was healthy for his spiritual development to experience church as a punishment. Her response was revealing: "I don't know what else to do. I can't handle him; and when I send him to you, at least I don't have to worry about him for a few hours."

Natalie was the youth group flirt. Her family was extremely active in our church, and she was present at everything we did. She wasn't overtly disruptive like Derek, but she was still exceedingly disinterested in anything other than constant chatting with friends, flirting with boys, and working on her next conquest.

In many ways, Natalie wasn't that unique—we had other girls (and guys) with the same values and behaviors. What made Natalie's situation stand out was her parents' perspective. One day they sat with me in my office, very frustrated, and asked, "Why can't you do something about Natalie? Why can't you change her? What's the point of our constantly bringing her to youth group if you can't fix her?" (To be fair, I'm not sure they actually used the word *fix*; but it was implied, even if they didn't use it.)

Of course, these misconceptions and challenges aren't merely in the minds of parents.

The church board was frustrated with me because:

a. We'd painted the middle school group's logo on the wall of our room. They'd given permission for this and even approved the design, but they didn't realize "it was going to be SO BIG."

b. The church van had been returned, once again, with a candy wrapper behind one of the seats and a slight hint of vomit clutching to one inside corner or another.

c. It had been discovered that we'd played Sardines (reverse hide-and-seek), and the kids had used...the sanctuary (intro ominous musical underscore).

But the final straw, and the grievance that got me called into a meeting, was that we'd used the gym (*with* all the prerequisite forms and permissions) for a large outreach event, and then used the adjoining fellowship room (without the prerequisite forms and permissions) when our attendance turned out to be larger than we'd anticipated.

I tried to tell them about the amazing event we'd had—how we'd invited a dozen smaller churches to join us, how we'd expected a few hundred young teens and ended up with close to a thousand, how kids had really connected with the speaker—but they couldn't (or wouldn't) hear it. With a passing and patronizing,

"Well, that's nice," they insisted it was my responsibility to "contain" the middle school ministry to the space provided for us.

(But wait! There's more!)

How about the senior pastor who referred to young teens as "pre-people"?

Or the search committee (for a role I didn't take) who told me they were looking for someone to create a "holding tank" for young teens during their turbulent middle school years until they could get to the high school group where lots of great stuff was happening?

Or my own proclivity, over and over again, to create programs to keep kids busy, programs to entertain (usually under the value banner of "creating a positive group image"), and programs—if I was truly honest, which I likely wasn't—to justify my existence and our budget?

(Okay. That was fairly negative and a bit ranty. Sorry about that.)

But let's face some facts: The gap between the perception of middle school ministry and the actual potential is a fairly universal gap. Some of this is our own doing, to be fair. But much of this gap has to do with complex cultural misunderstandings—even fear—of young teens and (let's continue being honest) middle school ministry.

We can't tell you how many times, over the years, we've been told by well-meaning church members and leaders: "God bless you for working with those kids; I sure couldn't do it." Or, "You must really be called to work with those kids because I can't understand how you do it."

The fact is, many of you reading this book feel as we do: That ministry to young teens is one of the most important and life-changing ministries in the church, an amazing opportunity to connect young teens to Christ for a lifetime of spiritual significance (or an amazing opportunity to completely blow it in the opposite direction).

A Little History (Very Little, Actually)

Focused ministry to young teens is a fairly new phenomenon in churches. And there's good reason for this. Until about the last 50 years or so, young teens weren't really considered "teens" at all.

Let's back way up. For thousands of years, in pretty much every culture around the world, children were children, and adults were adults. The line between these two worlds was clearly marked and not very wide. Children participated in family and culture at large in culturally accepted, boundaried ways, and were encouraged to look toward and aspire toward (and prepare for) the day they'd cross the line into the adult community (which was usually around age 14 or 15 for girls, and 15 or 16 for boys).

Historically, every culture had some sort of rite of passage that marked the transition from childhood to adulthood.[5] Rites of passage are fairly nonexistent today. Ask teens how they know they become adults, and they'll cite various responses, such as, "When I get my driver's license" or "When I have sex for the first time" or "When I graduate from high school." Ask parents, and the responses are just as mixed and usually fall along the lines of "When they're responsible for themselves."

This response from parents makes sense, really. Since adolescence was first identified in the early twentieth century, "being responsible for oneself" has been the working definition of the end of adolescence (and the beginning of adulthood).[6] Adolescence was originally considered an 18-month window of time, a bit of a culturally endorsed holding pattern in which "youth" were allowed an opportunity to wrestle with adolescent issues. At the time, these issues were called "storm and stress" and were a simplified version of the independence issues we might characterize today. Over the years, while using various terminologies, they've sifted down to these three adolescent tasks: Identity ("Who am I?"), autonomy ("How am I unique, and what power do I have?"), and affinity ("Where and to whom do I belong?").[7] The shift that's taken place over the last hundred-plus years isn't really in the *definition* of adolescence, however. It's a shift in the *duration* of adolescence. And this has a direct impact, on many levels, on the existence and importance of middle school ministry.

I (Marko) was a middle schooler (then universally called "junior high school," with a hat tip to a preparation for high school mindset) in the mid-1970s. My church hired its first youth pastor about the time I entered middle school, but he worked exclusively with the high school kids. We middle schoolers were still stuck in a wing of the Christian Education department. But by the time I was in high school, my church had hired a full-time junior high pastor. This was indicative of the lengthening of adolescence that was happening in culture at large.

By the time the 1970s had rolled around, adolescence was considered to be five years long (six school years)—from the commonly understood starting age of 13 to the normal graduation from high school age of 18. Let's stop to think where these numbers came from, because they've been burned into our cultural consciousness for so many years.

Between the time when adolescence was first identified as an 18-month window, from 14.5 years old to 16, both the lower and upper ends of adolescence had expanded. Upper expansion was cultural, to be sure, but was directly tied to the normalization of high school education. In the earliest parts of the twentieth century, only a small percentage of older teenagers were in school. In fact, if older teens were in school at that point, most were already off to college; and this was primarily reserved for wealthier families.

High schools became more commonplace toward the end of the first half of the twentieth century, to the point that it was compulsory through 16 years old and often through 18 years old. By the time youth culture came into its own, in the 1950s, high schools were the norm. High schools, of course, became the furnace of the new youth culture and quickly aided in raising the age at which adolescents were expected to be fully functioning contributors to society (the upper end of adolescence).

But the lower age also expanded. At the turn of the twentieth century, when adolescence was first talked about, the average age for the onset of puberty was 14.5 years old.[8] This became the *de facto* lower boundary for adolescence. But between 1900 and 1970, the average age for the onset of puberty dropped by about a year-and-a-half, to 13 years old.

But to say the expansion of the lower boundary of adolescence was purely physiological would be incomplete. As youth culture found anchoring and validation, preteens (who were 12 and 13 at the time, even 14) aspired to be a part of what was ahead of them. Soon enough preteens were considered young teens, both physiologically and culturally.

Now, this may not be a surprise to you, but things have changed dramatically since 1970. We could write a separate book about how the world has changed, how adolescence has changed, how education has changed, and how physiology has changed over the last four decades. We'll keep it short, but let's start with the older end of adolescence.

Since the 1970s, the expected age of integration into adult life has continued to grow older. There are economic reasons for this,[9] cultural reasons for this,[10] and physiological and psychological reasons for this (and probably others).[11] It's hard to nail down an exact age, as high school graduation provided us. But those who study it commonly understand adolescence to extend well into the mid-twenties now.

But this book isn't about older teenagers. So let's look at the lower boundary of adolescence.

The average age of puberty has continued to drop. These days, girls begin developing breast buds and pubic hair as early as 9.5 or 10 years old, and they often experience menarche (their first period) around age 11 or 12. For our purposes, it's fair to say that puberty now begins around age 11.[12]

We'll talk about *why* this has happened a bit more in chapter 3. But for now, let's deal with this reality: Adolescence begins around 11 years old. And that's just physiologically. Culturally, young teens have become fully ensconced in youth culture at younger ages also, creating a calcifying edge to this new, younger definition of a teenager.

In fact, the lengthening of "teenage" to a 15-years-plus journey has caused many to start talking about the adolescent experience in three phases: Young teen, mid-teen, and older teen (or emerging adulthood).[13] Add to this the "youthification" of preteens (often called "tweens" by the media these days), and it would be fair to say the adolescent journey is closer to 20 years long—a full fourth of life. Now *that* should reshape our thinking about youth ministry in general, and ministry to young teens specifically.

A Rare Opportunity

So what makes the years from 11 to 14 so unique? Why have we (Marko and Scott) continued to give our lives to this age group?

The two of us meet annually with a group of veteran middle school youth workers. When we first began meeting, back in 2002, we met to draft an open letter to the church about the importance of young teen ministry. Here's the content of that letter.[14]

> "Anyone who works in the church knows that junior high may be the single most pivotal period for spiritual decisions in the lives of our children." —*Rick Warren, senior pastor of Saddleback Church*

"Every church needs a strong Junior High ministry. It's top priority. Can't wait."[15] —*Leith Anderson,
president, National Association of Evangelicals;
pastor, Wooddale Church, Edina, Minnesota*

Barna Research claims that the overwhelming majority of Christ-
followers date their "conversion" prior to 13 years old;[16] indeed,
after 13 years old the likelihood of conversion drops drastically.

This evangelistic openness is just one example of the responsiveness of children and young teens. Young teens experience
change in every aspect of development: Physical, emotional,
cognitive, relational, social, and—of course—spiritual. With their
brand-new ability to think abstractly (a developmental "bonus"
of puberty), Christian young teens, thanks to this God-ordained
developmental phase, inevitably reexamine their childhood belief systems. This faith-evaluation is normal and good.

When we combine the "responsiveness" data presented by
Barna (and confirmed by thousands of observations by the writ-
ers of this letter[17]) and the unique capacity for spiritual development among young teens, we see an extremely narrow opportunity for lifelong impact.

RETURN ON INVESTMENT

Effective church ministry to young teens has a significantly high
spiritual return on investment—much more so than in other age
groups. It's a "return" in many areas: Spiritual understanding,
faith commitment, vocational calling, maturity, and leadership.

In addition, many churches are finding that middle school
ministry affords a collateral benefit as an effective outreach vehicle to families. The president of a large Internet company, along
with her husband, began attending a church in the Silicon Valley
as a result of the transformation they observed in their junior
high son through a church middle school ministry.

So what is the "investment"? Well, it's all the stuff churches already allocate to other valued ministries: Prayer, focus, exposure,

facilities, finances, and—perhaps most powerful—people. Since effective ministry to young teens must be relational, quality adult staffing (paid and volunteer) is a vital factor in many ministries.

HOW SHOULD I RESPOND?

We ask you to exercise your leadership potential to encourage a healthy young teen ministry in your church.

- If you are a senior pastor or a board member, consider hiring a full-time youth worker for young teens. Any church with 40 young teens, or the potential for that many, should have a full-time youth worker dedicated to young teens only (any church with a dozen or more young teens should have a distinct young teen ministry, separate from the older teens). Hire a professional, someone who feels specifically trained and called to work with young teens. Many churches make the mistake of hiring a low-wage intern—often just out of high school herself—to lead this critical age group.

- Churches should reexamine the old pattern of hiring a qualified, trained youth worker as a "student ministries pastor" who really works with high school students and for whom junior high ministry is a side project or afterthought.

- Encourage longevity in your paid and volunteer junior high ministry workers (and think long term yourself). Youth workers are often not in their prime until they've been at it a few years or more with young teens. They have much to learn about this age group in order to be truly effective—and there is no substitute for experience.

- Allocate funds for your young teen ministry: Funds for leadership training; funds for programming; funds for resources.

- Pray for your young teen ministry and especially for its leaders.

- Give them positive exposure. If you, as a leader in the church, talk positively about the young teen ministry, the church's perspective will begin to change for the better, and so will the health of the ministry. Check yourself against making sarcastic or joking comments (even well intentioned), like the pastor who habitually calls young teens "pre-people."

We firmly believe that your church will be a healthier, more effective ministry if you have a healthy young teen ministry. You will attract more families, raise future leaders, and connect with kids of an age that is possibly the most receptive to lifelong change and commitment to Christ.

That highly condensed argument kinda sums it up for us. The young teen years, when understood in the light of the physiological and cultural shift of adolescence and combined with the spiritual readiness of young teens (not just for conversion in the classic sense, but for conversion to living in the way of Jesus), are the crossroads of life. We're so passionate about this critical ministry, so excited about the potential for impact, and so giddy that you're interested enough in the lives of young teens to be reading this book. (Hold on, we need to take a few deep breaths.)

Okay. Let's move forward. Middle school ministry certainly is not baby-sitting.

SECTION ONE
On a Need-to-Know Basis

CHAPTER 2

It's All About Change

First off, we gave this section of the book the goofy, pretentious title of "On a Need-To-Know Basis" because, well, this is stuff you absolutely need to know if you're going to engage in ministry to young teens.

We're always a little bit surprised by how many middle school youth workers have never read a book about early adolescent development. Maybe it's because we youth workers *tend* to be shoot-from-the-hip leaders. In fact, it's crazy-hard to be a by-the-playbook person in youth ministry. We all learn— even if it's not our normal predisposition—to wing it. We learn to adjust on the fly, to accommodate interruptions, to redirect our plans based on new information.

So maybe that skill has a dark side? (We're just thinking out loud here—well, if you read that last part aloud, then it's actually "out loud.") Like, we're wondering if our wing-it skills result in us assuming that our anecdotal observations of middle schoolers alone provide us with all the input we need.

Anyhow, it's really, really common for middle school youth workers—paid and volunteer—to not know much about early adolescent development. Yet we're convinced that understanding middle schoolers is the *second most important thing you can do to increase your effectiveness.*

Yeah, it's the second most important thing. So we'll return to it in a couple of paragraphs.

The *most* important thing you can do to increase your effectiveness with middle schoolers is to deepen your connection to God. See, middle school ministry flows out of who you are, not what you know. You can have all the best tricks, the most rockin' games, a deep understanding of middle schoolers, and the relational ability of Oprah Winfrey, but if you aren't authentically and deeply connected to God, how would you stand a chance of pointing kids in God's direction?

We'll even go so far as to say the time you spend with God isn't just preparation for youth ministry—it *is* youth ministry.

But this chapter is really about the *second most important thing* you can do to increase your effectiveness with middle schoolers. And that, of course, is to understand them. Deeply.

The two of us have been working with and studying young teens for—collectively—about 40 years. And we can honestly say that while we've learned a ton about kids in that time, we still feel as though we're always learning new stuff.

Early adolescence is a profoundly unique segment of human development. Really, it's just astounding how much is going on and how unique it is from other developmental life stages.

Where most people go wrong (especially those who don't work with young teens or don't care about them) is in making one of two assumptions. And historically, most cultures have erred in one of these two directions.

The first extreme is to assume that young teens are just little adults. (Or, as lots of youth workers would tweak that, they're little versions of high schoolers.) Young teens seem like teenagers in many ways, and they certainly want to be treated like teenagers and want adults to stop perceiving them as children. So we capitulate to culture—and to the premature desire of kids themselves—and assume they're slightly miniature versions of ourselves (or slightly miniature versions of their older siblings).

Historically, the United States, Canada, and the United Kingdom have treated young teens this way (at least for the last couple hundred years). And with a media culture that serves up more of what young teen consumers want, this perception has deepened in recent decades.

The other extreme, of course, is the assumption that young teens are really just oversized children. This, for many reasons, seems to be the default in lots of churches. We believe this often comes from a desire to protect young teens from rushing into adulthood and adult-like behaviors. In some ways, this is a good motivation, and it carries some developmentally appropriate freight. But it can also be misguided—an overprotection that stunts the growth of kids during this critical transitionary time of life.

The dealio, as we've clearly tipped our hand, is that neither of these extremes is especially helpful. We'll get to this a bit more in chapter 10, "The Overlapping Transition."

One-Word Definition

If we asked you to summarize the young teen experience in only one word, what would you choose? We've asked this question from time to time during seminars and conversations, and we've heard the following responses:

- Stressed

- Immature

- Confused

- Impossible

- Annoying

- Fun

- Potential

- Eager

- Emerging

- Spontaneous

- Unpredictable

- Challenging-but-full-of-possibility (People always try to get away with strings of hyphenated words when you ask for just one.)

If you asked us (c'mon, ask. Say, out loud, "Marko and Scott, if you were to describe the young teen experience in one word, what word would you choose?"), we'd respond calmly and in perfect unison: "Change."

CHANGE

That's it in a word. The life of a middle schooler is *all about* change. As we previously noted, it's the second most significant period of change in the human lifespan. Stepping into puberty, and the two or three years that follow, brings about cataclysmic change in pretty much every area of life. It's a deeply radical seismic shift that upends everything that was and ushers in a period of profound instability.

Think of a significant change you've experienced in your adult life—maybe a move or a new job. Remember how you felt during that time? There's often a combination of uneasiness (from fear of the unknown) and excitement (from the prospect of what could be). That's very much akin to the experience of early adolescence.

But the difference between a significant change that you may have experienced as an adult and the significant change young teens are slogging through is this: Your feelings associated with change are mostly due to external factors. You likely experienced all kinds of internal stuff as a result of the external factors. But for young teens, the momentum of change is largely internal (although most young teens experience a host of external changes—such as a new school, new youth group, new friends, new freedoms—that further radicalize the internal stuff). The massive tsunami of change in the life of a 13-year-old is developmental, stemming from physical, cognitive, emotional, relational, and spiritual changes that are taking place in their bodies and minds.

Back in the '70s, a psychologist named Stephen Glenn came up with a helpful little description[18] of this change that we've found useful and have modified here:[19]

Birth to 2 years old = **Sampling**

3 to 7 years old = **Testing**

8 to 10 years old = **Concluding**

Puberty

11 to 14 years old = **Sampling**

15 to 19 years old = **Testing**

20+ years old = **Concluding**

Let's unpack that a bit. Glenn suggested there's a parallel between the childhood years and the teenage years when it comes to acquiring, processing, testing, and making conclusions about the world. Babies are intake experts. They're constantly sampling the world around them by watching, listening, touching, and, of course, inserting everything that can possibly fit—as well as some things that won't—into their mouths. For them, the world is a sampler platter.

Then there are those wild, middle childhood years. (By the way, the age brackets on this model are not hard and fast—they're fuzzy and vary from kid to kid.) If you have your own children, or if you've been around other people's kids much, you can see how they shift into a phase of testing. It's not quite as simple as their taking the information they've gathered for two years and sending it off to the Research and Development department in their brains. But it's close.

You can see this testing work in the following examples:

- Pushing parents on boundaries and rules

- Testing different approaches to getting things ("Now I'm demanding what I want" and "Now I'm the sweet kid, charming you into compliance")

- Making gregarious, exclamatory comments to see how people respond

- Jumping on everything, knocking things together, pulling things apart

But in late childhood, there's a dramatic shift. The pre-adolescent, pre-abstract mind begins to be amazingly self-impressed. Preteens have the brain equivalent of a high-end horse and buggy in the early 1900s. The age of the automobile was just around the corner—but the horse and buggy was at its peak, in terms of technology.[20] That's what's going on in the minds of young teens: They have the concrete thinking thing down. They wrap up their testing phase and move full-bore into concluding.

For example, ask a 10-year-old to give you input on a complex societal issue—such as racism or poverty or foreign trade—and, if she understands the question, she'll have a solution. What you will *not* hear is, "Well, that's complex, and I'm not sure I have a solution." What you *will* hear is something that starts with, "They should just...." Of course, it likely won't be a workable solution, although 10-year-olds can be surprisingly insightful (since they don't get bogged down in the hip-deep mud of complexities).

The same thing goes with spiritual stuff. Preteens are famous for drawing conclusions about all things spiritual. They really should be employed as marketers because they're fantastic at making overly simplistic, conclusive, fiat statements. Their spiritual conclusions (which are appropriate for their age, so this is not about immaturity) sound like bumper stickers.

But then (insert theme music from *Jaws*) along comes puberty, sneaking up on confident and worldly wise (in their minds, anyway) young teens. And all that beautiful conclusiveness gets annihilated.

In an era before we used the word *tsunami* as a metaphor for everything that changes, middle school ministry pioneer Wayne Rice described this onslaught as a tidal wave, wiping out all that hard work of sampling, testing, and concluding, and forever changing the landscape.

And then the three-step process starts all over again.

The young teen years—parallel to the earliest years of life—become, once again, a time of data collecting. Sampling. (It's interesting that these two stages of life, as mentioned earlier, are the two most dramatic times of change in a lifespan.)

The world is all-new to a young teen, thanks in part to new ways of thinking, new freedoms, increased access to information—including increased access to the world of adults—and an expanding worldview.

Mid-adolescents—or high schoolers—move into a phase of testing that's observationally obvious, right? And older adolescents, or what adolescent experts are starting to call "emerging adulthood," relaunch a long effort of drawing conclusions about the world (and everything in it) beginning around the age of 20.

Middle schoolers' new-again phase of sampling and information-gathering is directly tied to the massive change that's going on in their lives. Again, think of a significant change you've experienced as an adult (a move, a job change, a significant new relationship). Let's say you start a new job. Those early days of change are spent in information-gathering mode. *What are the workplace norms? How do I get from here to there? Who really has the power? Where are the paper clips stored? How do I fill out these forms for Human Resources?*

Even though much of this sampling and information gathering takes place internally, we can see tons of it working out in external ways:

- What kinds of clothes do kids my age wear so we don't look like little kids?

- How am I supposed to interact with my parents and friends?

- What sports and other hobbies might I be interested in doing or good at doing?

- Which subgrouping of youth culture might be the right fit for me?

Last night at my (Marko's) 6th-grade-guys small group, we were talking about what it means to be a man. We compared stereotypes of manliness with a look at true manhood. (Really, we were talking about wearing masks.) While filling out a silly "manliness quiz," we got talking about a sex question. Well, actually, it was a question about bragging about sexual experience.

I have four guys in my group—and they were split right down the middle, revealing a perfect snapshot of this age group. Two of the guys were extremely nervous to even talk about this subject. They stopped making eye contact, didn't joke around at all, and gave answers that would be parent-approved.

But the other two guys were nuts! Seriously. They went off, saying things like, "When am I *not* having sex?" doing little hip thrusts and giggling maniacally.

Since I was in the process of writing this section of the book, it dawned on me—right in the middle of that discussion—that I was witnessing two of those stages. Two of the boys were very much in the "concluding" mindset of upper elementary. And the other two boys were clearly experimenting with information gathering. They were "sampling" the responses of the other guys in the group and sampling the responses of my co-leader and me. They were sampling what it felt like to be a guy who talks about sex in over-the-top ways. (Neither of these guys actually had any sexual experience, by the way, they were just playing a role—a role created to gather information.)

Don't misunderstand this example: We're not suggesting that conclusion is about giving acceptable responses or that sampling is about bragging about sexual proclivities. That's not the point.

This sampling phase can be wonderful, full of opportunity and possibility. But it can also be (and almost always is, for most kids, at one point or another) scary and overwhelming. That's why this next section is so important.

NORMALIZING THEIR EXPERIENCE

We're convinced that one of the most important ministries you can have with young teens is to normalize their experience. Here's what we mean: *Every* young teen, at one time or another, feels abnormal. They feel as though they're physically developing in the wrong way. Or they feel as though they're the only ones experiencing emotional swings. Or they feel as though their spiritual doubts are aberrant and unique.

WHY I DO THIS

It was the fall semester of 1984; I was dressed in my short shorts and high socks, just getting ready for P.E., when Cody Owens, a fellow 7th grader, proudly showed us his one armpit hair—that was 12 inches long. A foot long! He said he was thinking about trimming it. The guys in the locker room all yelled, "No way! It's amazing! Leave it alone!"

I had another friend who had a full crop of hair in his right armpit, but in his left armpit? Completely bald. Ah, middle school.

I guess that's why I've spent so many years as a youth worker with this age group. I love the passion, the naïveté, the drama, the energy, the innocence, and the...well, the insane lack of good judgment.

As a young youth pastor I took a group of middle school students to Palm Springs, California. When we arrived, I knew I was in big trouble. We'd rented condominiums that were way too nice for a middle school retreat. Immediately I had a pit in my stomach and told everyone that if anything bad happened to these beautiful condos, they could very possibly lose their salvation.

Within an hour, all you-know-what broke loose. The pastor's son, a curious and creative 8th-grade boy with a serious lack of good judgment, came out of the bathroom and threw what appeared to be a paper lunch sack at his buddy (who, by the way, was standing right next to me). When the bag hit his friend, brown stuff exploded all over him, me, the wall, and the ceiling. We soon found out that the brown stuff was excrement (yep...).

Immediately a fight broke out between these two 8th-grade boys, one of whom was covered in poop. The pastor's son couldn't believe that his friend whom would get so upset (like I mentioned, brain damage). I said, "Dude, you threw poop at him!" Within 20 minutes all was good. They made up, and later that night at program we played the chocolate pudding in the diaper game. Fun times. By the way, the poop-thrower is now a middle school pastor in a church. (He's not a kid anymore.)

The reality, though, is that I love this age. I love what God does in the midst of chaos. I love that I feel so out of control; I love how God surprises me; and I love how God changes the hearts of kids who, I swear, have never sat still a day in their lives. I love the dreams and who the passion and the vulnerability.

You know, it's funny: I really need middle schoolers in my life, maybe even more than they need me. Every time I hang out with middle school students, their zeal for life seems to rub off on me. I need what they have, and I wish it came naturally to me. I guess we kind of need each other, don't we? They need our wisdom to get them through the chaos, to guide them into life and true living. And we need them to guide us back to passion, to stir within us curiosity, to be reminded how to play again, and to revisit the calling of childlike faith.

I'm blown away by how God has changed my life through the most unlikely of people. I'm so moved by how God has opened my eyes and softened my heart through these ragtag misfits. And what's amazing is that I've discovered that *I'm* actually the misfit and they've taken *me* in.

Brock Morgan is a youth worker in Salem, Oregon, where he recently launched a ministry to teenagers in the city. He's also a member of the YS One Day presenter team.

Don't trivialize their experience. (For example, don't say something like, "Don't you realize that you're *not* unique? *All* kids your age are going through what you're going through.") Instead, help them realize that their experience of change is normal—even good.

Recently, I (Marko) had an opportunity to normalize the emotional experience of my then 13-year-old daughter, Liesl. Here's how it happened.

Liesl and I were sitting at the kitchen table and having dinner together. (I'm not sure where my wife and son were.) In casual conversation, I asked about her homework.

She freaked. She exploded with, "Why are you yelling at me?"

A bit taken aback, I calmly responded, "Liesl, I'm not yelling. I'm just asking you about your homework."

Liesl escalated even more to a shrieking frenzy: "Stop yelling at me! I don't know why you're yelling at me!"

Now she was pushing my buttons, and I felt my own emotions starting to rise. I wasn't sure whether I should step into the role she was projecting on me and actually start yelling ("I'll show you yelling, if that's what you want!") or start laughing at her. I also knew, in a rare moment of parental insight, that neither of those responses would be helpful. But I could tell we weren't going to get anywhere at the moment, and we both needed a little space to cool down.

So I said, "I need you to go to your room. When you've calmed down, we can talk about this."

Liesl flew up from the table, stomped across the house, stomped up the stairs to her room, and slammed the door, yelling the entire time: "You're always yelling at me! It's so unfair!"

I waited, picking at my food.

Not three minutes passed before I heard her door open. Then I heard Liesl coming down the stairs, crying. "Daddy," she said, "I'm sorry." (*sniff, sniff*) "I don't know why I was yelling at you."

I now saw a window of opportunity to normalize Liesl's experience. I asked her, "Would it be okay if I tried to explain to you what just happened?"

"Okay," she said through self-flagellatory sniffs.

The conversation went something like this:

"Liesl, do you ever feel like your emotions are out of your control?"

"Yeah."

"Do you sometimes feel like you're depressed, and you don't know why?"

"Yeah." (*sniff*)

"And do you sometimes get totally excited but don't know where that came from either?"

"Totally! Emily and I get in trouble all the time at school because we get so excited we can't stop talking!"

"Here's what's going on. When you were a kid, you had emotions, too. But your brain was a kid's brain, and you were only able to experience certain emotions. It's like you had a small set of emotional options, and you knew them well. But now that you're a teenager, your brain is changing. And because your brain is changing, you're able to experience many emotions that you couldn't before. But these emotions are new to you, and you're not used to them. It's like getting a pair of new jeans that aren't broken in—they're still a little uncomfortable, and they feel like they don't belong to you yet."

I continued, "But here's the cool thing. Jesus promises us, in John 10:10, that he came to give us 'a full life.' In order for you to really experience a full life, you need to have a whole range of emotions. This change you're going through with your emotions is a change that God invented. It's a little awkward while you're going through it; but it's all a part of God's love for you."

Liesl and I talked about it for a bit more, and then we moved on to something else (maybe her homework?).

We must always be ready to slip "It's okay," "It's normal," and "It's good" into our teaching and conversations with young teens. These statements constantly remind young teens that their changes are normal and good and that they'll turn out great. And they really do need to be reminded of this over and over and over again. (Of course, they'll only hear it when they need to hear it, which is why we need to say it with regularity.)

In the coming chapters (in this section of the book), we'll unpack in more detail how these different changes play out in the lives of middle schoolers.

CHAPTER 3

Walking Hormones?
(Physical and Sexual Development)

The setting: A tiny, hot, fart-drenched small group room at church.

The context: Marko's middle school guys' small group—all 6th graders.

The conversation:

Marko: "So Potiphar's wife..."

Shane: "Oh! I've heard this! Isn't she the one that said Joseph raped her?"

Marko: "Yeah, that's right. She wanted Joseph to have sex with her..."

Matt: "We're starting sex ed. next week in school."

Shane: "We did it in our class a few weeks ago."

Zack: "You *did* it in sex ed.?"

(Giggles all around.)

Zack: "That must be a new teaching method!"

Shane: "Ha! No, I don't think our teachers have a license to do that."

Zack *(very serious, to me)*: "You need a license to have sex?"

Marko: "Yeah."

Zack: "Really?"

Marko: "You have to apply for one down at the DMV."

Zack: "Really?"

Marko: "No. Back to Potiphar's wife…"

The guys joked about needing a "sex license" for the next three years that we were in a small group together.

Hormones Are about More Than Sex

Lots of people characterize the teenage years as when we're taken over by hormones. We've even heard people refer to young teens as "walking bundles of hormones." There's some truth in this. And there's some inaccuracy also.

First, the truth: While we don't believe that middle schoolers' physical changes are the most significant changes they're experiencing (especially in terms of the implications for middle school ministry and faith development), the physical changes are still a *huge* deal. And, chronologically, they're the first of many interdependent buckets of change.

Physical change starts with hormones.

Actually, that's not completely accurate either. Puberty starts in the brain. At some moment in time, the early-adolescent brain says, "Now seems to be the time to open the hormonal floodgates." The brain signals the testes (for boys) or the ovaries (for girls) to start creating and releasing hormones.[21]

This is the launch point of the tsunami of change we've been talking about. And so begin the physiological changes (all the body and brain stuff) and the results of those physiological changes (cognitive, relational, emotional, worldview, and faith).

So, in a sense, yes—the change of early adolescence is about hormones.

But in another sense, it's really not about hormones—at least not in the way people popularly interpret that. When most people talk about hormones and the changes they bring, they're really only talking about one aspect of adolescence: Obsession with sex.

We believe it's wrong (and unfair) to characterize young teens as being sex-obsessed, and we believe it's really important to realize when we're doing it. Because when such a caricature infiltrates our thinking to the point where we believe it's the whole story, it diminishes the importance of other, nonsexual changes that are going on in middle schoolers' lives.

The Scope of Physical Change

Young teens are intrigued—even proud—while also nervous, sheepish, and confused about the changes going on in their bodies.

Young teens *want* to grow up (at least most of them do). And they *want* to have the bodies of adults—or at least their idealized notions of what an adult body is like.

Sure, they're experiencing physical change in their girl parts and boy parts (or as we've heard boy parts referred to as their "hanging down parts," their "junk," their "stuff," their "crotchal region," their "package," and many other inventive phrases not fit for printing here), but their physical changes are, of course, much more than that.

HAIR IN NEW PLACES

During the earliest phases of puberty, hair starts growing in places where young teens have never had hair before—the pubic area, armpits, face, and legs. This process usually continues throughout adolescence.

It seems to us—and we haven't done research on this—that the hairiness thing levels out in mid-adolescence for girls and older adolescence for guys, then comes back for a mean-spirited second round during middle age, as both of us are starting to find hair growing in places where we'd just as soon not have any hair: Nostrils, ears, nipples. Ah, the joy of being middle-aged.

I (Marko) remember this hair-growing thing quite vividly, due to a rather unfortunate assumption I made. In about 7th grade, I'd noticed that I had a good amount of dark hair growing on the lower part of my legs, between my knees and ankles. I thought this was completely cool and totally manly, and I wanted to do anything in my power to assist the process.

This being the 1970s, I wore those tube socks that came up just about to my knees. And, since I didn't have any leg hair growing *above* my knees, my early adolescent mind drew the conclusion that leg hair must grow best "in the dark" (where my legs were shielded by my glorious socks). There must have been a bit of leftover memory of a botany experiment we'd done in elementary school, where we found that a plant kept in the dark of a classroom closet grew really fast but didn't last.

I grew up in Detroit, and the summers were notoriously hot and muggy. But I went through an entire Detroit summer wearing jeans—not shorts—because I was convinced I needed to keep my legs "in the dark." The funny thing was that my leg hairs—even above my knees—did grow in that summer. And I thought, *I made it happen.* I was very proud of my accomplishment, and it took every bit of restraint I had not to prance around my school that fall in shorts, while pointing to my legs and saying, "Look what I did this summer!"

While this hair-growth thing might be something guys (more so than girls) are proud of when it comes to armpits and upper-lip peach fuzz, both girls and guys tend to have polarized responses to pubic hair. They want it, but they're a bit freaked out by it. Spending time with middle schoolers on retreats and camps, wherever they have to get dressed in a communal environment, will reveal that they tend to have one of two extreme responses.

Those who develop a little later will usually be shy (we've seen hundreds of guys get changed *inside* their sleeping bags). Kids who develop a little earlier than their peers are either equally shy or they swing the pendulum (no pun intended) to the other extreme, walking around naked like proud lions and casually showing off their new-found glory to anyone and everyone.

Because the "hair thing" is such a visible change, it can also become an area of teasing (either for "too much" or "too little" hair). Quick point: Don't allow this. Be vigilant in allowing kids privacy and hold to a strict zero tolerance on teasing. And remember to normalize.

BODY SHAPE AND HEIGHT

Of course, the physical changes are about much more than hair growth. The young teen's body shape changes (shoulders, chest, waist, muscle mass, and so much more), in addition to experiencing crazy spurts in height.

The whole area of vertical growth is another sticky one. Boys who grow taller are usually pleased with this, to a point. Some of the tallest boys are sometimes concerned that they're too far outside the bell curve and quickly tire of being known only as "the tall guy." Shorter guys start to obsess over their height and can really suffer a bit of a young teen identity crisis over what it means to be the short guy.

It's so easy for even the most well-meaning middle school youth worker to occasionally crack a sideways joke about a short kid. Remember, this can be seriously damaging. We need to be passionate about affirmation and normalization—not allowing for even a peep of teasing. What seems like a harmless off-handed tease to you can easily compound their suspicion that something is wrong with them.

Guys tend to be more concerned with being too short because our culture tells them guys are supposed to be big, tough, and macho. Girls, on the other hand, tend to be more concerned with being too tall because our culture tells them they're supposed to be diminutive and petite. Much of this stems from the fact that girls, on average, hit puberty 18 months prior to boys. So they start growing taller at an earlier age. Add to this the fact that girls usually reach their full adult height by upper adolescence, while boys often continue growing taller well into their young twenties. Girls who will eventually be above-average height are almost universally taller than their male peers in 6th and 7th grade. This is rarely something they're pleased with, and they're often teased about it (at worst) or have it constantly pointed out (at best). Have we talked about normalization yet?

BREAST AND PENIS SIZE

Let's get the easier of these two out of the way first: Guys obsess about the length (or lack of length) in their penises. Anyone who receives email spam about miraculous penis-lengthening solutions knows this doesn't seem to be isolated to the adolescent experience. But because a guy's body is changing so dramatically, he knows he's supposed to get an adult-sized penis—whatever that is. It's not uncommon (in fact, it's the norm, rather than the exception) for middle school guys to be very aware of the length of their penises, both in a flaccid and erect condition. Their trusty school ruler becomes a measuring stick of choice.

But there are three reasons this is less of a deal when it comes to working with middle school guys than breast development is for middle school girls.

1. Guys are secretive about this, and they usually lie when they aren't being secretive. They'll talk about penis length, but normally it's in third person or in the form of a lie.

2. Guys are less verbal than girls are, which means lots of guys never talk about this kind of stuff with anyone.

3. The length of a guy's penis is almost always hidden (which is part of why communal changing and showering, such as at a camp setting, can be such a big issue for guys), while a girl's breast development is pretty much out there for everyone to see, despite clothes to provide cover.

Girls know that breast development is a big part of their changing bodies (clearly boys know that, too). And, boy howdy, does it ever cause drama, concern, fear, obsession, and plenty of visual inspection. Here's a condensed and oversimplified rule: Girls want to be in the middle of the normal distribution. Developing breasts too early or too large can bring all kinds of unwanted attention and teasing. (Although the attention is occasionally desired, which often points to other issues about the girl's relationship with males in general.)

As with most physical changes in young teens, it's pretty hard to find a girl who believes her breast development is normal. Our culture (and their own culture) really puts them in a catch-22 on this one. They've learned that having breasts of a normal or slightly-larger-than-normal size is a culturally desirable thing. But girls with breasts too large, too soon are often made to feel abnormal, as if they should be ashamed. Peers (guys and girls both) will assume they're loose—as if that has something to do with breast development. And then there's the ever-present concern (for girls—guys don't notice this, as they don't normally have access to this level of inspection) that one breast is larger than the other and that they'll always be "deformed" or lopsided.

This issue was highlighted for me (Scott) at a middle school camp. We had a week designated for guys and a separate week for girls that year, and we traveled all the way to Michigan's upper peninsula. This camp was incredibly remote: No electricity, no running water, not even a slight cell phone signal. The idea was to take kids far away from their normal routine and distractions to hear God's voice and contemplate life. In fact, the camp's slogan was "Room to Grow." During the girls' week, I was talking to the camp director, and he mentioned they weren't selling very many T-shirts in the camp store. Even though I wasn't very concerned about the issue, I asked him to show me what the shirts looked like (I figured maybe the design was lame or something). But when I saw the T-shirt, I immediately laughed out loud. The design was cool enough—it had small letters at the top that read *Camp Paradise*. But in larger letters right underneath were the words ROOM TO GROW. I told the camp director that I didn't know very many young teen girls who'd want that phrase emblazoned across their chests.

The intensity and concern is only a fraction less intense for girls who develop breasts later than their peers. Being "flat chested" brings teasing from boys and girls alike and is a constant source of worry for these girls. Their concern (and, for some, full-on obsession) about their lack of breast development would be an issue for them *even if there were no teasing*. But the teasing thing—which is an almost universal experience for late-blooming girls—ratchets this issue up one-hundredfold.

Obviously, female leaders can have more opportunity to speak directly to this with middle school girls, affirming their beauty, encouraging them that they'll catch up, dismantling (to the best of your ability) our cultural obsession with body shape (in general) and breasts (in particular). Male leaders can play a role here also—we just have to be much more careful about what we do and don't say.

And then there are those girls who really just want to be one of the guys. Some young teen girls see puberty and their changing bodies as a nuisance. They can tell that guys are looking at them differently and are starting to *treat* them differently. And this isn't a welcome change. They enjoyed the more level playing field of the preteen years, when they were able to be friends with boys without sexual identity playing a significant role in the relational mix. They don't want to be seen as objects, or they don't want to be one of those girlie girls, obsessed with outward appearance. They want to be equals on the soccer field and in the classroom, as well as in friendships. Physical development—particularly for girls—can completely disrupt this equilibrium, and it's not welcome.

This is a tough one because, as leaders, we can't undo it. We can't change the reality that young-teen male-female relationships are shifting, and that some of this shift is due to physical changes. What we *can* do is affirm their desire to downplay the change. Affirm their attempts to have nonsexualized friendships. And be extra-careful not to make little comments that imply they should be "more feminine," thereby playing into the cultural stereotypes and rushing their fragile developmental transition.

A disclaimer: After about 40 years of middle school ministry experience between the two of us, we can't say we've had conversations with girls about breasts. We shouldn't. We don't. (Got that, men?) But we still play a key role, since girls are taking *tons* of cues from all the males in their lives about who they are and who they're becoming. Treat them equally. (In other words, don't allow *any* difference to creep in as to how you look at, speak to, or relate with girls of differing developmental swiftness.) Affirm them like crazy—but not about physical stuff. Affirm their character, personality, and questions—affirm anything and everything you can. Help them see that men find there's more to them than their physical exterior. This can have a huge and profound effect on their identity formation, including their sexual identity formation.

Women youth workers: This is one of those areas where, when the time is right, you absolutely must normalize the experience of middle school girls. You have to talk about this stuff. We're not suggesting you schedule appointments with your girls to have a "breast talk." This means you take advantage of natural opportunities in teaching and small group discussion, *and* it means that you're ever ready to slip this discussion into casual conversation with a group of girls or a one-on-one conversation. Of course, if you notice a girl is struggling with this—either because she's flaunting or because she's getting teased—take the opportunity to bring up the subject in a discreet and appropriate context.

CHANGING VOICES

We tend to think of changing voices as being a guy thing. But both girls and boys experience changes in the tone of their voices during the young teen years. If you listen to a 5th-grade girl talking with an 8th-grade girl, you'll hear it. The shift is just more pronounced in boys.

And a shifting voice doesn't seem to be an area of concern for girls. (Thank God for one area of physical change that doesn't cause them distress.) But for guys, this one is right up there with height—it's a big one!

Observationally, we'd say this change in guys is one where the bell curve (or normal distribution) doesn't apply. In other words, you'd be hard-pressed to find a guy whose voice lowered on the younger end of the curve, and it bothered him. All guys want their voices to change—unless they're a top performer in a boys' choir. And when they do, boys are thrilled with the new resonance, and they enjoy hearing themselves.

There are, of course, two kinds of boys for whom this shift is traumatic: Those whose voices change late, and those who are in the middle of the change. Guys whose voices haven't begun dropping yet are often embarrassed by the way they sound when they talk. So it's not uncommon for these guys to talk less often because it's a constant reminder that they're "abnormal" (at least in their own thinking).

The universally common experience, of course, is the boy whose voice is stuck in the transition between a boy's voice and a man's voice—between the upper registers and lower registers. Enter the voice break—that warbling sound that causes instant giggles from anyone within listening range. That cartoon character voice that sounds like a flip-flop between normalcy and falsetto.

Now, we're not trying to say that breast development for girls and vocal change for guys is the same thing. But there are some similarities in at least two ways.

First, this change can be massively diminishing to boys, making them feel awkward, broken, abnormal, weird, and embarrassed. Unlike girls and breasts, this period of change is relatively short-lived for guys.

A second similarity is how we, as caring adults, should respond. Female leaders, we'd encourage you to pretend as though you don't even notice the way a boy's voice sounds. Don't make comments such as, "Oh, that's so cute!" or even "You'll be fine." Even though such statements are positively motivated, they become verifying statements to guys, telling them that everyone notices this horrible, awkward thing.

Male leaders, on the other hand, can play a slightly different role. In general, ignoring voice breaks (especially in mixed company) is best. But since this is a universal experience for guys, it can be helpful to give an affirming comment about how cool it is that their voices are changing. There's an art to knowing when this is appropriate and when it isn't. But in general, make this kind of comment only when the relational environment is safe for the guy (in a one-on-one conversation with you, or in a small group where the guy feels comfortable). And don't say something if the boy doesn't indicate that *he* noticed it. But if he pauses or laughs at himself or gives some other indication that his voice break is on his radar, it can be good to offer an affirming, normalizing comment.

MENSTRUATION AND NOCTURNAL EMISSION

Okay, here we go.

If this were a book *for* middle schoolers, this would be the second section they'd turn to, right after the parts about breast size and penis length. Oddly enough, for adults it's probably one of the *last* parts you want to read.

In educational theory, there's this idea called "the null curriculum." It's the stuff we either never talk about or avoid talking about. And the idea is that our null curriculum teaches our students a lot. For example, if we never talk about homosexuality in our youth groups, we inadvertently communicate that we have nothing to say on the topic, that God has nothing to say about the topic, and that kids should merely go along with whatever information they hear from other sources in their lives.

The same holds true for these highly personal subjects of menstruation and nocturnal emissions. When we don't talk about them, we compound middle schoolers' notions that they're bad or dirty or wrong. Therefore, we have to talk to our students about periods and wet dreams, thereby ending the myth that they're bad or dirty or wrong. They're a beautiful part of God's brilliant design—even though we sometimes treat them as a part of the fall, rather than part of creation.

Both menstruation and nocturnal emissions are, at least in the public consciousness, seen as physical markers that puberty is happening. This is especially true with menstruation. Developmental experts usually refer to breast bud development as the first physical marker of puberty in girls; and many girls are well into puberty before they have their first period. But the marker remains strong.

It's almost like those Google Map or MapQuest directions that tell you how long it'll take before you get to a particular city. No one can remember if the predicted duration is to the city limits or to the city center. (It's to the city center, by the way.) So when we get to the city limits, we start thinking, *Well, we're kinda here*. But when we get to the city center, we *know* we've arrived. The same is true with a girl's first period and a guy's first wet dream. There's plenty of puberty happening prior to those physical events (they're already within the city limits), but those markers make it exceedingly clear that this puberty thing is fully upon them.

So, menstruation. You all know this, right? You know that a period is the natural release of the uterine lining (and accompanying blood) at the end of the monthly fertility cycle. Usually three to five days long, two to seven days is still considered a normal length. During menstruation, it's common for women (and girls) to experience loads of unpleasant physical and emotional side effects, including cramping in the uterus, abdominal pain, headaches, depression and emotionality, feeling "bloated" (which is due to premenstrual water retention), and a host of other not-so-fun realities. Of course, the severity of these side effects varies from woman to woman, and from period to period.[22]

And, of course, the reason menstruation is tied to puberty is because puberty brings fertility. Menstruation is merely the outward sign that a girl's body is now pregnancy-ready. (By the way, *menstruation* is the name of the process, *menses* is the correct name for an individual cycle, and *period* is the colloquialism for menses.)

There are lots of middle school ministry implications of menstruation, although they're mostly for the female leaders:

- On overnight trips always bring along an extra starter pad or two. Remember, most young teen girls don't use tampons at first, so pads are the way to go. There's nothing worse than being on a retreat and having a girl start her first period when no one is prepared to help her.

- Talk to girls about their periods. They'll likely get some of this information during their health class at school, and—hopefully—from their moms. But you can't assume this to be the case. Even when those other sources of information are in place, girls often don't feel comfortable asking the questions they have. Again, normalize it—create a safe environment to talk about this normal and good part of being a woman. (Ha! We're sure some of you women who are reading this right now are thinking, *Good?*)

- Be especially sensitive to girls who don't have a mom living in their home or another female caregiver who seems engaged enough to have this kind of personal discussion with them. Go out of your way to schedule a time to have a private conversation with these girls, answer their questions, and make sure they know they can come to you with any questions or concerns.

For guys, one of the only things we need to remember is that it's okay for a girl to want to sit out of a game or other rough-and-tumble activity. And make sure that the women on your ministry team are prepared and proactive about this subject.

Okay, so, on to wet dreams! (Are we having fun yet?)

Nocturnal emissions (also known as "wet dreams" or "spontaneous orgasms") seem to be discussed even *less* frequently than menstruation. Maybe that's because girls have to *do something* about their periods, so parents are—in a sense—forced to engage. But there's not much that needs to be done about wet dreams, so we stay silent. And this silence creates all kinds of confusion for boys. It's that "null curriculum" we talked about earlier—our lack of conversation about this topic teaches more than we know or are willing to admit.

First, let's talk about the technical stuff. Nocturnal emission is the spontaneous ejaculation of semen while sleeping. It's often accompanied, though not always, by an erotic dream. It sometimes results in waking up, but not always. It's usually accompanied by a tingling sensation, which, for many young teen boys, feels akin to urinating. (This is why they'll often wake up the first few times and believe they've wet their beds.) For men (and post-pubescent young teen guys), semen buildup is a continual process. So nocturnal emission is the body's way (read God's design) to release the excess buildup.

We'll say this plainly: Most of us in the church have lingering baggage about wet dreams being somehow sinful. This may be a holdover from Jewish purity laws. Or maybe it's a holdover from Augustine's belief that nocturnal emission is connected to a lustful mind. (He referred to it as "the glue of lust," an unfortunately vivid description, to be sure.) Or, more likely, it's all that combined with the reality of the oft-accompanying erotic dreams, which we'd like to believe are "controllable."

But the reality is that a teenage guy can no more control whether or not he has wet dreams than he can control his changing voice or growing taller. Wet dreams are just part of the package, so to speak. The only guys who don't have many wet dreams are those who regularly find *another* means of releasing excess semen, through sex or masturbation.

Women, since it's not appropriate for you to talk to boys about this stuff (that's obvious, right?), please make sure there are men in your ministry who are.

Men, let's not make this part of our null curriculum. We're continually amazed by the lack of information and total confusion guys have about this subject—not to mention guilt and embarrassment. Just recently, one of Marko's small group guys said, "Oh, yeah, that's when you pee in your sleep." And another guy responded, "No, it's not pee! It's your baby-makin' stuff, and it happens because you have a dirty mind!"

And talk to parents about this matter as well. If their young teen boy wants to wash his own sheets (a common practice, born out of embarrassment), they should let him. And don't make a big deal about it. (Although having the dad mention to the boy that he doesn't need to launder his own sheets and that his parents see this as a normal part of becoming a man can be helpful, too.)

Oh, and we can't forget about spontaneous erections. This subject, um, became a topic of discussion at my guys' small group recently. (Marko here: First I was going to say "came up" and then "arose." I find I'm tiptoeing all through this section—every phrase I write sounds like an entendre. I can just hear my middle school guys giggling!) I was a little surprised by how my guys were willing and able to talk about this experience. It was as if we tapped into a little safe zone where they finally felt they could share their awkwardness.

Let me pause the story here to offer a teaching point for the women. Since spontaneous erections are just part of being a teenage guy, and they *don't* always happen because a guy is thinking about sex, make sure your girls understand that, too. Spontaneous erections are quite frustrating to almost every guy. And, man alive, the fear of being "discovered" or having to stand in front of a group while having one is sheer horror. So many things can cause spontaneous erections, and often the source is not obvious to the boy.

Back to the story: All the guys started sharing how annoying it is, how they bend over at their school desks (hoping to stay anonymous), how they decline being called out, how they make up lies to cover why they can't stand up. One guy said, "We have to wear these shorts in gym class, and they kill me! Every time we run, I get a boner! It's horrible. I have to tuck 'it' between my legs and just keep running!" (This brings out shrieks of "Isn't that painful?" and "I know what you mean!" from the other guys.)

Two ministry implications here that should be obvious:

1. Male leaders, talk about this with your guys. *They all* have had this experience, and they all wonder if they're freaks or if there's something wrong with their penises or if they're just overly dirty. Help them understand that it's normal, it's part of the changes they're going through, and the frequency of them will subside over time. Female leaders, make sure you have men in your ministry who are willing to talk about this stuff with your boys. (It will *seriously freak them out* if you talk to them about it.)

2. Just as you should give a girl who might be dealing with menstrual pain some space and the permission to opt out of activities, be sensitive to guys as well. If they say they don't want to stand up—don't make them. Just let the moment pass on by.

MASTURBATION

This is an extremely challenging section to write, and we expect some people won't agree with our comments. To that end, we strongly encourage you to do more reading from other sources (those you trust and those who share a different perspective than what you already hold to).

Let's start with this: The subject of masturbation is very different for guys than it is for girls. But there are definitely some aspects of this discussion that are relevant to both genders.

First, the social acceptance of masturbation has shifted in the last 20 years. What was seen as a somewhat taboo practice (even in the locker-room talk of guys) 20 years ago is now considered normal. Morning drive radio DJs talk about "taking it out on the Internet." And didn't everything change once *Seinfeld* aired that episode about "being the master of your domain"? Suddenly, almost with a collective national sigh, it was normal and okay to talk about this previously closeted activity.

This also means that the even-more taboo subject (and practice) of girls masturbating has become culturally normative.

Another factor that has implications for both genders is the Internet-created access to pornography. There are still young teens who haven't been exposed to porn, but they're the exception, rather than the rule. Even "good, churched kids" with an active faith and engaged parents have been exposed to more porn, and significantly more *graphic* porn, than any of us adults were at their age. This adds both to the "normalcy" of masturbation and to the urge. (It's almost impossible for a teenage guy to view Internet porn and not get an erection.) And we know both from studies and experience that even the most quickly viewed graphic images can get locked into our memories to be easily retrieved at a later time—whether they're welcome or not.

One more commonality between guys and girls: Masturbation often starts, for young teens, as experimentation and getting to know their suddenly foreign bodies. If kids are willing to talk about this, they'll usually admit that their first attempts at masturbation were more about discovering what was and wasn't possible, about feeling new things, about checking out the plumbing.

But here's where the parallel tracks for the genders part ways, at least from our perspective. Guys—with their constant buildup of semen, brains that are more naturally attuned to think about sex on a regular basis (as opposed to intimacy, which is more the line of thinking, daydreaming, and longing for girls), and the constant fear of spontaneous erections—have a more urgent physiological "need" for the release that comes from masturbation, wet dreams, or—hopefully not for many young teens—actual sexual encounters. (We've both talked to boys who've been so sexually active as young teens that they had no use or need for masturbation.)

There's a fine line here, and we all know this. Masturbation can easily (and often, for guys and girls alike) become an obsession, something that rules them. And it can often become inseparably linked to other practices of the mind, such as viewing porn and fantasizing, that are horribly destructive to their sexual identity development, relational development, and faith development.

Yet even conservative family author, radio host, and psychologist Dr. James Dobson talks about masturbation for boys as being a normal activity and not harmful in moderate use: "It is my opinion that masturbation is not much of an issue with God. It's a normal part of adolescence, which involves no one else…if you do [masturbate], it is my opinion that you should not struggle with guilt over it."[23]

Our experience with boys tells us that the boy who "never, ever" masturbates is a mythical creature. And those boys who tell you otherwise are likely lying. They might feel massive guilt about it, and their guilt might decrease the frequency; but they still masturbate.

It seems weird to talk about masturbation in terms like "all good things in moderation." But there's a sense where this is true. For boys, masturbation, in moderation, is part of the growing-up experience. Masturbation, in moderation, can actually help a guy obsess about sex and fantasize *less* often because it releases built-up sexual pressure.

This is challenging for even the most gifted youth worker to talk about with guys because the line between helpful and "in moderation" on one end and obsessive and "fueled by lust" on the other end is extremely difficult to nail down.

So, let's leave it at this for now:

- Masturbation, for guys, is a normal part of the adolescent experience. We need to talk about it in sensitive and spiritually appropriate ways.

- Masturbation, for girls, is becoming a normal part of the adolescent experience, due to shifting cultural norms and messages. We (well, female leaders) need to help them think about what they're really longing for.

- Masturbation for both genders can quickly and easily become a destructive obsession, especially when fueled by porn, and we need to talk about this also, offering them examples of lives ruined by porn and obsessive sexual behavior.[24]

Okay, so that was a touchy subject. (C'mon, we had to slip in just one entendre!)

PERIOD PARTIES AND RITES OF PASSAGE

Remember, adolescence is a *recent* cultural phenomenon. And also remember that it was only about 100 years ago that the term came into popular use.

Prior to the last 100 years, the shift from childhood to young adulthood didn't have the "holding period" we provide today. And, as such, the transition wasn't the ever-widening gap that it is today.[25]

When the shift from childhood to young adulthood was "gapless," it *appeared* to be a point in time (although reality was more gradual, of course). And—get this—almost every culture around the globe (historically speaking, that is) had some kind of ceremony or rite or marker to acknowledge this transition. Often referred to as a "rite of passage," these family or community acknowledgments have almost completely faded away. We see remnants of them in the Jewish bar mitzvah and bat mitzvah[26] (rites of passage and inclusion into the world of adults for boys and girls, respectively), the Latin Quinceañera[27] (a girl's fifteenth birthday party that traditionally marks her "coming out" as a young woman), stories of Native American boys going on a "spirit quest," and even the debutante balls of the moneyed American South.

In North America the only rites of passage we seem to have these days are less about pomp-and-circumstance and celebrating the teenager than they are about giving them some new permission:

- Getting a driver's license (around 16 years old in most states)

- Graduating from high school (at approximately 18 years)

- Gaining the right to vote (at 18 years)

- Gaining the legal right to possess alcohol (at 21 years)

It's interesting that these new "rites" are not only about permission, but also tend to fall at the *end* of adolescence, rather than at the beginning of puberty—when rites of passage traditionally occurred.

Historically, rites of passage were (and remain, in some subcultures) public spectacles of rejoicing, honoring the young subjects, and welcoming them as fully identified members of the community. In many primitive cultures, a girl's first period was cause for great celebration. It signaled the coming of age and birthing-readiness of the young woman, and this was cause for celebration because it indicated fertility, which was critical to the future existence of the people group. The tribe would come together and celebrate with the newly fertile young woman as the person of honor. (Perhaps this was the one time in her otherwise male-dominated life when this would occur.) She'd be acknowledged as no longer a child but a woman—and with all the privileges (and responsibilities) due a woman in their culture.

We don't know about you, but we haven't been to a good period party in years.[29]

Actually, this isn't wholly true. In my (Marko's) home, we had a period party, of sorts, for my daughter. We'd already talked with her (my wife more than I, but both of us) about all the changes her body was going through. But when she had her first period, we decided to make it a bit of a celebration to mark this transition point in her life and celebrate who she was becoming. We took her out of school for a day, let her get a new haircut and a manicure (something she'd been begging for), had a masseuse come to our home to give her a private massage, and had a special family dinner, complete with gifts. My son, Max (then about 9), was a little confused by the whole thing. But Liesl felt like a princess. My wife also planned a small gathering of women who'd been chosen by Liesl because they were the kind of women she'd like to be like. They gathered for a women-only tea and spoke words of blessing to Liesl about what it means to be a woman.

There's been a small resurgence of interest in rites of passage in the Christian community, and in culture at large, with helpful books and articles readily available.[30] This is a great thing, and we couldn't more highly affirm this trend. Our strong encouragement is to think, along with parents, about how you can plan some meaningful rites of passage for girls and guys (and their parents) in the context of your ministry, as well as encouraging parents to do things with their kids on their own.

Since adolescence sprawls in front of young teens as a more-than-a-decade span of transition, current rites of passage aren't about saying, "You're now an adult." Instead, they're more about acknowledging that the young teen is now *on the road* to adulthood. Good stuff.

The Shifting Age of Puberty

In chapter 1 we wrote a tiny bit about the plunging average age in the onset of puberty. Really, it's such a fascinating change.[31]

A little recap of what we wrote earlier: In the early 1900s, the average age for the onset of puberty (in girls) was about 14 and one-half years old.[32] By the 1970s, this average had dropped to somewhere around 13 years old. Realize that the couple of decades prior to then were when youth culture was becoming clarified in the collective conscious of the Western world. So the notions about young teens that developed during the '60s and '70s have, in many ways, stuck with us. The notion of "junior" high school (notice the connotation in that phrasing) became the normative educational model, replacing the previous system of

K-8 schooling.[33] With this, the concept of the teenage years being ages 13 to 18 became a cultural norm. (Remember: Adolescence is normally understood to start with puberty and end when the emerging adult is ready to assume adult responsibilities. And, at that time, high school graduation was when our culture expected adult engagement.)

The notion that the teenage years begin at age 13 has lingered. In some ways, it's a redefinition of the beginning of adolescence, since 13 *is* no longer the age at which puberty strikes. If 13 is considered the start of adolescence (which it's not and, we'd contend, it shouldn't be our mindset), then it's purely a cultural construct, since puberty no longer starts at 13.

Okay, we were ranting there for a bit. Back to the shift. The average age for the onset of puberty has continued to drop. The most recent research shows puberty somewhere in the 11-years-old range. Some studies say it's as early as age 10 and a half. And African-American and Latino girls tend to hit puberty up to a full year earlier.

Why has this happened? For years, there were three competing theories:

- Some proposed that the drop in puberty age was due to our diet and, more specifically, the additives and preservatives in our less-organic, more modified intake of food.

- Others proposed that the drop was also diet-related; but conversely, it was because we have a *better* and *more well-rounded diet.*

- Still others suggested that the shift was a physiological response to the cultural expectation that kids act older at younger ages.

We believed, and taught in seminars, that the reason was some combination of the three. However, in more recent years, research (and common opinion among developmental specialists) has firmly landed on the first notion.

So it's preservatives and additives in our diet that have brought on this shift. But here's the really weird thing: In cultures where the diet does *not* include modified food, there's still been a drop in the onset of puberty—not as drastic a drop, but a drop nonetheless. And no one has a good explanation for this. It's also not clear if this trend would be reversible, were we to eat only unmodified, preservative- and additive-free food. Certainly, there still seems to be a cultural component at work.

The church has—in large part—been oddly resistant to acknowledge this shift in the age of onset for puberty.[34] We believe much of this comes from a good motive (even though it lends itself to a bit of the proverbial ostrich-head-in-the-sand syndrome). Churches, and engaged parents in general, have wanted to protect their kids from rushing into adolescent behaviors that are beyond their maturity. But to disavow the shift, or somehow believe we can change it, is to discard the opportunity for age-appropriate ministry and adult input.

With all this reality in place, we simply have to acknowledge that adolescence begins around 11 years old. Whatever the best approach to schooling, and hundreds of other responses to the issue, we must be responsive to the adolescent experience of 11- and 12-year-olds and not wait until they're 13 or 14 to deal with the real world and body experiences that our young teens are living in.

But this lowered-age thing brings up all kinds of new complications, which we'll get into a bit deeper in future chapters. For example, what does it mean for an 11-year-old girl who's slightly ahead of the curve (in terms of her physical development) to be ogled by her male peers and adult men? She has 11 years of life experience and a barely usable third-person perspective.

In our opinion, the lowering of the average age of puberty greatly compounds the reasons why middle school ministry is so crucial, and why it's a make-or-break time in the psychological, emotional, relational, and spiritual development of a human being.

Restating Middle School Ministry Implications

We've tried to weave implications throughout this chapter, as we do throughout this entire book. Our desire is for *Middle School Ministry* to be all about implications, rather than a dissertation on development.

But we want to restate a few of the notions we've harped on multiple times already:

- The physical changes of early adolescence are truly massive and world changing. And they bring with them universal concern and fear. Every young teen feels abnormal at one point or another.

- Because of this universal concern and fear, young teens need caring adults (parents and others) who can walk with them through this turbulent change, who are affirming and willing to talk, who will answer their questions without inducing guilt, and who can help them feel normal.

- Helping young teens feel normal (and even good) is one of the most important aspects of effective middle school ministry.

- Great middle school ministry calls for courage because it's awkward to talk about lots of this stuff.

CHAPTER 4

Mind Warp
(Cognitive Development)

One Sunday morning I (Marko) was teaching on God's forgiveness in my church's middle school ministry. Partway through the teaching time, I used a few mini case studies to check for understanding.[35] I read a short blip that went something like this:

Charlotte is a committed follower of Jesus, and she usually makes decisions that reflect that desire. But she also wants to be popular. Last weekend, Charlotte got invited to a party with a bunch of cool kids from school. And, not sure how to act in this setting, Charlotte ended up having some alcoholic drinks. Now Charlotte has tons of guilt. She feels like Jesus could never forgive her and that she must not be a Christian anymore.

I asked the kids what they'd say to Charlotte if she confided her feelings to them. Hands went up.

The first kid I called on said, "I'd tell her that alcohol is stupid!"

Okay.

I tried another student who said, "I'd say, 'Jesus still loves you, but it's too bad you're not a Christian anymore.'"

Uh...

The girl in the front row was thrusting her hand in the air and making an "ooh, ooh, ooh!" sound. I reluctantly asked her what she'd say to Charlotte. With a huge grin and a basketful of confidence, she responded, "I'd tell her that my name is Charlotte, too!"

I believe my face fell a bit. At this, the pastor's daughter raised her hand with a look on her face that said, *I'll help you out here, Marko; I know what you're looking for.*

"Bethany?" I pleaded. With a bored voice that simultaneously mocked both her fellow youth groupers and me, she flatly sighed and said, "I'd tell her that Jesus forgives her."

Ah, the minds of middle schoolers. It's the combination of innocence and a willingness to verbalize any thought that makes middle school ministry such a wild ride at times.

Stage Theory

In the early 1920s, a French dude named Jean Piaget, proposed a theory of cognitive development[36] that's been widely tested and accepted, as well as built upon.[37] Piaget suggested that children go through several stages of development[38] in terms of how their brains process and understand information.[39]

While the physical changes of early adolescence are the most visible and tend to be the ones most people focus on, we don't believe they're *the* most significant changes. We've found that the shift in cognitive thinking brings the most dramatic changes of the middle school years, particularly when we consider the ministry implications. Cognitive change has an enormous impact on all the other areas of change in the life of a young teen (all the chapters on development that follow this one). It really is, in simple terms, the determinant factor that separates children from young adults.

The final two stages in Piaget's theory of cognitive development are Concrete Operations and Formal Operations. In laymen's terms—concrete thinking and abstract thinking.

Concrete thinking results in a rigid, black-and-white understanding of the world. A world without nuance or paradox. We can readily see this in preteens, right? They have a wonderfully "concluded" worldview, with their little systematic theologies all worked out and their worldview encased in plastic wrap. Ten-year-olds have a confidence in their opinions born out of a general, limited belief that everyone sees the world and everything in it just as they do. Preteen thinking is concrete, linear, pragmatic, tangible, and simplistic.

But puberty really messes that up, just like the mother eagle stirs up the nest in order to prepare the eaglet for change when it's time for the baby bird to learn how to fly (Deuteronomy 32:11).

Around the onset of puberty, the brain begins a transition in how it processes information. This brings on a long trek into useable abstract thinking. And this trek is far from concluded during the young teen years. In fact, some research shows that adolescents are postponing the use of abstract thinking well into their teen years, and often well into their twenties.[40]

We like to view abstract thinking as God's "puberty gift" to young teens. If they *did* have period parties, God would show up with a card and inside the card he'd write, I LOVE YOU, AND I'M

PROUD OF YOU. AS A GIFT, I'M GOING TO CHANGE YOUR EN-
TIRE WORLD BY GIVING YOU THE GIFT OF ABSTRACT THOUGHT.
HAPPY PUBERTY!

This isn't an overnight change, of course. It's not as if they're
concrete thinkers one day and abstract thinkers the next. The
change is gradual, and young teens slowly start to bump in and
out of abstract thinking. If one could take a median of abstract
thought use over a period of years, the progress would be seen.
But in everyday life, the experience is much more hit or miss.

THUMBS UP

Now, abstract thinking isn't a muscle, of course. But being visual
dudes, we find it helpful to use a muscle as a metaphor. In that
light, abstract thinking is like a brand-new muscle that kids receive
when they're young teens. But it's undeveloped, and they have
no idea how to use it.

I (Marko) had a bad run of thumb injuries in late adolescence.
As a high school junior, I worked as a dishwasher in a Chinese
restaurant. But I'd often help with food prep also. As such, I was
usually the guy who had to chop the cabbage. We'd take a large
crate of cabbage and, using a butcher's cleaver and butcher block,
whack it into quarters, which could then be fed through a massive
food shredder. One time, I made the mistake of challenging the
cook to a race to see who could quarter a case of cabbage heads
first. In hindsight, I can see how this was a race to be lost.

When attacking one particularly large cabbage head, the
cleaver didn't go all the way through, and I tried to yank it back
out. Fearful of the extremely sharp blade when it came flying out,
I reacted by bringing it quickly back down—on my thumb.

Luckily, I didn't chop off my thumb. But I cut all the way to
the bone, between the knuckle and my hand. And worse, I cut
my tendon in half.

A few days later, a hand surgeon stretched what looked like a bloody rubber band out from my thumb and said, "This is your tendon!" I remember feeling the tug and responding, "Great, please put it back in my thumb."

Internal and external stitches followed, as did a plaster mold around my thumb and all the way up to my elbow, which was held up by a sling. I had my hand in a six-week-long "thumbs up" position. I felt like a dork.

Two years later I was a college freshman, and I was working in a pizza joint, slicing mozzarella on a circular meat slicer. Wicked sharp things, those meat slicers. So when the tip of my thumb got too close, I lost it—right into the edge of, and a little into, my thumbnail.

A few days later I was having a skin graft taken from my inner hip and sewed onto my thumb tip.[41] Repeat: Plaster mold around my thumb and all the way up to my elbow. Repeat: Sling. Repeat: Six weeks in a thumbs-up position. ("I'm doin' great! How you doin'?")

In both of those situations, my thumb was immobilized for six weeks. In both of those situations, I had the same experience at the end of the six weeks: The doctor removed the splint, wiggled my thumb, checked out a few things, and said, "Everything's great. You're good to go."

And in both cases, I held my newly freed "thumbs up" thumb in front of my face and stared at it. I commenced sending massive quantities of brain signals down through my arm and directly to the muscles in my thumb, commanding it to MOVE! But it wouldn't move. Not one little tiny bit. "Everything was great," but I had no muscle memory of how to use it. My thumb had no recent history of movement, and it had atrophied.

Later that day, I could wiggle my thumb a tiny bit. After a few days, I had about half the full range of motion. And after about a week, all was normal.

These thumb experiences have stayed close to me over the years because they're such great snapshots of what's going on with young teens and their new abstract thinking ability. They have it—they're theoretically capable of formal operational thinking. But it's a foreign land of the unknown. They have no idea how to use it, no experience of the process, no "muscle memory" of how.

What Is Abstract Thought?

Abstract thought can be described, possibly in an overly simplistic way, as thinking about thinking. In more expanded terms, abstract thinking includes the abilities to consider—

- Third-person perspective

- Self-awareness

- Nuance and gray areas

- Paradox

- Systems

- Speculation and inference

But what does this mean for a young teen with a newly acquired abstract thinking ability? Most of us (as adults) have been utilizing abstract thinking for so long that it's easy to forget what it's like *not* to have this ability or at least not have it function well. We can't overemphasize how important it is for middle school youth workers to understand this stuff.

HYPOTHESIZING

Abstract thinking allows teenagers (and adults, of course) to create multiple scenarios—real or imaginary—of "what might be." Teenagers are just beginning to consider likely, and unlikely, down-the-line results of various actions and choices—both their own and others'. Of course, they're also really bad at doing this because it's a new ability. But they have the basic cognitive tools to do it.[42]

WHY I DO THIS

I'm absolutely crazy about middle school students, and I have been for a long time. I find myself constantly thinking about this specific age group, their development, and their behavior.

People ask me all the time, "Why do you do what you do?" I always begin by saying it's a calling God has put deep inside of me and a passion to come alongside early adolescents and help them connect to Jesus and the family of God.

I'm amazed at how much I continue to discover about this age—and I want to learn more each day. That could almost sound as though I see them as research, rather than people. I don't. I see them for who they are and what they bring to this world at this season in their lives.

I love spending time with them and living in their world. To sit down with them and talk about everything or anything is so much fun. I really enjoy listening to what they have to say and what they actually believe about life, school, friends, parents, teachers, politics, games, movies, music, and God.

Middle schoolers are, at times, brutally honest about what they think about you or others.

What's even more fun is to play with them. As I've gotten a little bit older, I can't play with them as long, but I sure enjoy the time I do play.

I love how they're beginning to think abstractly and how they begin to wrestle with faith issues. They're learning for the first time to own their faith and pursue the Christian life. It's a privilege to journey with them and their parents, and, in partnership with the Holy Spirit, to help shape and influence them in their faith development.

At this age they're still very moldable and shapeable, and they're looking for adults to speak truth into their lives. And, no, they don't verbalize this, but it's a desire they have. They can be genuinely excited about pursuing their relationship with Jesus, or at least the possibility of a relationship with Jesus.

To sum up: Middle schoolers are an incredible gift to the church and to this world. They have so much potential and ability that, if tapped, can and will change the world and advance the kingdom of God. In my opinion, middle schoolers are one of the most valuable gifts and natural resources in the world.

Alan Ramsey is the pastor of Student Ministries/Middle School at Fellowship Church in Knoxville, Tennessee.

SPECULATING

Closely linked to hypothesizing, speculation is directly tied to decision making and is the practice of thinking through likely outcomes. We adults do this quickly (most of the time) and intuitively. When presented with a choice, we immediately (again, in most cases) speculate about the likely outcomes of the various options. We might call this "making an informed decision." Again, children and preteens aren't capable of making an informed decision, as they don't possess the ability to speculate.

EMPATHIZING

I (Marko) live near Tijuana, Mexico, which is an area filled with poverty. If I take my two children to visit families who live in a Tijuana garbage dump and scavenge for food and sustenance, then my children will most likely have two very different experiences. Max, my 11-year-old—a naturally sensitive boy—will experience deep sympathy regarding the plight of the children and families he encounters. He'll feel bad for them and want to help. However, Liesl, my 15-year-old daughter, will likely experience empathy. She'll also feel bad for the children, but she'll take it a step further. She'll empathize as she imagines (even "feels") what life would be like for an impoverished child. She'll place herself in a child's shoes and perceive life from the child's perspective, a perspective that's completely third person and outside herself. Liesl might also wrestle with abstract questions, such as, "Why was this child born in this place and to this poverty? And why was I born into the comfortable life that I have?"

DOUBTING

Doubting, of course, occurs when we internally question our beliefs. This is a very abstract thought process, and it's not possible prior to adolescence. But it's absolutely essential to faith development and a wonderful developmental gift in God's design.

EMOTING

Emotions are abstract. And since children don't think abstractly, they're significantly limited in their emotional options. I like to think of this as if children go through life with emotional "painter's palettes" that contain a limited number of colors or emotional options—just the primary colors and a few simple secondary combinations. But with the onset of puberty and the gift of abstract thinking, that small palette is replaced by a massive new emotional palette with hundreds of nuanced and complex emotions, as well as a massive glob of black to add dimension, broodiness, and all other things emotionally dark.

SELF-PERCEIVING

Preteens don't have the ability to think of themselves beyond what they see in the mirror or what others say about them. But abstract thinking brings the ability to think about oneself and to speculatively perceive oneself from another's perspective. Once again, teenagers—especially younger ones—are notoriously bad at this. They often incorrectly perceive how others see them and assume everyone is "checking them out."[43]

IDENTITY FORMATION

It would be wrong to say that identity formation *begins* in adolescence. Our identities are being formed from Day One. All the messages we take in from family, friends, and the culture at large form our self-perception. So the shift that occurs during adolescence—thanks to our friend, abstract thinking—is that young teens suddenly acquire the ability to take charge of their own identity formation. Since they gain self-perception (and all the other outcomes just discussed), they can begin directing the course of their identity formation. They make choices and see the implications of who they are and who they're becoming. They begin speculating about who they want to be, not only in regard to what careers they'd like to have someday, but also what kinds of people they want to be and they want *others* to identify them as being. In other words, adolescence provides the opportunity to choose who one becomes.

This is why identity is such a major task in adolescence. The reality is that by the time an adolescent reaches her mid-twenties, her identity will be mostly formed. (And, remember, this is the whole point of culture giving teenagers a respite between child-hood and adulthood.) Sure, we all continue to shape and refine our identities throughout adulthood, but the core formation work is done. The course is mostly set.

Two Stories

Since this is such an important issue for us to understand, we'd like to tell a couple of stories to help flesh it out a bit. First, a story about concrete thinking; then a story about abstract thinking.

A friend of ours was speaking at a camp for middle school kids. Central to the recreational offerings of the camp was a pond that the kids could swim in. On one side of the pond stood a two-story-high tower, and suspended on a cable stretched across the middle of the pond was a trapeze. The challenge was to climb the tower, jump out over the pond, and try to grab the trapeze. If one succeeded, the reward was a few moments of hanging there, as well as some cheers from those watching. Of course, the gnarly misses resulting in sideways two-story drops into the pond were what everyone was really hoping to see.

Many of the middle schoolers at the camp found this little test of courage to be the coolest thing they'd ever experienced. But, as you might guess, many others would have nothing to do with it and stayed well away from the tower's ladder.

Late in the week, our friend had been asked to share the gospel and offer kids an opportunity to respond. At one point in her talk, she was trying to describe "taking a leap of faith." Being a seasoned middle school youth worker, she was well aware of the fact that this is a very abstract concept. So she wanted to find a way—on the fly—to illustrate the idea. The tower and trapeze sprang to mind (a great concrete example). She explained that taking a leap of faith is kind of like jumping off the tower down at the pond. "It's a little scary. You're not completely sure what's going to happen or what grabbing that trapeze is going to be like—but you jump."

(Just as a side note: We're not sure our friend realized it at the time, but another way this metaphor works is how kids who were into the tower jump often did it over and over again, just like how middle schoolers often believe they need to "become a Christian" over and over again, typically when they're at camp.)

After the meeting time was over, an incoming 6th-grade girl approached our friend. She was shy, and she held back until the other students had walked away. Then she said, "I have a problem. I think I want to do what you talked about—become a 'follower of Jesus.' But I'm way too afraid to jump off that tower."

At this point the speaker thought the girl was speaking metaphorically—that she meant she was afraid to take a "leap of faith." But the girl continued, "Do I really have to jump off the pond tower if I want to become a Christian?"

Ah! This wonderful little concrete thinker had completely missed the metaphorical nature of the speaker's illustration, which is ironic since it was an attempt to make an abstract idea more concrete. She actually thought she had to jump off the tower by the pond in order to follow Jesus.

So they took her down to the pond and threw her off the tower. (We're kidding!)

This is a great example of a preteen thinking in *very* concrete ways. It's an extreme example, in many ways, as many preteens—even those utilizing concrete thinking—would still catch the metaphor in that example. But this is the kind of thinking that many of your middle schoolers are locked into—especially when they're thinking about subjects that are truly abstract (such as taking a leap of faith).

This second story shows the other extreme.

I (Marko) took a group of middle school kids to Mexico on a short-term mission trip. We stayed at and worked with an orphanage and one of the local churches it was connected with. During our trip our students were involved in four tasks: Helping around the orphanage, building a few small houses for people in the community, running a "kids club" (like a Vacation Bible School) for children in the community, and going into the community with members of the church to talk to people. This last task was, by far, the most intimidating for most of our kids.

We'd prepared our middle schoolers for months, and we always had them take a backseat in the discussions, especially since they had to rely on a translator. But the conversations were often naturally geared around why this group of American teenagers was in their community, which often led to spiritual discussions. We were careful not to build an expectation of lots of "conversions," but we wanted to work alongside this church in their efforts to reach out to their own community.

One of the students on the trip was an 8th-grade guy named Garrett. He'd been reasonably active in our middle school group for a few years, but he'd been one of those kids who kind of blends into the crowd. He hadn't shown any particularly elevated leadership ability or even spiritual interest—prior to this trip.

But while we were in Mexico, it became obvious to all of us that Garrett had the spiritual gift of evangelism. While the other middle schoolers nervously avoided this face-to-face ministry, Garrett was never found on the construction sites or at the kids club. He was always grabbing a translator and someone from the church, walking around the community, and, in a beautifully innocent way, leading people to Christ. The church we were working with more than doubled in size during the week we were there, and all the adults could see that it was because God was doing something pretty amazing through this middle school kid.

When we returned home, we had an opportunity to give a report to our church during a church service. Now, if your middle school ministry is anything like ours, much of your communication with the church at large comes in the form of a request ("Please, we need more leaders!") or an apology ("We're sorry about that stain; we know blood is difficult to get out of carpeting, especially when mixed with eggs and marshmallow cream.").

So—I'll admit—I saw this as an opportunity to score some points for our middle school ministry. (I have a tendency toward manipulation—but all for the glory of God, of course!)

I know, this wasn't a completely pure motive on my part. But I had these visions of Garrett sharing and all the blue-hairs in the church thinking, *Oh, what a wonderful boy! Our middle school ministry must be wonderful! Let's double their budget!*

Yeah.

So when I asked Garrett to share as part of our trip report, I said, "Be sure to tell everyone how you led all those people to Christ."

I stood in front of the church and gave an overview of the trip, calling out a few highlights. Then I asked Garrett to talk. He stepped up to the mic, not nervous at all (more from being clueless than from being confident), and started talking. I was standing a few feet away from him with cartoon-like, budget-increase dollar signs cha-chinging where my eyes would normally be.

When Garrett got to the "rope 'em in and bring it home" part of the story, he paused. Then he said, "Marko wanted me to tell you how I led a whole bunch of people to Christ."

My smile stiffened, and I thought, *NO! You're not supposed to tell them I told you to say that!*

He continued, "But that's not what really happened."

Now I was in full-blown panic and trying with everything in me not to show it. Thoughts flew through my head of yanking him off the stage before he could say something really stupid. I had absolutely no idea what Garrett might say next.

Garrett paused for what seemed like a few minutes (although it was probably a few seconds). He tilted his head sideways, like a puppy trying to figure something out. Then the thought hit him, and he went with it. With a big grin on his face, Garrett said, "What really happened was, God led a bunch of people to himself through me!"

I was stunned. I was thinking, *Dude! I barely understand that!* I started to wonder if I should ask Garrett to disciple *me*.

That flash of abstract thinking even caught Garrett by surprise. And it was a stunning moment of clarity on a deeply abstract spiritual plane.

YOU NEVER KNOW

So here's the challenge of middle school ministry.

It would be difficult enough if you simply had both the concrete-thinking tower girl and Garrett in your middle school ministry. You'd know that you had to include both of them when talking about abstract things. Maybe you could put all the concrete thinkers on one side of the room, and all the abstract thinkers on the other. Then you could tell the abstract thinkers to hold on for a minute while you explained something abstract to the concrete thinkers.

Or you could put all the concrete thinkers in one small group, and all the abstract thinkers in another, and really focus your discussions in ways that were perfectly tuned to their thinking abilities.

Ah, that would be nice. But it's not reality.

The reality is that every young teen pops in and out of abstract thinking. Sure, the younger ones (6th graders) are more likely to think concretely. And yes, the older ones (8th graders) are more likely to have *some* ability to grasp abstract ideas. But reality isn't that clean.

You *never* know what students are actually hearing when you talk about abstract stuff. (By the way, this pretty much includes all spiritual stuff—which we'll talk about more in chapter 8.) Their abstract "thinking muscle" is so new and tiny that it's better to assume they aren't utilizing it and go the extra mile at concretizing abstract stuff.

Good luck with that! We feel your pain.

Abstract Thought as a Gateway

We already wrote that we believe this cognitive shift has the biggest implications for middle school ministry. But it's not only because of the cognitive shift in and of itself and isolated from other implications. Instead, it's because the next several chapters all *flow out of* this brain shift.

Emotional development is directly tied to abstract thinking. Emotions are abstract. Children and preteens have limited emotional arsenals from which to draw because they're concrete thinkers. Abstract thinking opens up entire new vistas of emotional possibility and experience. (More on this in the next chapter.)

The massively changing relational landscape of early adolescence is also directly tied to abstract thinking. As young teens begin to think in new ways, they start to become more self-aware. This—along with other factors—brings about a shift in how they form friendships and what's important to them in the friendships they do form. (More about this in chapter 7.)

We all know that part of the teenage experience is gaining some independence. In fact, we've heard good parents encapsulate their roles as "helping their children become independent." This is a great perspective, and *all* young teens struggle, in one way or another, with this shift (as do most parents). We'll talk about this more in chapter 7.

Then, of course, there's spiritual change. Wow. This is the thing that keeps the two of us passionate about middle schoolers. Young teens are in the process of completely reinventing their worldview (no matter what their worldview is—Christian or otherwise). They're questioning the very things they've "concluded" in their preteen years and the things they've inherited from parents, churches, and other input. It's an extremely fragile and potent time of spiritual opportunity, and it's directly tied to the cognitive changes that are happening during their young teen years. (We'll address this, at length, in chapter 8.)

Other Brain Stuff

There's been a slew of new research on adolescent brain development in the last decade, revealing some fascinating stuff with huge ministry implications.

For hundreds of years, the medical community assumed that the human brain was fully developed in childhood. While it still needed more experience and data, it was thought that the raw goods were considered "all there." This was mostly based on the physical inspection of actual brains (both during surgery and postmortem).

But new advances in technology provided for real-time three-dimensional brain scans of live brains. This provided an unprecedented opportunity for scientists to look at teenage brains *while still in* development. This book doesn't have space for a super-detailed dive into all of this (although reading more about it would be highly recommended).[44] But we'd like to provide a short overview, as it's captured quite a bit of our imagination in the last couple of years, and it's been the subject of lots of deep implication-oriented conversations between the two of us and the middle school ministry peeps we hang with.[45]

In short, the primary discovery was that the brain isn't fully developed until the mid-twenties.[46] There are three aspects of this we'd like to discuss a bit more:

FRONTAL LOBE DEVELOPMENT

This is the biggie of this research and the one component that's received the most attention. Real-time brain scans of teenagers have revealed that the frontal lobe (more formally called "the prefrontal cortex"), which is the part of the brain behind your forehead, is significantly underdeveloped in teenagers and isn't fully developed until the mid-twenties.

What's particularly critical about this discovery is that it shines a light on many teenage behaviors. The frontal lobe is responsible for a bucket of astounding brain functions. Often called "the executive office" of the brain or the "decision-making center," the frontal lobe is responsible for processing things, such as—

- *Focus.* Teenagers have a hard time focusing on things and not being distracted by everything else in the room.

- *Forethought.* Teenagers find it difficult to predict consequences to real or potential behavioral choices.

- *Impulse control.* Teenagers don't have a developed "governor" that helps moderate their impulses.

- *Organization.* Teenagers often do poorly at organizing tasks, time, relationships, and other things.

- *Planning.* Without this, we live in the here-and-now. It's hard for teens to make decisions based on what's coming in the future and the need to plan for it.

- *Judgment.* It's challenging for teenagers to discern the best choice in a particular situation, as they often don't possess a fully developed ability to make good judgment calls.

- *Empathy.* Teenagers struggle to see how their choices might impact others, as well as seeing something from another person's point of view (a distinctly abstract thinking ability).

- *Insight.* Teenagers have difficulty speculating about other peoples' behaviors and motivations and often draw wrong conclusions (as if *this* is something we adults have all worked out).

- *Emotional control.* Closely related to impulse control, teenagers will often act out a negative emotion instead of controlling the emotion.

TEMPORAL LOBE DEVELOPMENT

Also underdeveloped in teenage brains are the temporal lobes, which are found behind the temples. The short story on the temporal lobes is that they're responsible for (among other things) emotional interpretation. This means that teenagers have a physiological reason for not always understanding their own emotions and for being notoriously deficient at interpreting other peoples' emotions. (Guys, by the way, are significantly worse at this than girls are; and in addition to the latter physiological reasons, it's cultural.)

MYELINIZATION AND NEURON WINNOWING

A third new finding is exceptionally fascinating to us. Neurons are the "wiring" of the brain. They're the microscopic conduits through which electrical pulses of information bits are transmitted throughout the brain. Bundles and pathways of neurons form into what are referred to as "neural pathways"—superhighways of thought, in a sense. Two remarkable things occur during the young teen years with neuron development.

The first is the process of myelinization. Myelin is a "sheathing" that coats the outside of a neuron, both protecting it, and—even more so—accelerating its performance. This sheathing process occurs during the teenage years. We asked an adolescent brain specialist to give us his guess at the percentage of increased performance as a result of this process. He was reluctant to say. So we pushed him and asked, "Does it, like, *double* the speed at which information travels on neural pathways?" He responded, "Oh, no! It's more like a 200-times increase."

Then there's this crazy thing that happens with neuron development prior to and after puberty that's left us digging for implications in our ministries. In the two years prior to puberty, the brain switches into a growth mode where it develops *millions* of additional neurons—way more than will be needed or even exist in the eventual adult brain. But at puberty the process reverses itself, and a multiyear winnowing process takes place.

The leading scientist on all this new brain stuff is a guy named Jay Giedd. He calls this winnowing a "use it or lose it" process.[47] In other words, the process by which the brain begins to reduce the number of neurons present in the brain (remember, neurons make up the pathways by which the brain processes information) is based on use. Those neurons and neural pathways that are well used in early adolescence remain. Those that are underused are eliminated.

This has *enormous* implications for those of us who care about the development of young teens. Giedd (as well as the adolescent brain specialist we met with over a period of days) confirms that, in a sense, by mid-adolescence a teenage brain is "hard-wired" for the way it will function throughout the rest of life.

This is a very important issue for us to consider, as many middle school ministries have traditionally taken an approach to formation that emphasizes cramming kids full of as much "information" as possible, in the hope that it will "stick" and become a guiding force in their lives.

But what does this "use it or lose it" principle tell us? It's essential that the young teen years be about learning how to think. Process, "What if?" and "Why?" are all critical. Discovery is the best learning mode (for spiritual or academic learning). If young teens exercise this part of their developing brains, then it will positively impact their lifelong thinking, their spiritual growth (remember, spiritual stuff is abstract), their emotional health, their relational maturity, and their desire to continue growing and learning.

So make room for "Why?" and "What if?" Those are questions of speculation (that brand-new but wimpy ability in young teens). Encourage discovery. Don't be threatened by questioned values and boundary-pushing. This is the best stuff of early-adolescent brain development.

Can you see why the two of us are so passionate about young teen ministry? We believe science has confirmed our calling *and* our experience with real middle schoolers. High school is too late.[48] Middle school ministry is make or break, baby.

At our junior high pastors' summit a few years ago, we asked that adolescent brain specialist how we can help teenagers develop their brain capacity. He listed three things: Lots of sleep, good diet and exercise, and living with the consequences of their choices. Wow. Our ministries have often sabotaged the very outcomes we hope for in our kids.

What This *Doesn't* Mean

As this brain research has reached a popular level, it's often been misunderstood and misapplied. An example of this was a full-page ad by a large automobile insurance company that ran in many newspapers a couple of years ago.[50] The ad showed a cute line drawing of a brain. There was one little puzzle-piece section missing, and it was shaped like a car. The copy at the top of the ad said, WHY DO MOST 16-YEAR-OLDS DRIVE LIKE THEY'RE *MISSING A PART OF THEIR BRAIN?* BECAUSE THEY ARE.

The copy went on to describe a cursory overview of frontal lobe underdevelopment in teenagers, and how they aren't capable of good judgment. Really, this whole thing was a poorly veiled attempt to justify higher insurance rates for teenage drivers; a way to placate the impact on parents' wallets with a come-alongside tone.

The ad was a cheap shot, in our opinion. And it typifies the wrong thinking that can come from these new discoveries.

Yes, there are physiological reasons for what we've always observed in teenagers—they struggle with judgment, they're impulsive, they have a hard time prioritizing, they're not good at emotional interpretation or control. But these realities aren't an excuse to conclude that teenagers (and young teens in particular, for our purposes here) are *incapable* of these things. Our conclusion should be just the opposite.

Since we have scientific support for many adolescent behaviors, we should be patient and sympathetic. But we should also be *that much more* committed to helping young teens exercise these deficient, *but not absent*, life skills. Puh-leeze! This gives us a reason to step it up, not get fatalistic. The brain, including these underdeveloped parts, gains efficiency and ability through *use*. It's not that at some magical point in their mid-twenties, their brains suddenly have fully developed frontal and temporal lobes and young adults can now make great choices and prioritize well and become experts at emotional interpretation.

THINKING ABOUT MATURITY

Our adolescent brain specialist friend also gave us a helpful framework for thinking about maturity. He said, roughly:

- Physical Maturity comes to fruition between ages 16 and 18. This is when the body's full potential is in place. Practice can make it better, but the potential is there.

- Knowledge Maturity peaks at ages 18 to 20.

- But Wisdom Maturity peaks at age 25. Car rental companies won't rent a vehicle to anyone under 25 years old because they know this little fact.

This raises some challenging questions for us about middle school volunteers (and paid staff) who are in their upper teens and young twenties. (Now, if you're in that age group, don't be offended by this. We believe older teen and younger twenties middle school youth workers are fantastic in so many aspects of ministry.)

But here are some of the implication questions we've wrestled with as a result:

- Do we let older teens and young 20-somethings drive vans and cars full of middle schoolers? If so, what extra precautions should we take?

- How do we coach and mentor young paid and volunteer staff? How can we come alongside them with a bit more wisdom to help them be successful?

- What about pairing younger leaders with more seasoned leaders, especially for small group leadership?[51]

- Are we ready for the young youth leader to make mistakes? What are our expectations?

- What about using high school students as middle school leaders?

- Should we offer additional training for younger leaders?

A Wrap and a Toss

We hope you can see that we're passionate about all this brain stuff—both the development of abstract thinking and the new brain research information. We find that it affects *everything* we do in middle school ministry, from planning schedules, to teaching topics, to the language we use in teaching and conversations, to small group discussions and personal conversations, to counseling parents, to training volunteers, and everything else. Really, there's just no way to be super-effective in middle school ministry without some consciousness of these critical developmental issues.

All this cognitive development stuff is *constantly* in the backs of our minds, at all times, as we go about our ministry with young teens.

And, as we wrote earlier, it directly brings about much of the additional changes that middle schoolers are trudging through, such as the emotional changes we'll address in the next chapter.

CHAPTER 5

Roller-Coaster Freak Show

(Emotional Development)

My (Marko) wife went through an *Anne of Green Gables* phase a number of years ago, reading all the books in the series and buying the movies and a few Anne knickknacks. As a result, I watched the movies, too. (Uh, more than once, if I'm being totally honest.) There were two movies, and both were originally made as a TV miniseries. And they're both really long. They're from the VHS era, and both movies are two tapes each. This meant that when a person watched them straight through, it took about seven hours to observe this little Newfie (a playful term for someone from Newfoundland, in Eastern Canada) orphan work through her adolescence.

Anne is a classic external processor—we never have to wonder what she's thinking. Her character is really a wonderful little snapshot of a pure adolescent experience, but without the cultural stuff of living as an urban or suburban teenager in the twenty-first century.

One of the most notable things about Anne is her emotional volatility. Any woman reading this (and a few guys, like me) knows that Anne is regularly over-the-top giddy. She'll talk a blue streak of possibility and excitement, palpably thrilled with her prospects. But just as quickly as that effervescence comes on, Anne has some negative internal or external experience that plunges her into (c'mon, Anne-fans, say it with me) "the depths of despair!"

Last week at my (still Marko) middle school guys' small group, a normally quiet and even-keeled Zach couldn't sit still. But it wasn't merely a classic early-adolescent case of the wiggles. He was downright plucky. He had a perma-grin on his face, and he kept drumming his fingers on anything and everything.

I knew he'd started attending a new school that day—an experience that would be challenging for most kids. So I asked him how it went. His response: "Well, I didn't get called a motherf---er even *one* time today!"

Same small group time: Bryson, the kid who has more energy and randomness than just about any middle school boy I've ever met, told us—at a completely random point in our small group time—about the deep pain in his family because of his dad's partial paralysis after a motorcycle accident several months earlier. Our group has been meeting for only about six weeks, and I didn't know Bryson's family. So this was brand-new information to me.

The funny thing about Bryson's tale was that he shared it with a chipper smile on his face and in a lighthearted tone. Sure, he's most likely got some deeper emotions that he wasn't willing to reveal at that moment. But he didn't appear to be wearing a mask. It was just that his emotions didn't match his story; and he didn't have a clue about that reality.

You don't have to be in middle school ministry for long before you'll experience most, if not all, of the following:

> The girl who bursts into tears because when you mentioned your childhood pet cat, it reminded her of her neighbor's cat that died in a tragic road-crossing incident four years ago.

> The boy who broods in the back row, but then suddenly comes alive and forgets his coolness while getting caught up in a fun game.

> The girl who believes you're the coolest leader EV-AR and always wants to be near you; but who suddenly, and for no apparent reason, decides you're the biggest dork to ever walk the planet.

> The girl who, on the first day of camp, talks non-stop about being "in love with Tommy," then plunges into a broody depression as a result of being spurned (according to a friend who told her so) on the second day of camp, and then—later that evening—bounces back into "I'm a free agent" land now that it's clear "Tommy is such a loser."

> The boy who holds his emotional cards very close, like a sunglasses-wearing professional Texas Hold 'Em player, but innocently lets a little grin squeak out from time to time.

> The girl who goes through a phase where she frequently hugs everyone and says, "Love ya!" to pretty much everything that moves.

These are all external examples of the massive internal shifts taking place in the minds and hearts of young teens. Their emotional landscape is undergoing a brutally thorough renovation, and it's confusing, messy, costly, intrusive, and harrowing.

Please know this: We didn't write the previous examples with disdain or condescension. And while the emotional roller coaster of early adolescence presents all kinds of interesting and unique challenges for those of us called to this ministry, we find it absolutely gorgeous and see the fingerprints of God all over it.

The Expanding Color Palette

Being visual dudes, we believe the emotional shift going on in the lives of middle schoolers is akin to a painter receiving a larger palette of colors.

Children and preteens, with their limited cognitive options (meaning, their more literal, concrete thinking), are like painters holding color palettes containing the primary colors and one or two others.[52] Sure, they can mix colors on the canvas, but those brush strokes are often unintentional at best.

Emotions are abstract. More accurately: Thinking about emotions, or being self-aware of one's emotions, is even more abstract. A nine-year-old can certainly identify "I'm mad" and "I'm happy," but any more nuance than that gets a bit challenging. When concrete thinkers *are* able to identify the sources of their emotions, they'll usually assume an external reason ("You made me mad" or "The puppy made me happy").

Recently, my (Marko here again) family moved locally. We'd been in our house for almost seven years, so it was the only house my 10-year-old son, Max, really knew. And it was a great house, with lots of room and an awesome pool. The day we finally moved, Max and I were the last two from our family at the house. The new owner was poking around downstairs, and I was running around checking things out for a half-hour or so. When it was finally time to drive away for the last time, I realized I hadn't seen Max for that half-hour. I walked around looking for him.

I found him upstairs in his empty bedroom, lying spread-eagle in the middle of the floor, his eyes a little moist from emotion. I lay down next to him and asked him what he was doing. He was silent for a bit, then he whispered, "I was just talking to my room, telling it how much I liked it."

Max and I talked about the strong emotion he was feeling over leaving our house. But he just didn't have the words to describe it. He's a very sensitive kid, and he feels strongly. But other than saying he was "sad" because we were leaving this house, he couldn't identify the details of what was going on in his heart—he only knew it was there and it was strong. It even frustrated him that he didn't know how to explain it better.

With the cognitive development we wrote about in the last chapter, and the acquisition of a new, tiny, abstract-thinking "muscle," the options for *experiencing, understanding,* and *articulating* emotions expands dramatically.

Imagine that preteen painter with her little limited color palette. Then, without her actually realizing it, someone takes that color palette away and replaces it with a significantly larger palette, one that's preloaded with a huge assortment of colors. New colors, new shades, new combinations.

And she starts painting.

But she has no prior experience applying these new color options to the canvas of life. So for a while, her painting is extra bold or extra muddled. She's creating art with patches of bright primary colors in one area of the canvas and subtle, nuanced shades in another. The combination is not attractive, and sometimes it's even jarring. But this experimentation is necessary to get her to a place where she can effectively *experience, understand,* and *articulate* these new emotion-color options.

Here's another metaphor.

I (Marko) am *not* what anyone would consider a handyman. Other than replacing light bulbs and hanging pictures, I'm fairly useless when it comes to home maintenance or fixing things. And for years, the only tools I had were old hand-me-downs from my dad and grandpa: A few assorted screwdrivers, a couple of hammers, and a few other tools for which I could only guess a purpose.

But a few years ago, my wife and kids bought me a new toolbox for Christmas. It's a cool plastic jobby with trays and little compartments that open together to reveal neat little storage areas for various hardware bits. It came with, and I subsequently procured, a wad of new tools: Different kinds of wrenches and grips, drill bits and fasteners, strippers and pokey-things. I like my toolbox. I'm even proud of it—its presence on my workbench in the garage makes me feel a bit manlier.

But I still don't really know how to use much of the stuff in the box. I'm no more "handy" than I was before receiving my "now you're a real man" toolbox.

For young teens, it's as if they've strapped on a massive tool belt, one that would make a contractor proud. They're walking around with all these tools at their fingertips. They like wearing it. They like having the tools there. They even pull them out from time to time and show them off or play "Bob the Builder" with them. But they don't really know what all the tools are or how to use them. They don't *understand* them. And they're likely to try hammering a nail into the wall with a wrench, or poking a new hole in a leather belt with a Phillips screwdriver.[53]

EMOTIONAL WHIPLASH

Of course you know what whiplash is—that painful neck condition brought on by a sudden and dramatic stopping or starting, usually in a car. And, of course, we use *whiplash* as a nontechnical, metaphorical word in lots of other ways (for anything that brings with it a sudden, unexpected change).

With that framing, there's almost no better metaphor for young teen emotions than whiplash. It's not that every kid experiences every emotion suddenly and without warning. But this emotional whiplash is a common experience in the young teen years. And, unless they have an emotional disorder that brought on this kind of rapid emotional change during childhood, it's a new and not-very-welcome encounter with their feelings.

Just as with physical whiplash, emotional whiplash can leave kids with pain and a bit of disorientation. Because their abstract thinking is new and underdeveloped (and because, as we note in the last chapter, their underdeveloped temporal lobes leave them a bit short on emotional interpretation), they have very limited knowledge of how to understand or control these feelings. It's very common for young teens to feel blindsided, or even betrayed, by their emotional experiences.

It's essential that we understand this if we want to be effective in ministry with and for middle schoolers. It's essential that we understand this if we care about them at all.

Parallel, in a sense, to the reality that their lack of cognitive ability shouldn't cause us to assume they're *incapable* of making good choices, prioritization, or speculation, we do them a disservice if we assume that their whiplashy emotional experience is just something to be tolerated in a fatalistic way. Instead, it becomes part of our mission to walk with them through these emotional blindsides, acting as emotional tour guides and emotional language tutors.

FEAR OF THE UNKNOWN

As with so many of the changes going on in the lives of middle schoolers, emotional change brings with it great opportunity and possibility, as well as fear. We all have a tendency toward fear when we're enmeshed in an experience of the unknown. Depending on individual personality, this can sometimes be a positive fear (such as the person who loves the fear associated with bungee jumping), or it can merely bring abject terror (a different person bungee jumping).

Most middle schoolers will tell you, in moments of honesty, that they don't understand why they're feeling such emotional intensity at times, or why particular emotions snuck up on them so fast or lingered so inexplicably long. They just don't have the experience or language to interpret this stuff.

Think about something that causes you fear or has caused you fear in the past.

We pause for a moment here, for a semi-related story of young teens trying to put words to their fear. While working on DCLA, the large student training event, my (Marko) friend John was preparing several student presenters who'd be co-leading a room full of middle schoolers in understanding evangelism. For this exercise they were to ask all the middle schoolers in the room to identify any fears they had in relation to talking about faith with a friend. And the student presenters were supposed to seed this discussion by sharing their own fears. John asked his student presenters to talk about this in their prep time. Realize, these were 8th-grade student leaders—kids who were chosen for this role because of their maturity (in every way).

Two of John's student presenters "got it" immediately and shared things such as the fear of rejection or not knowing what to say. Then it was Bassam's turn to share. He simply said, "Bees."

Surprised, John said, "What?"

Bassam repeated his answer, "Bees. I'm afraid of bees."

John said, "Um, these are supposed to be fears about sharing our faith."

Bassam said, "Yeah, I know; but I really am afraid of bees."

Classic.

Now, back to your fear. Psychologists tell us that the root of fear is the unknown. When we don't know what will happen, or we can picture a negative outcome, we may experience fear.

Therefore, we experience fear when we wonder if ending a relationship might bring pain. We experience fear when we stand at an ATM in the dark, wondering if we might get mugged. We experience fear when we're unsure what the outcomes of a particular choice might be, especially if some of those outcomes are perceived as negative.

But when we gain understanding of the unknown, or we move past the potential of negative outcomes, the fear dissipates.

Most adults don't experience fear *because of* our emotions (unless we're afraid of what our emotions might lead us to do). But remember, young teens are seriously impeded in their ability to project outcomes. This can bring *less* fear at times (when standing at that same ATM in the dark, they might not think of potentially negative outcomes); but it can also bring a greatly heightened, although unarticulated, experience of fear.

Here's Normalization, Again

We realize we're starting to sound like a broken record on this normalization thing. But the reality we've observed is that helping middle schoolers normalize their experience is counterintuitive to most of us. It's our own "tiny muscle" that needs exercise and lots of use before it becomes part of our ministry norm. We have to choose, over and over again, to be *conscious* of normalizing before we'll be good at it in a more *subconscious* or *unconscious* way.

So how do we normalize emotional experience? We wrote about this a little bit in chapter 2, where I (Marko) shared the story about the conversation I had with my daughter, Liesl, regarding her emotional outbursts. But let's review a bit here.

Normalizing, when it comes to middle school emotions, starts with acknowledging emotions in healthy ways. The two unhealthy ends of the spectrum (which all parents of middle schoolers are well familiar with from their own challenging experiences with their kids) are—

- *Acknowledging emotions, but in a diminishing way.* Because we have more experience with emotions and we understand them more fully, it's easy for us to see that a particular strong display of emotion (positive or negative) is often way out of proportion to the experience generating it. And often our knee-jerk reaction is to tell them they're overreacting, or they're being ridiculous or they're being immature.[54] (Remember, maturity is behavior that's appropriate to development and age—so a young teen's emotional outbursts are actually mature.)

- *Ignoring emotions, especially extreme or unpleasant ones.* Since we know, or assume, the emotion isn't warranted—at least from our adult perspective—we're quick to dismiss it by ignoring it. While this approach isn't ultimately all that helpful, it's understandable, since we've seen how these extreme emotions often pass so quickly.

Unfortunately, neither of these extremes is connected to a "come alongside" approach. If we envision our roles as emotional tour guides and emotional language tutors, then our response shifts to a more helpful place. This requires us to live with a challenging engaged-but-disengaged tension. We want to be fully engaged with middle schoolers in the midst of their emotions, even joining empathetically *in* their emotions. But at the same time, we need to remind ourselves that "this is not about me." Their emotions can quickly affect *our own* emotions, which is fine and good when we're aware of it. But it's not helpful when we react against them or become a peer.

The acknowledgment of emotions that we need starts with a calm response, something along the lines of "You're feeling pretty strongly about that, aren't you?" Often, it can be helpful to acknowledge through a question. "Hey, you seem pretty down. What are you feeling?" "What are you feeling that's making you so happy today?" Try to ask questions that get them to describe the feeling more, not just the external factors producing the feeling. (This is key, and it takes some practice.)

When young teens are willing to let you in a little (or a lot) on what they're feeling, it's great to make comments such as, "I've felt like that before," as long as that's a truthful statement.

Slip emotional acknowledgment into conversations and small group discussion and teaching times by saying things such as, "That might cause you to totally freak out!" or "You've probably felt like this before." Pepper your conversations and teaching with this kind of generalized emotional acknowledgment.

And, of course, when appropriate, it's wonderful to *enter into* an emotion with a middle schooler. If she's mourning, even if it's a situation where her emotional response seems out of proportion to the incident, then mourn with her. If he's uncommonly happy and chatty, then match that emotion and go with the flow. This will be a very different experience than kids usually have, as they're quickly growing used to adults responding to their emotions in one of those two extremes we wrote about a few paragraphs back.

Talk about this emotional development stuff, head on. Make it a teaching topic or a small group discussion. Approach it the same way you might approach a conversation about physical change or sexual development—with sensitivity and frankness.

Actually, we like to take the normalization of emotions a step beyond, well, normal. We like to take it to "good." So often, normalization can come off as "grin and bear it" or as suggesting that this is an unfortunate phase of life that you can only hope to emerge from. Instead, we want our normalization attempts to point kids to Jesus, to the Creator God who loves them so much that he wants them to fully experience life (John 10:10). We want them to see that this crazy emotional roller coaster they're experiencing is all part of God's loving plan to give them a rich and meaningful life that's full of great emotion. Really, how terrible would life be without emotion?

Controlling Versus Understanding

Just a short rant here.

We've often heard people say that kids need to learn to "control their emotions." Of course, there's a sense where this is true, and it will come, in time. But what we've observed is that the call for helping teenagers control their emotions very rarely comes from a place of caring about those teenagers. It's usually about the inconvenience of teenage emotions on the adults who are voicing this desire for "control." *And*, if we can push this a bit, it often comes from adults who have somewhat lost the ability to really be present in the midst of their own emotions. They equate their ability to stuff emotions with controlling emotions, and they assume that everyone else should do the same.

If we think back to Stephen Glenn's model of sampling, testing, and concluding (in chapter 2), we remember that the young teen years are all about sampling. Testing and concluding will come, eventually. No reason to rush into them.

So we should be more interested in helping young teens *understand* their emotions than helping them control them. Remember, thinking about emotions is a new thing for them, and it's really hard work.

And when we consider that "hard wiring" thing in regard to neuron winnowing (in chapter 4), we'd much rather spend our energy helping their brains develop the ability and practice of understanding, than the ability and practice of control.

In our opinion, control is overrated. And without understanding, control is wrongly fueled.

Rant over.

Differences Between Boys and Girls

Most of these developmental areas we're talking about indicate differences between guys and girls (as was clear in the "Physical and Sexual Development" chapter). Some of the "mechanics" are the same for both genders in various realms of developmental change; but how they play out is often subtly or massively different for both physiological and cultural reasons.

We've seen some research that seems to say that emotional development has some physiological reasons for gender difference.[55] But there's still a lot of work to be done in this area. Certainly, we know that boys are 18 to 24 months behind in lots of developmental changes, including the brain functions that allow for, regulate, and interpret emotions.

But there also seem to be some strong cultural factors at play here. In Western cultures (especially in the United States), girls are taught from a young age to externalize their emotions, and boys are taught to internalize their emotions.

Group pressure, media, parental influence, sibling influence, and lots of other stuff conspire (consciously or not) to tell guys it's not manly to cry or be emotionally expressive. It seems we tell our guys that anger is the only strong emotion that's acceptable to express. So boys quickly learn that they're expected to stuff their emotions, not express them.

There's lots of fear attached to this for middle school guys. Not wanting to run counter to any of these developmental norms, guys who feel strongly find ways to mask those emotions. In fact, some talk about "the guy code" that's all about an "I'm fine" attitude.

Girls, on the other hand, are told to see their emotional expression as a means to an end. Externalized emotions often get "used" as a way of getting friends or keeping the ones they have. In a bit of a catch-22 risk, girls observe that strongly emotive girls are either wildly popular, or seen as freaks. It's a tough choice they have to make, and you can literally watch as middle school girls test their hypotheses about this. When girls shrink away from their emotions, it's often because they don't believe they have what it takes to use emotional expression as a means to a positive end. (In other words, it's often the result of a lower self-image.) Girls who *do* express their emotions are either confident in the result that this expression will bring, or they're merely rolling the dice that it will bring a desired result. (In some cases, especially for younger girls, they're merely clueless about how others perceive them.)

Do you see how this all connects with the abstract-thinking ability of perceiving how others see us? Middle schoolers aren't very good at this third-person perspective, so they (both boys and girls) often miscalculate the expected response from others. In the midst of a response that's different than what we *adults* would hope for, we usually change gears and regulate our emotions. But kids are not only underdeveloped at "guessing" how their emotions will be received by others, but they're also pretty weak at gauging real-time responses. So in the midst of a response that's different than what they expected or hoped for, they'll often "turn it up to 11" with the notion that more is better.

We'll talk more about this in the chapter on relational changes (chapter 7), but it's also important to realize that girls' friendships are formed with a high expectation of intimacy and self-revelation. Emotions, and emotional expression, are 100 percent essential to these expectations. As a result, expressing emotions in the context of friendships—or potential friendships—becomes a subconscious "tool" (we don't necessarily mean that in a negative way) that girls wield as relational glue. Boys, on the other hand, well, not so much.

Deeper Issues

We've written about all these emotional issues at a very popular level, as they pertain to the in-the-trenches middle school youth worker working with average kids. But emotions are tricky things to generalize. As soon as we make one generalization or characterization, it's easy for you to find an exception.

Here's what you need to hear from us about exceptions: Not only *are* there exceptions, but good youth workers *look for* exceptions.

In this case—emotional development and expression—an exception falls into one of many possibilities. But in general, a kid who shows outside-the-norm emotions—either too much or too little—may be tipping his hand to the fact that there are other serious issues that need to be addressed. Therapists call this a "presenting issue." These are the face-value issues we see; but they're often only an outer onion skin to deeper issues that have very little to do with the presenting issue.

Also, even "normal distribution kids" (when it comes to emotional expression) can have much deeper issues that need to be explored and may need to be dealt with by someone other than you. This is another reason for middle school youth workers to engage with young teens in the whats and whys of their emotions.

We can't make that potentially harmful assumption that their moodiness or low-grade depression or even super-happiness is merely the stuff of early adolescence. Emotions are clues to us, and they point us toward deeper conversations that may reveal abuse, clinical depression, or difficult life circumstances.

It's always wise for youth workers to have a professional "go to"—a therapist or psychologist with whom they can have a chat about a particular kid. Most of us (the two of us included) aren't trained to deal with serious issues. We can't assume that our empathy and compassion will be enough for young teens with serious emotional issues. Ask for advice and know when to refer.

Tom and Joanne, two caring and

CHAPTER 6

Best Friends Forever!
(Relational Change)

engaged parents, sat in my office (Marko here). With them was Christopher, their 7th-grade son. "Topher," as he'd recently asked his friends to call him, was slouching in his chair, arms crossed, with a look on his face that radiated, "I'd rather be anywhere than here" behind a thinly veiled attempt at looking bored.

Joanne started talking. "I'm very concerned about our Christopher."

"Topher," Christopher mumbled.

Joanne ignored this and continued, "We're not even sure who he *is* anymore. It seems like just yesterday he was this sweet kid who wanted to be around us and loved family time. He was help-ful around the house. And he was consistently happy."

Topher rolled his eyes.

"But he's so withdrawn now. And the thing that really scares us is that he seems so committed to swapping out all his good friends for new ones—and these new 'friends' aren't the kind of kids we want him hanging around. They're not a good influence on Christopher." (She actually made air quotes with her fingers on the word *friends*.)

"Who says they're not a good influence, Mom?" Topher shot back. "You don't know them. You just want me to hang around that loser, Sean!"

"Honey," Joanne turned to her son, "Sean is not a loser. He's been your best friend since kindergarten. You've played together for *years*. And he still wants to be your friend. But you're *so mean* to him now. It just breaks my heart."

"Mom, Sean was fine as a friend when we were little kids. But *everyone* knows he's a loser now. And if I hang around with him, everyone will think I'm a loser, too!"

Obviously, there were lots of issues swirling around this little exchange. Christopher was wrestling with new emotions he didn't have words for; he was struggling to gain some new indepen-dence from his parents, and they were struggling with how much independence to give him. (More on that in the next chapter.) But Christopher was also articulating the relational shift that occurs in the lives of young teens.

Like the other shifts happening in their lives, this relational shift is often fraught with confusion and fear, with desperation and failure, with experimentation and discovery.

Christopher was explaining, in the words of a young teen,

that the reasons one chooses a friend in childhood don't often hold up in the world of early adolescence.

Proximity Versus Affinity

Like many of the changes going on in the lives of middle schoolers, these relational changes are directly tied to cognitive development. As their brains begin giving them peeks into abstract thinking, young teens begin exercising a different set of criteria for friendship selection, a set of criteria that's much more adult in nature.

To oversimplify: Childhood friendships are normally formed around proximity. Children choose friendships based on those they're near most often. Of course, this is a generalization and other factors play in. But because children are less differentiated and don't possess an external perception of themselves (at least not an articulated third-person perception), they're often fine forming friendships with a neighbor or someone they spend a lot of time with (like the child of a family friend), even though they may have extremely differing personalities and interests as they grow up.

Put five seven-year-olds in a room with a pile of Legos, and they'll usually find a way to play together just fine. Their interests are less diversified. And their sense of self is rather unarticulated.

But put those same five kids in a room together five years later, as 12-year-olds, and the situation is very different. They "dance" around each other, trying to find alliances and political influences. It's suddenly a game of *Survivor* with all the drama and second-guessing and questions of "Who can I trust?"

Instead of proximity, middle schoolers begin to form friendships based on affinity.[56] They want to form friendships with those who share their interests. Of course, this is a big challenge, since they rarely have a clear sense of their own identity and what their interests actually are—they just have a sense of what they'd *like* their interests to be.

Christopher, in our example at the beginning of this chapter, was talking, quite clearly, about this shift. He might be fine hanging out with Sean if he knew no one would ever know. But his perception that others consider Sean a loser carries such enormous weight in Christopher's own attempt to define himself that he can't risk being defined by his affiliation with Sean. Sean would drag him down and relegate him to loser status.

This shift often brings a literal change in friendships during the young teen years—jettisoning formerly meaningful childhood friendships, while reaching out for new, and often tenuous, attempts at friendship. Of course, there are kids who maintain childhood friendships throughout their teen years; but it's very normal for those childhood relationships to simply be unsustainable in adolescence.

Multiple Affinity Groups

While young teens are wrestling with what it means to form friendships around affinity, they often dabble in multiple affinities. This is all a part of that discovery mode we've mentioned several times. They're very unclear about who they are, and, as a result, they find it very challenging to align with any particular affinity group.

My (Marko) daughter, Liesl, now 15, seems to have three different personalities. When she's with her school friends, she adopts a particular set of values, language, preferences, and behaviors. When she's with her small group from our church, she adapts and embodies a slightly different set of values, language, preferences, and behaviors. And when she's with just our family, there's a third set of values, language, preferences, and behaviors.

As a high school freshman, Liesl's three sets of "norms" are already less differentiated from each other than when she was 12, as she's becoming more comfortable with who she is.

It's the wrong question to ask which of these is "the real Liesl." Were she an adult, we'd correctly assume that one is real and the others are not (or that they're all a mask and the real Liesl is something still other). But this isn't the case with young teens. *Those three manifestations are all Liesl.* She's trying them all on, like different wardrobes, in an attempt to discover more about herself.

It's very normal to find young teens playing with multiple affinities and switching styles and personalities along the way. One week a boy will clearly want to be perceived as a skateboard dude, with the accompanying clothing, music preferences, language, and attitudes. A month later, this seems to have been shelved and an attempt is being made to be *uber* soccer guy. Or the proto-emo. Or sensitive artsy guy. Or chick magnet. Or wannabe gangster hip-hop brutha. Keeping up with these shifts can be exhausting.

And when, from our adult perspective, we see the short-lived, not-fully-embraced nature of these passing affinities, it's easy to dismiss them. But a dismissive attitude isn't any more helpful than fully assuming these outward manifestations are the whole story and the real kid. We need to affirm their quests, while also looking through and beyond the externals to the real kid behind the often temporary multiple affinities.

The Role of Self-Perception

We've hinted at this a bit already, but it bears fleshing out a bit more: A big reason for these relational changes is the new influence of self-perception.

As we wrote in earlier chapters, it would be wrong to say that identity *begins* forming in early adolescence. Identity is being formed from Day One of life, and childhood relationships, roles, expectations, observations, and media intake play a gargantuan role in forming aspects of our identity. But the shift that occurs with the onset of abstract thinking is enormous: It's the first time in life that we have the ability to think about our own identity formation. It's the first time we can really say, "This is the kind of person I want to be, and these choices will move me in that direction."

In other words, puberty brings with it the abstract-thinking skill of self-perception. A preteen's ideas about how others perceive her can be based only on observation (how others treat her, what others say about her). But an abstract thinker can now perceive herself *from* another person's perspective.

Let's be clear about this because it's an important difference:

Nine-year-old Tammy might have a sense of what her friend Jenna thinks about her. But this perception is solely based on external indicators, such as—

- Jenna's desire to spend time with Tammy, both face- to-face and in the virtual world

- Jenna's willingness to share secrets with Tammy

- Jenna's comments that Tammy is fun, pretty, and more adventurous than Jenna is

Now compare that to 14-year-old Tammy's experience. She now has the ability to exercise an empathetic perspective. She can place herself in Jenna's shoes, so to speak, and think about what life is like for Jenna (who Tammy perceives to be a great friend, but a bit quiet and reserved). And Tammy can ruminate on thoughts, such as—

- *Since Jenna is quiet, she probably wishes she were more outgoing like I am.*

- *Since Jenna is less adventurous than I am, I'm the leader in our friendship.*

- *Jenna really likes to IM and text a lot. This is probably because I'm one of her only friends. I can choose to abuse that or manipulate her, or I can honor that special place and protect Jenna.*

Tammy might not be quite as mentally articulate as we've described here; however, loosely formed third-person thoughts about herself, from her friend's perspective, become a shaping force in Tammy's identity formation and self-image.

And, to take it one step further, young teens start to subconsciously understand that they can influence others' perceptions of them and—in essence—change or direct who they are. In fact, this growing realization can either be energizing or shattering. Tammy might find great confidence in realizing that she has a real responsibility in how Jenna perceives her. Or this new awareness can bring a sense of helplessness if she begins to believe she *should* be able to influence others' perceptions of her but can't influence those perceptions in the direction she desires.

Remember, this abstract-thinking ability is new, and it's weak. Kids jump in and out of abstract thinking for years. So the reality is that Tammy will continue to rely on her nine-year-old indicators while she's starting to develop some of these self-perception abilities.

And in many ways, this is a lifelong struggle for most of us. We vacillate between a self-perception based on external input from others, and a self-perception based on what we know about ourselves or who we desire to become.

Of course, with these new self-perception framing abilities, it's super-important that we middle school youth workers talk about identity issues all the time. Constantly ground your discussions about who young teens are and who they're becoming in creation (rather than the fall). Remind them of who God made them to be and that their identities should ultimately be informed and formed in the context of God's perfect love for them. Help them see themselves as part of a community that needs them. Remind them that God didn't mess up when he made them.

WHY I DO THIS

When I was a teenager, my parents were the church bus drivers. Not *one* of the bus drivers, mind you; they were *the* bus drivers. That meant they came along for the ride on every church function where the bus was required. Let's just say that from my teenage perspective, that was not a good thing.

I decided to go into youth ministry because I grew up a church brat who found a vibrant faith in high school as a result of adults who invested in my life. As a 17-year-old kid, I knew I wanted to go into vocational youth ministry. I really wanted to change hearts, and my focused passion was for church brats who were going through the Christian motions. My desire was to help students find a faith they could call their own. However, I also knew that when I eventually was given a ministry to oversee, I was convinced I wouldn't have the parents involved. As far as I was concerned, parents weren't helpful; they were part of the problem.

My real zeal for young teen ministry came after working with them for a few years. I loved their honesty, their quest for life, and their mode of discovery.

As for parents and ministry, somewhere along the way I decided that parents weren't the enemy but a great resource. After that, parents were involved in the ministry I led in a variety of contexts.

Today, I still love the same things about middle school students that I loved 18 years ago; and I still get a thrill over watching them discover what it really means to be an apprentice of Jesus. Yet, the older I get—and now that I have middle school kids of my own—my heart is changing. And the spark of passion I've begun to experience for parents has slowly grown into a small fire.

I no longer see parents as the enemy or even as a resource, but rather as a partner. I love middle school ministry today because of the kids, yes, but also because of the parents.

Ministry to middle school students will continue to expand and become more successful over the long haul if we're investing in the adult leaders who will be with these kids for a lifetime: Their parents.

Alan Mercer is the pastor of Middle School Ministries at Christ Community Church in Leawood, Kansas.

Girls' Friendships

Fairly significant gender differences seem to emerge in early adolescence concerning how friendships are formed. Some of this is physiological, or rooted in gender differences regarding how women and men connect with others; but lots of it is rooted in cultural expectations for how girls and guys are supposed to act.[57]

For instance, young teen girl friendships are deeply connected to girls' desire for intimacy. As a result, girls' friendships require a high level of intimacy, commitment, perceived trust, and transparency. Middle school girls often form friendships *based on* shared intimate or transparent shared experiences.[58] This is (duh!) not the case with guys.

So middle school girls tend to form intense, highly vulnerable, and intimate friendships, bonding deeply and strongly and quickly. And, we've observed, middle school girls tend to have these intimate friendships with one or two other girls (forming a friendship group of two or three girls). Girls *love* having BFFs— "best friends forever!"

But a friendship group of four or more middle school girls usually can't sustain its own emotional weight. Gossip and insecurity are enormous factors. And since they're in a discovery phase of life, young teen girls are playing with their identities and these intense friendships are often short-lived and transitory. A friendship group of four middle school girls will usually split into two groups of two or a group of three (where the fourth girl moves on to another friendship group or is forced out).

So it would be fair to say that middle school girls form small, intense friendship groups with high expectations of exclusivity, intimacy, and commitment; but these friendships are often temporary. This isn't true with all girls, of course. Some form friendship bonds with another girl or two that last throughout early adolescence (and, occasionally, into the older teen years). But some ebb and flow in this transitory landscape of friendships is normal.

It's important for us (and especially for female middle school youth workers) to help young teen girls understand the value of friendships that aren't temporary or dependent on developmental changes. But of course this means helping them understand the skills required to stick with a friendship through the challenges that are natural to all friendships: Disagreements and fights, perceived or real betrayal, changing interests, and the place of other friends (which are usually perceived as competition).

Guys' Friendships

Middle school guys' friendships are very different from the relationships of their female counterparts. Part of the reason for this is physiological. As previously noted, guys tend to be a good 18 to 24 months behind girls in pubertal development. This means they're behind in the development of their abstract thinking, which means their self-perception and ability to speculate on third-person perception is also lagging behind the girls'.

But the larger reason for this difference in how guys form friendships is connected to our cultural expectations about what it means to be a guy. Guys learn to internalize their emotions (whereas girls often live with their emotions on their sleeves) and wear the mask of "the guy code" that says, "It's cool; I'm fine."[59]

In the United States and the U.K., particularly where we have a marked low-trust culture and a high expectation of individual rights and personal autonomy, guys grow up in a substantially more isolated world than many girls do.[60]

We've observed that middle school guys tend to fall into one of two extremes when it comes to friendships. The first is what we like to call "the wolf pack." This is a large-ish affinity group of guys—four to eight in size, usually—that forms around external affinities, rather than personal sharing and intimacy. And along with that organizing force there may come a whole raft of language, clothing, values, music, behaviors, attitudes, interaction styles, and boundaries.

We're the guys who are into skateboarding.

We're the guys who are bored and brooding.

We're the guys who are consumed by gaming.

We're the guys who are into soccer above all other things.

We're the guys who are proto-emos.

We're the guys who are still into Legos and Awana.

These affinity groups—wolf packs—often define everything for boys. Remember, as we wrote earlier in this chapter, they may not stay in the same affinity group for their entire early adolescent experience. And they're sometimes dabbling in multiple groups at the same time (although, usually only one group in a setting: School, church, sports).

There's a synergy that happens in these groups, and they're often collectively single-minded, destroying everything in their path as they amoeba toward a goal of conformity.

The other extreme that we see in so many middle school guys is the loner. This is the young teen guy who really doesn't have any significant friendships. Our observation is that this "classification" is increasing: More and more middle school guys have no real friendships. They may have a guy or two whom they consider a friend, a guy they occasionally game with, or a guy they went paint-balling with once (and both of them now perceive that they go paint-balling with each other all the time). But they live in a relationally isolated world, masking their feelings and hiding their interests in the fear of being shunned.

We're convinced that good middle school ministries need to be intentional about helping guys form meaningful friendships. This needs to be done in partnership with parents, by the way, by exposing parents to these issues, encouraging a proactive stance, and providing opportunities for friendships to form. We need to talk about the attitudes and skills of a friend. And since guys usually form friendships by *doing things together* (rather than by sharing things about themselves), we need to provide opportunities for this shared experience that fosters friendships. We need to encourage potential friendships, fertilizing the relational and emotional ground that's often untended.

Here's a startling fact: Teenage girls, on average, use approximately 20,000 words a day.[61] They connect by talking, form relationships through verbal interaction, and process their feelings by talking about them. Adolescent guys, on the other hand, use approximately 3,000 words a day.

Simply put: Girls form friendships by talking; guys form friendships by doing. While we shouldn't play into these norms blindly, and we should still provide opportunities for guys to use words and learn to express themselves, we also need to be aware of the natural inclinations that exist in their worlds.

CHAPTER 7

I Can Do It, Just Don't Leave Me

(Independence)

Long ago, I (Marko) discovered that middle schoolers believe hotels are extremely cool. It doesn't have to be a fancy hotel—any roadside roach bomb will do. And many of the more family-friendly national chains have a "kids under 18 stay free!" policy (which certainly wasn't created with youth workers in mind, but, ya know, it's a nice loophole).

For many years I utilized the occasional hotel for a middle school ministry trip or event. (For instance, when en route to a mission trip or staying in town with a group of boys for an all-night video game fest.) When I did, I created a couple of guidelines for myself and for the ministry volunteers: Adult leaders couldn't share a bed with a kid (either the leader could sleep on the floor or the kids could), and we always had one leader for every two rooms of kids (with an open adjoining door between them).

But then I had an out-of-town event with too many kids for the number of leaders I had. There was no way to enforce my "one leader for every two rooms" rule (which usually amounted to about a 1:7 ratio). So my team and I came up with a new hotel security measure that allowed middle schoolers to stay unchaperoned in a hotel room. The security measure: Cellophane tape.

The kids were stoked about staying in this hotel and having a bit of freedom and independence. When it came time to herd them into their rooms for the night, we explained the limits of their freedom: They were in charge of themselves for the night, but we'd be accessible if they needed us. They could choose their own bedtime and decide when to get up. (We'd give all the rooms a wake-up call at some point.) They could order pizza if they wanted, but it had to be delivered to their room by midnight.

Because...

We told them we were going to place a small piece of cellophane tape between their room door and the doorframe at midnight. This little piece of tape—we assured them—would not "seal them in." If there were an emergency, their doors would open as easily as if the tape weren't there. But when the adults made a few rounds during the night and a final check at 6 a.m., we'd know if they'd opened their door for any reason at all. And for any door we found where the tape wasn't in place, all the occupants would have to sit out for two hours at the beginning of the next day—at a water park.

Of course, the response was the same as if we'd said we were going to shackle each of them with leather straps and straightjackets. They cried about how *unfair* this was, about how we didn't trust them.

Our response: "We *do* trust you, within the boundaries of your hotel room.[62] And we want to remove the temptation to try something stupid outside of your rooms, which would create problems for all of us."

The first time we tried this experiment, a few kids "checked" to see if the tape was there. This was a hard lesson, as they quickly learned there was no way to reapply the tape from the inside. In subsequent years, we never had any doors opened, and the groaning morphed into a happy acceptance of this boundary. With big smiles they'd ask, "Are you going to tape us into our rooms again?"

This example is both a literal illustration and a metaphor. It's a literal illustration of how to give kids both freedom and boundaries. It's also a metaphor of the tension that exists between the independence young teens *want* and the boundaries they *need*. The "boundaries," in this case, are the metaphorical walls of the hotel room and, more specifically, the little piece of tape that carries an inordinate amount of metaphorical freight.

The Point of Adolescence

Entire books could be, and have been, written about the point of adolescence. Since adolescence is a fairly recent cultural phenomenon and has since morphed dramatically in length and content, trying to say, "This is what it's about" is a tricky proposition.

In a simple sense, adolescence is the culturally approved pause button between the carefree life of a child and the responsibilities of adulthood. Marko wrote about this at more length in his book *Youth Ministry 3.0*.[63] But for our purposes here, let's look at it this way:

Carefree life of a child = Dependence

Responsibilities of adulthood = Independence

Adolescence is the space between those two states, and it lasts for however long the culture approves. To that end—while it's a little simplistic—the transition from dependence to independence is the whole point of adolescence. And since it's a transitional period, there should be a mix of both states.

If we look at adolescence as a line graph, with puberty on one end and emerging adulthood on the other, we could see the shifting mixture of dependence and independence along the way. In other words, the young teen years *do have* and *should have* more dependence (and less independence) than the older teen years.

Whatever the mixture (more on this in a bit), the reality is that young teens want more independence. This, once again, is directly tied to their cognitive abilities, as well as cultural factors.

First, their expanding sense of self (as described in the last chapter) provides the opportunity to see a direct connection between their choices and their identity—who they are and who they're becoming. They begin to see how they play a role in shaping themselves, that they have a choice in who they are and who they're perceived to be.

Second, they start to wrestle with a distinctly adolescent task: Autonomy.[64] The task of autonomy is about asking—and answering—these questions:

- How am I unique from others?

- What's the extent of my power to influence myself, others, and my world?

Struggling with these questions *requires* some amount of abstract thinking. There's really no way to think about one's uniqueness or the extent of one's power without some ability to exercise third-person perception.

Psychologists talk about the process of individuation.[65] This is a ten-dollar word for the process of becoming one's own self, and it includes self-knowledge and a somewhat functional understanding of autonomy.

We've heard it said that the goal of parenting teenagers is to help them become functionally independent. While we're sure there are other supplemental goals, this does seem to make some sense.

I (Marko) remember talking to a dad I deeply respected. I'd been so impressed with his kids, who were in high school at the time. I knew his daughter the best, who was then about 16 or 17 years old. So I was surprised when her dad said, "Really, my job is pretty much done. Of course I need to stay involved and continue to love her; but my years of influence, if I've done my job well as a parent, are mostly over."

This was reorienting for me in many ways. Not being a parent of a teenager myself back then (*now* I am!), I'd perceived parents exerting a large influence on their kids throughout adolescence. But if we're right about that changing mixture of dependence and independence (with puberty on one end and emerging adulthood on the other), then the latter end would be *mostly* independent.

Of course, this also means that the end of that continuum nearest to childhood should have *large portions* of dependence, even if middle schoolers don't appear to want it.

What Do They Really Want?

Young teens *need* boundaries. Yes, young teens want freedom, and there's a massive tension here. (Just imagine Mel Gibson's character from *Braveheart* shouting, "FREEDOM!") But the reality is, they believe they want more freedom than is actually healthy for them.

Young teens with too much freedom (read: too much independence) often flounder because they don't yet have the ability or perspective to make good choices with unlimited options.

WHY I DO THIS

Last week I went to a camp and shared a message with the middle school students who were attending. After the service, I sat at lunch with a few of them: Annie, Beth, Ben, and Dalton. (We were having a delightful and balanced meal of tots, pudding, and pizza bagels.) They were eager to get to know me, and the minutes that followed solidified my reasons for loving this age group.

Their conversations were like many that I hear every week as a middle school youth pastor: Full of drama, non-filtered, unashamed, and deeply believing each other's perceptions and exaggerations. As I listened to camp stories of staying up late and midnight pranks, I heard an honesty that an older crowd might hide in coolness.

I saw eyes lit with imagination that hasn't been hindered—yet—by the crowd. They commit the smallest details to memory and believe it's not a burden to share every detail with people they've just met. I love how they can hear you speak one time, hear a song, meet you once, receive a hug, or see you at school—and be able to say without an ounce of fakeness that they love you.

I love middle school people because they aren't afraid to freak out, cry, snot on your shoulder, or give you funny gifts that others might be ashamed of. I'll never forget the year I turned 26 and received 26 straws, 26 cookies, 26 pennies, 26 spit wads, and 26 packets of ketchup.

Middle school girls love you with their eyes and say it with their actions—always there, always listening (well, most of the time), and loyal as ever. Middle school guys are amazing because they aren't too cool to "oooh and ahhh" over babies, and they aren't afraid to laugh at themselves when they trip trying to clear a chair jump.

Sitting with middle school students makes me realize how great I've got it. Watching 6th graders walk into our program in the fall reminds me that teenagers are still moldable, they're listening, and they're watching. Seeing them grow faster than you can say "8th-grade graduation" reminds me of the short amount of time we have to listen, be there for, and make a difference in the lives of our students.

I love being a youth pastor, and being around middle school students makes the call that much sweeter.

Brooklyn Lindsey is the middle school pastor at Highland Park Church of the Nazarene in Lakeland, Florida, and the author of Confessions of a Not-So-Supermodel.

Remember, their abstract-thinking ability is very new and wimpy. And their frontal lobes—the decision center of the brain (see the end of chapter 4)—are still very underdeveloped. Limiting their options greatly increases their ability to exercise wisdom.

Think of it this way: If you put a puppy in an enclosed yard, it has the opportunity to experience a sense of freedom. There's plenty of room to explore, plenty of opportunity to go this way or that way, to run or walk or lie down, to bark or be silent. But place that same puppy in the middle of a massive open park, and the puppy will lack any kind of reference points for choosing where to go. It might end up running in circles and chasing its own tail; or it very well might run off and get completely lost, having no sense of the ramifications of running nonstop in any particular direction.

It's only with *well*-defined boundaries that middle schoolers are able to effectively exercise some sense of independence. A lack of boundaries creates confusion, fear, and danger.

Young teens *want* boundaries. This might seem counterintuitive. And you'd be hard-pressed to find a young teen who could articulate, "Please, give me more well-defined boundaries." But, ultimately, middle schoolers are more content and confident when they understand the extent of their control. And because they haven't worked out that autonomy task yet, their understanding of their ability to control is greatly limited and notoriously unreliable.

The goal is to slowly increase those well-defined boundaries. As a middle schooler gets comfortable with some freedom, she's ready to have the boundaries widened. This process should be repeated, gradually and continually, throughout adolescence.

"From everyone who has been given much, much will be demanded; and from the one who has been entrusted with much, much more will be asked" (Luke 12:48) seems an appropriate bit of Jesus wisdom here. If we (or parents) give too much independence, too quickly, then middle schoolers will crumble under the requirements.

Independence Isn't a Challenge for Kids Alone

Here's a no-duh reminder that still might be helpful: Independence isn't just something to be exercised; it's something to be given or granted. In other words, for middle schoolers to move out of dependence, *someone* has to give them independence. It's a transaction, in a sense.

We, as middle school youth workers, are involved in this "giving" of independence. But substantially more so, their parents are involved in granting and setting the boundaries of freedom.

And let's be clear here: This is one of the most difficult aspects of parenting a teenager. Even the best parents struggle to know where to set the boundaries. Thoughtful, engaged parents err in both directions, and they often feel a bit helpless in knowing how much independence to grant. We've heard countless parents express this to us over the years. And now that we have young teens ourselves, we live it every day.

As a youth worker who understands the importance of coming alongside parents, you'll have to remind yourself *not to assume* parents are intentionally drawing too-tight or too-loose when it comes to independence. Most of them are just trying to figure it out, and they can use all the support and grace we can muster.

That said, you'll run into two extremes in parenting styles that are equally harmful to the healthy development of young teens.

HARMFUL EXTREME #1: SMOTHER

The first extreme is the parent who draws the boundaries too small, not offering the opportunity for any real independence or decision making. This often comes from a good motivation on the part of the parent(s).[66] The good motivation, as we've seen it, is normally along the lines of desiring to create a space for their children to remain children as long as possible and hold on to their innocence, not rushing them into adolescence.

These "smothering" parents are usually well aware of the cultural pressure for young teens to act like older teenagers at younger ages and to participate in and be exposed to behaviors and options that aren't age appropriate. This is a good inclination, when it's set in the proper context and perspective.

My (Marko) wife and I made the difficult choice of moving our daughter from her public middle school to a more sheltered private school about six weeks prior to the end of her 6th-grade year. We made this choice because our daughter is a natural risk-taker (one of her strengths), and she was quickly drawn to all the behaviors, values, and attitudes of older kids as soon as she was exposed to them. In other words, her "boundaries" were massively expanding, beyond what she was ready for, and she was naturally inclined to rush all the way to the fence (and hang over it a bit).

We feel we made this choice just in time, as Liesl was able to rebound and rediscover some of her age-appropriate innocence. It was as if she'd started to play at older teenage behavior, values, and attitudes, but she hadn't fully taken them on yet. When we moved her into a more protected environment, she flourished with the more age-appropriate amount of freedom she was granted.

Of course, the extreme is not healthy or helpful. The extreme—and you don't have to be in a middle school for long before you'll find these cases—is the parent who doesn't allow her child any real freedoms and keeps her child's choices limited to those appropriate for a 5th grader.

HARMFUL EXTREME #2: TOTAL FREEDOM

The other extreme is just as harmful, or maybe even more so. And, certainly, we're seeing this extreme played out in greater frequency than ever before. This is the parent who says, "I don't know how much freedom to give. My son wants total freedom. And it sure seems as though his friends have that. So I guess, since he's a teenager now, total freedom is what I should give him."

Oof. The result is the lost puppy in the park.

This parent might be operating out of fear of losing a connection with her kid, or out of exasperation over constant fighting, or out of ignorance or disinterest. But whatever the case, we are regularly shocked by the number of 13-year-olds who seem to have almost complete freedom in decision making. Sure, they still rely on their parents for food, shelter, and rides to the mall. But they have no boundaries when it comes to time use, media consumption, food intake, texting and phone use, bedtime, room décor, friendship choices, and a host of other should-be-boundaried choice realms.

I (Marko) know a 6th-grade boy who can get a perfect score on the expert level of the video game *Guitar Hero*. That means he can play the songs on the hardest level and complete them with zero mistakes. And *that means* he's been allowed completely unboundaried access to countless hours of *Guitar Hero* play. Seriously, it's difficult to imagine the number of hours it would take to get that "good" at *Guitar Hero*. And I find myself asking, "Where are his parents?"[67]

Young teens with total freedom are often stunted in developing good decision-making skills. Because the playing field is so open and wide, they find it difficult to connect consequences with their choices. So, in a sense, this boundary-less freedom actually impedes the healthiest course of growing in wisdom.

Of course, this doesn't even cover the multitude of truly bad decisions young teens could make with total freedom, which could have significant long-term consequences. Then again, our observation is that parents who err in this direction also tend to be parents who err by removing the natural consequences of their children's bad choices, thereby doubling the error.

How to Help Parents

We have a whole chapter devoted to working with parents (chapter 18). But this independence thing is such a big deal and such a cause of sleepless nights and deep frustration for parents that we believe we need to toss out a few thoughts here.

First, you may have noticed that this chapter talks less about your role as a middle school youth worker than it does about parents. That's because this developmental issue is so strikingly connected to parenting. Sure, there are ministry implications in addition to parent stuff; but the parent factor in regard to this developmental shift is 100 percent inexorably integral. You might be able to consider the ministry implications of the physical changes kids are going through apart from their family system. But it's impossible to consider the quest for independence apart from the dynamic give-and-take being played out between middle schoolers and their parents or guardians.

Two main things we can do here:[68]

1. *Adopt a curious perspective when considering parents' motives.* Assume that they have a "positive intent" behind their approach to granting independence. That positive intent may not always play out in the most helpful ways, but we're out of line when we make negative assumptions based on our limited knowledge and insight. If you have concerns, then this second bit might help.

2. *Engage in dialogue with parents and host a dialogue between parents.* Seriously, this is a tough one for parents. Ask them grace-filled questions about their attempts to walk this fine line. Talk with them about the concept of freedom within well-defined boundaries, and about how those boundaries need to expand over time. Talk with them about what you've seen in kids whose boundaries are too tight, or those who don't have clearly defined boundaries. Engage them in discussions with other parents (*especially* if you're not a parent of a teen), so they can learn from each other. In the process, you'll not only be ministering to these parents, but you'll be dramatically increasing your ability to minister to their kids as you learn more about the familial context in which your students live.

The Challenge of Choices

Young teens need the opportunity to make choices if they're ever going to learn to make *good* choices. This means, of course, that they're going to make some *bad* choices. So it's critical that we create a middle school ministry context where a few things are present.

GIVE 'EM CHOICES

It's great ministry to give kids the opportunity to make choices within the context of your middle school group. This might include choices regarding their involvement, choices for ministry participation, choices for leadership opportunities and involvement in setting the direction on everything from small group discussions to calendar planning. Remember, we're tour guides to the young teen experience. That means we offer our students choices and then walk alongside them, giving input when sought and encouragement always.

IT'S OKAY TO TRY AND FAIL

Failure is a major part of learning. In fact, our contention is that most of us learn much more from failure than we do from success.

Recently, a group of seasoned youth workers was developing content for the Youth Specialties One Day training day. The theme was what real transformation looks like in teens, so they started by talking about significant times of spiritual transformation in their own lives. When the list was compiled, they realized that deep transformation seems to take place, most often, in four contexts:

- Community
- Perspective-altering experiences
- Victory and success
- Failure and pain

We've seen that most youth ministries have the first two on their radar. But very few middle school ministries are proactive about creating a ministry environment that's responsive to the last two. Particularly, we seem to dump on those who experience failure, or we ignore it. What would it look like for your ministry to be a place where it was *safe* to fail and to talk about failure?

DON'T LEAVE THEM IN THE PIT

We need to be intentional about walking alongside middle schoolers while they live with the natural consequences of their choices. Remember that adolescent brain doc we wrote about in chapter 4? Remember how he said one of the *only* things we can do to help the development of the decision-making center of the brain is allow kids to experience the consequences of their choices? Our natural inclination—because we love kids and because walking with them through their consequences is much harder—is to remove the consequences. But we do them and their development a disservice when we do this.

A quick first-person adolescent story before we move on.

When I (Marko) was 16 and got my driver's license, I convinced my dad to let me take the family Volkswagen Bug on a driving date. This was two weeks after I got my license. I picked up my date at her house, and then I drove a half-hour to a large new shopping mall where we had dinner and went to a movie. When the movie got out, the mall was closed. So we walked to the car in the back of the now-empty parking lot.

The mall had a huge parking lot surrounding it and a circle drive around the outside, like the glaze on a donut. I was driving around the perimeter, heading for the exit, when I remembered a math lesson: The shortest distance between two points is a straight line. But I was driving an arc. So I turned into the empty lot, cutting across rows of empty parking spots, and made a 50-mile-an-hour beeline for the exit.

Except, I didn't see the traffic island. I thought it was just a line painted on the ground. But just before I hit it, I realized it was actually a cement curb about 18 inches high and 10 feet across.

As I slammed the Bug into the parking island, I ripped all four wheels, both axles, and part of the drive train off the car. We skidded along the pavement on the other side before coming to a skewed stop.[69]

Long story, short: My dad was going to sell the car the next week. So he made me buy it from him for his full asking price. I made monthly payments to him throughout the following year. I was not happy about this. But in hindsight, I'm glad he didn't remove the difficult consequence of my actions because I've never driven fast through an empty parking lot again.

School Shift Comes Around: K8 to JH to MS to K8

Schools are wrestling with the best approach to this independence issue, too. And there are varied opinions about what's best for middle-school-aged kids.

Historically, kids in what are now considered the young teen years were in primary schools (now called elementary schools). There was no real separation of children until secondary school (now called high school).

As high schools became mandatory and the number of students in schools increased, "junior" high schools popped up, providing an intermediate space between elementary and high school, where age-appropriate learning, as well as freedoms, could be experienced. The middle school movement of the 1980s (and beyond) began to lobby for a schooling approach that was less about preparation for high school, and more about developmentally appropriate education and the "right" mix of dependence and independence. And this continues to be the dominant approach to education in both public and private schools.[70]

However, a new/old approach is getting a lot of buzz these days. It's the old K-8 approach, which keeps "middle schoolers" in a school with their elementary counterparts. This seems to be a mostly good attempt to allow them to be young longer, not rushing them into adolescence in a way that a 6-8 or 7-8 school (11- or 12-to-14-year-olds) seems to do. There's a bit of a *Lord of the Flies* vibe that takes place in a normal middle school; and the K-8 approach is an attempt to postpone that.

This shift usually means fewer freedoms for middle school kids in these K-8 schools; but conversely, it also brings more responsibility, as they're often called upon to play a mentoring role with the younger students.

We're intrigued by this direction (and Marko's kids attend a K-8 school). It will be interesting to see how this evolves as our culture at large continues to shift in its understanding of preteens and young teens.

A Fly in the Ointment: Independence and Community

One final bit here in this chapter—just a question to mess you up a bit.

Should independence really be our goal?

To state it another way: Is independence a *biblical* value or an American value? Certainly, it's an American value. But we believe you'd be hard-pressed to make a strong case for it being a biblical value. Community, yes. Independence...not so much.

So what do we do with this? Certainly, learning to take responsibility for oneself is at the core of the adolescent experience, at least in our culture. (And remember, there was no "adolescence" in the time when the Bible was written.)

We don't have a great answer to this question. We believe it's a tension we have to live with. We need to help kids develop independence (and help their parents with this challenging task), while remaining suspicious of our culture's obsession with independence. We are people of community, and our identity is one of being *the people of God*, not individual, disconnected, Lone-Ranger-like, sons and daughters of God.

Hmmm. Let's all think about that one a bit more.

CHAPTER 8

Operating System Upgrade
(Spiritual Development)

When I (Marko) was in 9th grade, I went on a two-week wilderness trip in the Appalachian Mountains. We carried everything in backpacks and spent the time hiking, canoeing, climbing, and learning about ourselves.

One day, after a long and arduous uphill hike through thick forest cover, we emerged just before sunset at a high promontory with a massive panoramic view of a valley bathed in early evening light. It was breathtaking; and we all stopped and stood in silence, just taking in the view, the fresh air, the warm feeling of accomplishment, and a shared experience.

There was lots of work to be done for the evening (camp to set up, meal to cook, plans to talk about for the next day). And there was this lingering knowledge that we didn't really know where we were. (We were without our adult leader on this day, and we'd gotten ourselves hopelessly lost.)

But even with all this confusion and disorientation and added responsibilities, it was still a moment dripping with possibility, with greatness, with a new awareness of expansiveness.

This works as a metaphor for what's going on in the spiritual development of young teens. And, as is true with most of these developmental issues, the revolution of middle schoolers' faith is directly tied to their cognitive development.

Abstract Faith

Stop to think about it: What, if any, aspects of faith aren't abstract? Sure, children can have a very real and concrete faith. And that's good and age appropriate. But you wouldn't want to have a child's understanding of spiritual things. There's a difference between childlike faith (which Jesus praises[71]) and childish faith.

Choose a faith topic, anything from discipleship to the incarnation, from salvation to the Trinity: *They're all abstract.* And you can concretize something like the Trinity all you want (and as you should) with descriptions such as, "It's like an egg. There's a shell, white, and yolk; but it's still one egg," or "It's like water, steam, and ice—three forms of one substance." But these cute little efforts at concretizing the abstract concept of the Trinity still leave us substantially short of actually understanding the interdependence and relationality of a three-in-one God.

This challenge doesn't matter so much for preteens and children. They're fine with a simplistic, concrete understanding of faith things. They're fine with seeing a black-and-white version of an issue that's deeply and richly nuanced with color because the black-and-white version is all they're capable of grasping.

It works for them. But the new opportunity of abstract thinking that comes with the onset of puberty changes everything. It takes young teens to a surprising vista (not all at once—usually in bits and pieces) where everything gets reframed. In a positive sense, this shift is exciting (both for them and for us), as it opens up new opportunities for understanding, ownership, application, and implication.

Viewed from a more challenging perspective, this spiritual shift is disconcerting and confusing because it necessarily calls into question childhood beliefs that no longer work or no longer make sense. And remember, young teens *have* the ability to think abstractly, but it's a wimpy, underused ability. They don't toggle switch into full-on abstract thought one night while they're sleeping. So they tentatively step in and out of abstract thought on a regular basis, advancing and retreating.

You'll notice flashes of abstract faith understanding in your middle schoolers (like the story of Garrett in chapter 4). And if you check for understanding when talking about abstract spiritual stuff, you'll also notice that they're often squishing your abstract discussion to fit their thoroughly concrete childhood thinking models.

A New Operating System

The best way we've found to think about this shift is the operating system of a computer, which runs in the background and informs all the programs you use and see on your computer. You don't *see* the operating system, per se, but you use it with all the other programs.

I (Marko) am typing on a MacBook Pro right now (in my local coffee shop). I "went Mac" about a year ago, after well more than a decade of PC use. And just recently, I got an operating system upgrade to Apple's newest OS, commonly called "Leopard." (This will quickly date this book.)

But I still have plenty of documents (PowerPoint presentations, word processing docs, spreadsheets, and so on) saved on my laptop's hard drive from years past. Some of them are in a PC format, and some are in an older Mac format. When I open one of these older documents, my computer takes an extra second to convert the file into a format that my current operating system can utilize. Then, if I make any changes, a window pops up and asks me if I want to save the file in the old format or the new format.

In fact, one more element exists now that I'm using "Leopard": The new documents I create aren't readable in the old operating system. If I saved this manuscript in the new format and sent it to someone who was using an older format, they wouldn't be able to open it. I have to go through the additional step of *intentionally choosing* to save the document in a format that can be read by both the older and newer operating systems.

This is *exactly* what's going on in the spiritual development of middle schoolers.

THE CHALLENGE TO JOHNNY'S SYSTEMATIC THEOLOGY
Let's put this into a case study of a middle school kid.

All preteens, no matter what faith system they do or don't subscribe to, are in a time of concluding. And as such, they all have a somewhat concluded, worked-out worldview. You might even call it their systematic theology. They have an understanding (as wrong or simplistic as it might be) in which they have a good deal of confidence about how the world works, relational dynamics, power, and spiritual stuff. Ask a Christian preteen to explain the Trinity, and she'll have no problem. She'll even think you're a little weird or dumb for believing there's any reason *not* to understand this concept. Easy peasy lemon squeezy. I's dotted and T's crossed.

So meet Johnny. Great kid. Johnny has had a robust faith as a preteen, one that's beautiful and age appropriate and wonderfully childlike. Johnny is traveling through life with his little backpack of faith. And in that backpack, Johnny has stuffed his cobbled-together systematic theology, his fairly concluded understanding of all things spiritual. And it works for him.

One of the things Johnny has come to believe is that prayer works. (This is a great thing!) Johnny believes that God answers his prayers. Johnny also believes that if he asks God for something—and it's not selfish—then God will give it to him. (Johnny understands this doesn't mean he can just ask for a new skateboard, duh!)

But in the fall of Johnny's 7th-grade year, his favorite grandpa is diagnosed with advanced inoperable cancer and given a couple of months to live. While initially a bit disoriented by this (because Johnny also has a simple belief that good things happen to good people, and he knows his grandpa is really, really good), Johnny grows confident that if he asks God to heal his grandpa, God will do so.

Johnny prays and prays and prays. But his grandpa still dies. Suddenly, that faith bit is pulled out of Johnny's backpack of faith and examined.[72] Johnny considers the clash between his previously concluded faith bit about how prayer works and the reality he's just experienced. He now has three options:

1. Johnny can conclude, *Well, my understanding of prayer didn't quite work. But it's all I have, so it will have to do.* Then Johnny stuffs his simplistic faith bit about prayer back into his backpack of faith. Years of repeating this choice is what leads kids to the unarticulated, mushy faith that Christian Smith calls Moral Therapeutic Deism. And this is why most churches are full of adults who attend church and subscribe to a basic set of moral guiding principles but lack an articulated, active faith that affects their daily lives.

2. Johnny's second option is to conclude, *Well, this doesn't make sense anymore. But I don't have anything to replace it with, so I'll just chuck it.* This is why we have so many older teenagers and young adults who leave the church

or jettison their faith. By the time they actually walk away from the Christian faith, they've typically gone through years of discarding this faith—bit by bit. Their childish faith system just isn't sustainable in the real world of a 19-year-old. And, really, why should it be?

3. Johnny's third option is the most difficult—and it's why middle school ministry is so important. Johnny can go through the challenging process of evaluating this faith bit and working to find a new, more adult-like (abstract) way to frame his understanding of prayer. This work of faith evolution, of growing in understanding and articulation, is a bumpy, potholed road with plenty of opportunities for misunderstanding and frustration. And it's a process for which Johnny *absolutely needs* adult "coaches"—whether they're his parents, his youth leaders, or other adults— who walk alongside him and help him sort this stuff out.

The Role of Speculation in Faith Formation

There's a cycle we all go through when we're learning something new, and it pertains to spiritual stuff also: We consider a truth or an idea or the implications of an experience and it shows up in our lives as—

- A new behavior

- A new understanding

- A new value

- A new perspective

- Deeper faith

This "cycle of learning" has specific implications for middle school ministry, as there are a few steps in the process that are natural for adults but don't come easily for young teens.

WHY I DO THIS

We were driving to camp and 10 middle school boys, with the prompting of their college-aged leader, treated me to a "full moon" out the bus window. It caught me at the wrong moment. I was stressed out about leading my first big camp. I was worried about kids getting hurt or in trouble because of all the horror stories I'd heard. So there we were, on the ride to camp, and everything already felt out of control. It was the culmination of a frustrating introductory four months in middle school ministry.

I'd accepted the job of middle school director at our church somewhat reluctantly. I didn't even really want to be in youth ministry. My childhood dream had always been to announce professional sports. I'd work at church until I got my big break, although I wasn't excited about being on the "JV" team. Wasn't high school ministry where *real* youth pastors worked?

Meanwhile, the mooning incident pushed me over the edge. "I quit," were the only two words I could muster. I marched into my boss' office on the Monday morning after camp and did just that—no more "baby-sitting" for me.

Then God's sense of humor kicked in. Someone handed me a copy of a book I hadn't known existed: *Junior High Ministry* by Wayne Rice. I was stunned that people actually wrote books about middle schoolers, but I was even more amazed by what I read in the first two chapters. I read that caring for middle schoolers was not just baby-sitting. In fact, it's one of the most vitally important ministries of all. For someone who wanted people to know, love, and trust Jesus Christ, I had somehow stumbled upon the age group where faith often comes to life for the very first time.

Two years later, my wife and I were eating dinner when the phone rang. The voice introduced himself as the vice president of entertainment for the Colorado Avalanche and Denver Nuggets—two professional sports franchises in Denver, just 30 minutes from my home. He asked a question I'd always dreamed of hearing, "Are you interested in trying out for our open public address announcer position?"

Three weeks later I found myself in Denver trying out for my dream job—announcing professional sports for two of my favorite teams. I left the tryout with a strange certainty that I'd won. Then it hit me: People would admire me. I'd finally be doing something everyone thought was important. *I was going to be rich.*

But something unexpected happened. As I drove home, I literally got sick to my stomach. Announcing for both of these teams meant quitting middle school ministry. The faces of some of the kids I was working with flashed through my mind. How could I leave them? I started praying, and the message came through clearly: "Jim, you need to stay with those kids." *Are you kidding me, God?*

Later that day, the phone rang again. "Congratulations, Jim! You're the new announcer for the Denver Nuggets and Colorado Avalanche," the voice said.

Soon I was in a position I'd never dreamed possible—a professional sports franchise was trying to convince me to quit my church job with middle schoolers. And I was refusing.

"Wait," I could hardly believe what I was about to say. "I can't do it. I'm working with kids at my church...and I won't leave."

Silence.

The voice whispered back, "Jim, don't you know this is the big time?"

The Big Time. It sounded so good, but a bigger voice was vying for my attention.

"I can only do one team," my voice quivered. "If I have to do both, I won't do either."

We agreed I would announce full time for the Nuggets and substitute for the Avalanche, and not on Wednesday nights so I could lead our middle school ministry meeting. Over the next few years, something surprising happened. I learned that I loved youth work more than broadcasting.

When my first son, Joshua, was born, the juggling act overwhelmed me—I couldn't continue doing it all. My wife and I prayed, and we felt that we should keep ministering to kids. I would quit announcing.

I dialed the Pepsi Center. It was time to tell them I was quitting. But then I stopped. The "Send" button on my phone glared back, taunting me. I couldn't call. For three weeks I tried to call every night, but for some reason I couldn't.

Finally, I involved God: *Why can't I quit, God?*

You love broadcasting because people admire you for it, came the response. God was right, of course. I was in a vicious tug-of-war over my identity. On one side, God was calling me to keep following him in middle school ministry. On the other, my friends, church, and family constantly told me how great I was because I announced professional sports. The affirmation made me feel more important than being "just" a middle school worker. I would have never admitted it, but deep inside I thought, *I'm capable of more than working with middle schoolers at a church. I could be important.* I was struggling to reconcile God's calling on my life with the culture's definition of success.

Working with middle schoolers generally doesn't bring admiration or money, but I'm happy to report that God has changed my heart in a way I never would have expected. I realized the call to my dream job came long before the Nuggets and Avs. That call came when I started working with middle schoolers, but I hadn't seen it.

Middle school youth workers live the dream—we're called by God to love and care for some of society's most vulnerable and impressionable people. Wow. Do we believe that middle school ministry is the real "Big Time"?

(Portions of this article first appeared in the November/December 2006 issue of *YouthWorker Journal*.)

Jim Candy leads the children's, youth, and family ministry teams at Menlo Park Presbyterian Church in the San Francisco Bay Area.

Here's the cycle:[74]

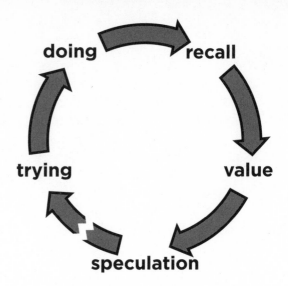

RECALL

The process of learning starts with recall (in other words, some bit of data). It could be a biblical truth in the context of teaching. It could be an experience. It could be a narrative of some sort. But something provides a data point of fodder for potential learning (and, in our context here, for spiritual growth).

Unfortunately, many youth workers wrongly make the assumption (or work off the assumption) that it's normal for us to go from information to a changed life. While we agree with Scripture that "the Word of God will not return void" (Isaiah 55:11 NKJV) and that the Holy Spirit can do whatever the Holy Spirit chooses to do, there are normally additional steps in the process of truth (in the form of the Bible, experience, narrative, nature, and other truth exposures) showing up as change in our lives, minds, and hearts.

VALUE

The second step of the learning process is one we don't often think about when it comes to middle schoolers, yet it's extra important. The "value" step is one of emotionally connecting or "adding value" to the data.[75]

At this very moment, you're crossing this hurdle as you read this book. You're adding value to the learning process of this book because you care about the subject material, and you care about middle schoolers. You're naturally incented to care about this subject, based on your interests and values as a middle school youth worker.

We'd like to believe that middle schoolers will attach value to the learning process (or any spiritual growth opportunity) due to their valuing of the subject matter itself. But no matter how stunning your exposition of the book of Numbers may be, the reality is that most middle schoolers are *not* going to attach value to a teaching experience based on the subject matter.[76] This is a little less true with data that comes from experience, rather than a teaching topic. But the valuing step is still a big hurdle.

Lucky for us, this valuing can occur another way: It can come from the learner (in this case, a middle schooler) attaching value to the learning *process*, rather than the subject itself. *And* this "valuing the learning process" can happen as a result of a middle schooler valuing her relationship with an adult leader who she knows cares about the learning process.

In other words, Kisha can be sitting in your middle school group and care very little about what Paul had to say about loving others (which is what you're teaching about up front). But three seats over from Kisha is Ellen. Ellen is Kisha's small group leader, and they have a relationship that's important to Kisha. Kisha knows (at least at a subconscious level) that Ellen cares about what's taking place in this room right now, that she cares about this stuff you're talking about, that she believes it's important. As a result, Kisha can attach value to the learning process simply because she knows Ellen values it.[77]

SPECULATION

The third step in the learning cycle is speculation. (Ooh, now we're gettin' to the good stuff of middle school ministry.) Speculation is simply asking the "what if" questions. It's the conscious or subconscious process of considering the data (again, a truth or experience or other input) and what implications it could have for her life.

Here are a couple of simple examples:

- Josh is in your small group, which is talking about what it means to be a good friend. Speculation is Josh merely thinking about the questions: "What does it look like for a middle schooler to be a good friend?" or, more specifically, "What would it look like for me to be a good friend?"

- Emily is standing at the head of the line at the soup kitchen where your youth group is serving breakfast. She's handing out trays to the homeless people as they enter the serving area. A homeless woman smiles at Emily and says, "Thank you, sweetie, you are an angel." Emily starts to think about what it would mean to change her ideas about homeless people.

Hey, if you haven't read the "Cognitive Development" chapter (chapter 4), then you really need to go back and read that now. It's impossible for us to talk about speculation and middle schoolers without framing it in the realities of how *new* and *challenging* the abstract-thinking process of speculation is for young teens.

Here's the harsh reality: The speculation step of the learning process (or spiritual growth process—there really isn't a difference for our purposes here) can't be skipped; but middle schoolers stink at speculation. Here's the "duh" point: We have to be extra intentional about what we like to call "taking them to the shores of speculation." We have to *help* middle schoolers exercise their speculation muscles.

Young teens are *capable* of speculation, but they rarely go there on their own. So a *huge* part of an effective middle school ministry (one that understands the spiritual development of early adolescence) is about constantly working guided speculation into teaching, small group discussions, and conversations.

THE KNOWING-DOING GAP

After the speculation step, you'll notice a little break in the next arrow. That's the gap between knowledge and action—or the "knowing-doing gap." Everything prior to that point was a cognitive activity. But on the other side, we try on new behaviors (much like trying on a shirt in a store to see if it fits you both in size and style). And beyond "trying" we move to "doing," where the behavior or understanding or value or perspective is now a part of who we are.[78]

This "knowing-doing gap" is a big challenge in middle school ministry. Helping kids speculate about what a new behavior (value, understanding, or perspective) might be and then *actually trying it on* won't come naturally to them.

Do you see how your growing knowledge of early adolescent development affects every aspect of the ministry you do with them? Whew!

The Importance and Beauty of Doubt

Tom and Barb, the parents of an 8th-grade guy named Stephen, sat with me (Marko here) at a coffee shop. They'd asked to meet with me to get some input on "what was happening to their son" (Barb's words) and to "join forces on a solution" (Tom's words).

Stephen had been a fairly regular part of our middle school ministry for three years, and he'd grown up in our church. He wasn't exactly a student leader or a kid who exhibited a passionate and articulated faith. But he wasn't a big problem in our ministry either. Until recently, he seemed to be nominally interested, at best, and blissfully ignorant of the fact that he was coasting into adolescence with a loose grasp on an inherited faith (the faith he'd picked up in his home, rather than one he owned himself).

But in the last couple of months, I'd seen a change in Stephen, and so had his small group leader. He was asking more questions about faith stuff. And because he was a middle schooler, Stephen was often asking these questions (or expressing comments that revealed a hidden question) in a way that was passive-aggressive or combative. Stephen's small group would be talking about some Jesus-y subject, and Stephen would pop off with a comment like, "I don't even know why we'd bother." And when I was teaching up front, I'd noticed Stephen dramatically roll his eyes a few times and cross his arms in defiance.

I'd had one quick conversation with Stephen about what was going on, and he'd said something like, "I don't know...I just have all this stuff I've heard my whole life, and I'm starting to have a hard time believing it's true."

Back to the coffee shop. Tom started: "Stephen has always been a good Christian boy. He's been willing to participate in our family devotions and to pray out loud at dinner. But he's shown a real change in the last few months, and we're greatly concerned."

I listened.

Barb interrupted by bursting into tears. They'd been leaking out of her eyes from the moment Tom began talking; but now they flooded out, and she momentarily held her face in her hands. When she caught her breath, Barb continued in Tom's place: "Stephen loved Jesus. I know he did! But do you know what he said the other night? Tom asked him to pray at the dinner table, and Stephen answered, 'I'm not sure I want to be a Christian anymore, so I'm not sure I should pray.'"

I'll admit that what I said next was not the shining moment of my middle school ministry years. I don't believe I was being very sensitive to the fear and concern that were very real to Tom and Barb.

I smiled (that stopped them) and said, "That's fantastic!"

There was a long awkward silence as Tom and Barb tried to sort this out, wondering whether I was the Devil incarnate or at the very least the newfound cause of their son's waning faith.

I continued, "Sorry, that was a bit abrupt. And I know this is very difficult and painful for you as parents because you love Stephen and genuinely want him to experience life in Christ."

Then I went on to talk about the absolutely critical nature of questions and doubt in the formation of early adolescents. Not that every middle schooler has to consider completely chucking her faith. But the journey from inherited faith to owned faith always goes through a process of questioning and often goes through a series of doubts.

In the church we have a tendency to guilt kids (or anyone) for expressing doubts, as if they're sinful. Not only is this theologically wrong, but it's harmful to the spiritual development of young teens. If we shun them or guilt them for expressing a doubt or question, they quickly learn—

- *It's not safe to talk about questions or doubts. Even if I have them, I should keep them to myself.*

- *It's wrong to have questions or doubts, and my only two choices are to "be a good Christian" (which must mean ignoring or stuffing my questions and doubts) or reject the whole thing.*

Obviously, we don't want those results. So we need to be willing to walk alongside kids as they express their doubts. We also need to reframe our own thinking about doubts and view them as a *good* thing and a *helpful* part of faith development, especially when young teens are willing to talk about them and give us the opportunity to process with them.

Of course, young teens don't always express their questions and doubts in healthy ways because they don't have the emotional maturity or clarity of thought to do so. So their articulation of questions and doubts often comes out in ways that can push our buttons and make us feel insecure. It takes maturity on our part to realize that their button-pushing statements usually have nothing to do with us, even if they seem to be directed at us. We have to learn to look past the "presenting evidence" and be present to the very real questions and doubts that drive those comments. This, of course, is easier said that done.

THOMAS WANTED PROOF

We like to consider how Jesus handled Thomas' doubt. You remember the scenario: Jesus had risen from the dead, and the Marys and a bunch of the disciples had seen him. But Thomas wasn't there. And when the others reported how they'd seen and talked with Jesus, Tom said, basically, "I don't believe it; and I *won't* believe it until I have physical evidence. I'll believe it when I can put my fingers in the nail holes in his hands, and my hand in the sword hole in his side."[79]

Then—uh-oh!—Jesus shows up again. Can you imagine what Thomas was feeling and thinking at that moment? Whatever doubts he had would have instantly vanished. We picture it going down like this:

> Jesus: *Thomas, I want you to come touch these nail holes and this sword wound.*
>
> Thomas: *Uh, Jesus, that's not necessary now. I can see you. I'm sorry I doubted; but I, uh, was kind of exaggerating when I said those things. You know, it was kind of like that language you use sometimes, like when you said we should pluck out our eye if it causes us to sin?*
>
> Jesus *(still serious, but with a twinkle in his eyes): Thomas, I'm serious—come over here now.*
>
> Thomas shuffles forward. He's uncomfortable that everyone is watching him and a bit grossed out by the impending reality of sticking his fingers and hands in those wounds.
>
> Jesus gently but firmly takes Thomas's hand and guides it to the wounds.
>
> Then Thomas verbalizes his belief: *My Lord! I believe!*
>
> Jesus *(with a smile and a little wink): Okay, we're done with that now, Thomas. You can put that doubt behind you.*

This is a great example for us. We acknowledge questions and doubts as real. We don't downplay them, dismiss them, ridicule them, or heap guilt on them. We use them as opportunities for interaction. We walk alongside young teens, guiding them as they process their doubts and questions. Then, once a resolve is reached (which doesn't often happen in one sitting, by the way), we help kids have confidence in what they've discovered.

Three Generalized Paths

Like Johnny and the examination of his answered prayer faith bit (played out in the earlier example), we believe there are three paths that middle schoolers can take in their faith development. We don't have our own research to back this up, although it seems to resonate with Christian Smith's work (referenced previously). And one might say it's based on the observational research we've conducted with thousands of young teens and middle teens over many years of ministry.

We believe that kids who grew up with some kind of Christian faith have to question and reevaluate that faith, coming to some sense of a revised, owned, semi-articulated faith by the time they're 15 or 16 years old. Otherwise, they'll likely move toward one of the two other options that Johnny had—cling to his childish faith or just chuck it altogether.

If middle schoolers (up to slightly older teens) don't rearticulate their faith, then it's quite possible that they'll move into a simplistic kind of moralization that's more about karma than it is about living in the way of Jesus. Or they'll simply jettison their faith as irrelevant, a holdover from childhood that no longer makes sense to their almost-emerging adult world (such as dolls and Transformers, stuffed animals and security blankets).

On the one hand, this is the weightiness of our calling. This is the crux of the importance of middle school ministry. But at the same time, we aren't the Savior (nor are we the Holy Spirit). Our role is *not* to make kids change or *force them* (as in, manipulate them) to change. Honestly, we're not capable of that; and any perceived "results" of those kinds of strong-arm tactics will be shallow and short-lived.

Instead, we walk with humility and compassion *alongside* middle schoolers as they trudge through this messy, disorienting, and beautiful transition in faith development. And as we do, we must be aware that what we think we see is often not the whole story.

CHAPTER 9

White-Hot Temporary
(Early Adolescent Culture)

Whenever we talk to adults about the early adolescent experience, we seem to find one of two extreme responses in their thinking. Either they believe *nothing* has changed, and today's young teens are basically the same, dealing with the same things they were dealing with in their 11-to-14 years. Or they believe *everything* has changed, and nothing is the same at all.

As you might expect, we believe both are true. Or, more accurately, since those two extremes don't allow for each other, we believe both are true in the sense that there is much about the early adolescent experience and young teen culture that remains constant, *and* there is much about the experience and culture of today's young teens that's markedly different than even 10 years ago.

What's the Same?

A few stories...

When I (Marko) was in 8th grade, my friends pushed me into asking a girl named Sue to "go with me." (That's what we called steady girlfriend-boyfriend relationships.) I'd liked many girls, and a couple of them even liked me back. But I'd never taken this step that I perceived to be *huge* and *life changing*.

One day Sue and I were together as our youth group went on a daylong outing—horseback riding. I remember being crazy nervous as she and I walked around the corral and I tried to get up the nerve and find the words. If my memory serves me, I'm pretty sure that I finally said something like, "Well, everyone thinks we should go together." (Romantic, huh?) Then, as my heartbeat rose to dangerous levels, I continued, "So, what do you think?"

My memory definitely serves me when it comes to Sue's response. She shrugged her shoulders and said, "Okay, I guess so."

And that was it! We were official. It lasted about a week.

Later that year, I acted on a crush I'd had on a girl named Kathy who was way out of my league (at least in my perception). She was popular, and she was...a cheerleader. She'd been "going with" a guy named Doug for a *long time* (which, in middle school time, was probably about six months). But they'd broken up, and she was on the rebound.

Through friends, we'd made our interest in each other known. I knew it was the expected time for me to act. So one night while I was baby-sitting, I called Kathy (after the kids were in bed). We made small talk for a while, and I tried to get up the courage to ask her to "go with me." Finally, in a burst of now-or-never courage, I got out the words, "I have something to ask you."

She said, "Okay."

And I froze. I mean, I completely choked! My mouth was open, but the words simply wouldn't come out. So I did what came naturally to me: I hung up.

I quickly dug around in the cabinets of the house where I was baby-sitting and found a tape recorder. (Remember those little cassette decks with the clunky buttons on the front? This was before boom boxes, by the way.) I used the tape recorder to practice asking Kathy out. I tried it a dozen ways, playing the recording back and listening for the right vibe and words. When I was convinced I had it nailed and I'd be the most suave and manly asker in the history of the world, I called her back.

I made up some reason for hanging up earlier (a kid was crying, or something like that, since this was prior to cell phones and the always plausible excuse that the call got dropped). Then I restated my intention, "I have something to ask you."

Again, Kathy responded with, "Okay."

And I froze again! I was trying to form the words and hear that cool stud muffin from the recording, but it wasn't happening. Instead, I uttered a few "acks" and other noises.

Kathy said, "Are you still there?"

Finally, in a moment of panic, I grabbed the tape recorder, held it up to the phone, and pushed play. Unfortunately, I hadn't set the volume for this scenario, and my tinny recorded voice came booming out at a ridiculous volume: "KATHY, I REALLY LIKE YOU..." At this point, I scrambled and started adjusting the little volume thumbwheel, which provided a wonderful scratchy sound as the volume plummeted to a whisper, right through my perfect sentence, "Will you go with me?"

She said yes, and we "went together" for two weeks. Then she broke up with me and got back together with Doug. (I toilet-papered Doug's house throughout high school.)

One more, just so these aren't all about girls!

In 7th grade my buddies and I went on a guys' weekend outing with our youth group. We stayed at a rustic camp an hour away from our church. I don't remember much about the trip—other than sledding straight into a tree and almost knocking myself unconscious. But I do remember what we did to my best friend, John, utilizing our brilliant (not!) speculation abilities, well-articulated judgment (not!), and massive need for discovery and experimentation (yes!).

One night—who knows where our counselor was—we grabbed John, who was substantially smaller than the rest of us, and shoved him deep into his sleeping bag. Whenever we tried to pull pranks on John, he had a way of not caring. This usually diffused the situation or infuriated us. But in this case, it worked to our favor. We picked him up, still encased in his sleeping bag, and hauled him outside like three little Santas carrying a large sack o' gifts.

The camp had a large flagpole near the dining hall. It stood about two stories high, and it had a little cement pad at the bottom. Since it was nighttime, the pole was barren. So we carried the bag-o-John to the flagpole, untied the ropes from their lashing points, and wound them around the end of the sleeping bag. The one thing we did right that night was tie great knots!

Then, with John now coming to life and starting to get nervous, the three of us pulled the rope, heaving and grunting and laughing as we raised John—inside the sleeping bag—to the top of the pole. He later told us he was very confused as he realized our voices were getting farther away, and he could tell he was hanging from something.

I *think* our plan was to tie off the rope and stand there laughing for a while, amazed at our own brilliance and unquestionable hilarity. But once we got John to the tippy top of the pole, we'd expended all possible gripping and holding power. Someone said, "I can't hold on any longer!" and we all looked at each other in panic, just as all three of us let go of the rope at the same moment.

We clearly weren't thinking things through; but at least we had the wherewithal to step back so John's plummeting body bag wouldn't land on us.

The good ending of what could have been the most horrible story of my young teen years: John broke his arm, nothing more.

Here's my point in telling these true stories from my own young teen years. I can totally see the middle schoolers I work with today living these exact same stories (except the tape recorder would be replaced by some newer technology).

What's the same about today's young teens is that they're still going through the early adolescent changes we've written about in the last several chapters. Yes, the onset of puberty is a bit younger; but the young teen years are still years of upheaval, disorienting shifts, and newness. They're still years of fear and concern. They're still years of questions.

A really significant sameness is the reality of the young teen years as being years of discovery and sampling. And while the *duration* of adolescence has significantly lengthened, the *content* of adolescence still has the same primary tasks: Identity, autonomy, and affinity.

We wrote about these a bit in earlier chapters, but here's a quick reminder:

- Identity is asking, "Who am I?"

- Autonomy is asking, "How am I unique?" and "What's the extent of my control?"

- Affinity is asking, "To whom and where do I belong?"

These three adolescent tasks have remained fairly consistent over the years of otherwise shifting youth culture.

WHY I DO THIS

I remember it like it was yesterday. As a 7th grader, I was a pretty good kid; but a series of bad decisions led my parents to send me to meet with a pastor at our church. As I sat in his office, I imagined the conversation we were about to have—condescending, hellfire and brimstone, time to grow up, the usual stuff adults say to middle schoolers.

Then Dr. Lown, an unassuming elderly pastor in a wheelchair, came in and threw all my expectations right out the window. He loved me just as I was—a goofy, awkward middle school boy who was struggling to find his path in life. Over the next several months, Dr. Lown began teaching me about the Bible and about God's deep and passionate love for me. As we explored the mystery and wonder of God, I soon found myself committing my life to following Christ.

Dr. Lown continued to disciple me until he passed away during my early college years. Near the end of his life, he struggled with great physical pain. But he still continued to meet with me in his home on a regular basis. After his death, his widow told me that he'd backed away from all his commitments except discipling me and one other person, the late Christian musician Rich Mullins. Dr. Lown changed my life because he took the time to invest in a goofy middle school boy. He made me feel valued, and he helped me understand that I have a place in God's kingdom. Even at the end of his life, he affirmed me by showing me the same respect and commitment that he showed to Rich, a hero of mine and an incredible man of God.

Following Dr. Lown's death, I had no doubt about what I wanted to do with my life. I wanted to minister to middle school students in the same way that Dr. Lown had ministered to me. I studied youth ministry in college, and I've been working with middle school students for a little more than a decade. It's an honor and a privilege that I don't take lightly, and I pray I'm blessed to be a part of it for a long time to come.

Sean Meade is the executive director of Stuck in the Middle, a ministry to middle schoolers based in Andover, Kansas.

What's Different?

Here's a partial list of the things that did *not* exist when we (Scott and Marko) were young teens:[80]

- Cell phones
- The Internet (meaning, Web sites and buying stuff online and everything else that's so completely normal today, including YouTube and Wikipedia and Google and so many other staples of life)
- Home computers, PCs, Apple, laptops
- Text messages
- IM
- Hybrid cars
- Social networking
- "Friends with benefits"
- "Bi-curious"
- Cable TV
- Digital Video Recording (or TiVo)
- Mp3s and downloadable music
- DVDs
- Hi-Def and widescreen TV
- Satellite radio
- Xboxes and Wiis and other amazing gaming systems (*Pong* was introduced when I [Marko] was a young teen, and *Space Invaders* had just showed up in the commons of a local community college.)
- email
- Spam (the email variety—we had the stuff in the can, though)
- Any kind of camera, video or still, that didn't need developing (other than Polaroids)
- Cordless phones
- Ringtones
- Call waiting and caller ID
- iChat or other video conferencing
- Snowboards and wakeboards
- Rollerblades

- An African-American president and a female secretary of state
- Starbucks
- Airport security (plus national security levels and terrorist threats)
- Internet porn
- Viagra
- Plastic soda bottles
- Cordless tools and appliances
- Game Boys (and PlayStation Portables and Nintendo DS and other handheld gaming systems)
- News—anywhere, anytime
- Seat belt and car seat laws
- Harry Potter
- Hip-hop
- Post-it Notes
- Self-service gas pumps
- X Games
- Energy drinks
- Home theaters
- *The Simpsons, SpongeBob, American Idol,* and a host of other dependable TV staples
- Reality TV
- Crack cocaine (and a host of more recent designer drugs)
- Minivans
- Global Positioning Systems (GPS)
- Voicemail
- Disposable cameras
- Disposable contact lenses
- The morning-after pill
- Doppler radar
- Space shuttles
- *USA Today*
- HIV/AIDS
- Paintball and Airsoft
- Laser tag
- ESPN

- MTV
- DNA fingerprinting
- Fantasy sports teams
- Cloning animals
- The Super Bowl as a kind of national holiday
- Suitcases with wheels on the bottom
- Body and face piercings (at least not commonly)
- Tattoos (on people other than bikers and carnies)
- McDonald's Playlands
- iPods
- Microwave ovens
- Pay Per View and On Demand movies
- Easy-Mac
- Home printers, scanners, and copiers

Let's add to that—here are a few more things that didn't exist when we were young teens. And while they seemed so revolutionary when they came on the scene, now they've faded away into, at least, partial obscurity:

- Fax machines
- CDs (Seriously, who buys CDs anymore? They're the Betamax cartridge of this generation.)
- Videotapes
- Internet chat rooms
- Really, we could put email on this list, since teenagers don't use email anymore, except to communicate with parents or teachers.
- Music videos played on MTV (and remember *TRL*?)
- The Walkman (pre-MP3, cassette, and CD players)
- Answering machines
- Dial-up modems
- Personal pagers
- Palm Pilots
- Popcorn popping machines (Remember those pre-microwave beauties where the butter melted on the top while the popcorn got blown out by hot air?)
- Laserdiscs

Uh, yes, things have changed.[81] And it's important for us to remember that these changes aren't all external. Sure, it would be easy to say that the Internet and a few other technologies are merely changes in how we do things, and that the things we do are still the same. But this just isn't true, and it doesn't line up with what researchers are finding.

Think of it this way: You, like us, probably grew up having access to an adult who could drive you somewhere. (Of course, this wasn't true for everyone; but it was the norm of North America during the '60s, '70s, and '80s.) This "technology" had an impact on how you, as a 13-year-old, interacted with the world when compared to the lives of your great-grandparents who grew up in a time when driving everywhere wasn't the norm. This mobility had implications for spontaneity, for the reach of friendships (and possible friendships), for free-time options, for sports involvement and other extracurricular activities, even for the context for schooling (as motorized vehicles meant schools didn't have to be within walking distance, which opened the doorway for more age-specific classrooms).

In the same sense, the technologies (and the nontechnological things as well) that are normative for our kids today shape their lives and experiences and behaviors and worldviews. These things change what it means to be a young teen.

We'll unpack this a bit more in a moment.

Three Epochs of Youth Culture

Another thing that we believe has shifted is the prioritization of those three adolescent tasks (identity, autonomy, and affinity).[82] Here's the gist of what we're seeing.

The modern era of youth culture could be broken up into three epochs with slightly different values and issues. These shifts have been driven by a combination of factors:

- The lengthening of adolescence (and the drop in the age of the onset of puberty)

- The acceptance (or other responses) of youth culture by culture at large

- Changes in technology that have impacted relationships and other human interactions

To oversimplify things a bit (these are generalizations), we could say that from post-World War II to about 1970 was the first epoch of youth culture; 1970 to the millennial turn was the second epoch; and we're now in the third epoch. In each of these time periods, our contention is that the priorities of those three adolescent tasks have shifted.

In the earliest days of modern youth culture, identity was the long leg of the three-legged stool. Youth culture was new and just beginning to gain some acceptance by culture at large. Identity trumped the other two tasks, as youth culture (if we can personify it for a moment) tried to figure out who it was.

Then at the end of the first epoch and the beginning of the second, people accepted youth culture and all the "stuff" that comes with it—norms and behaviors and attitudes, music, clothing styles, language—and youth culture shifted to a place of trying to differentiate itself from culture at large. This is the task of autonomy. You can see this most markedly in the countercultural youth movements of the late '60s and throughout the '70s. But we believe this autonomy priority continued to lead the way for a few decades.[83]

The third epoch arose, in a sense, because the second epoch was so successful. Youth culture (often with our help and the help of marketers interested in getting into the minds and pockets of teenagers) found ways to be extremely "other" than the culture at large, even while the culture at large was starting to adopt a popular level of youth culture as the dominant shaper of the adult world. Thus, youth culture splintered into multiple subcultures, and it went underground.[84]

This splintering and subterranean nature of today's youth culture has created a belonging vacuum and once again shuffled the deck of adolescent tasks. Affinity, we believe, is now the long leg of the three-legged stool. It's not that identity and autonomy aren't important anymore—they are! But today's teenagers are using their desperate need for belonging as a *pathway* to inform the identity and autonomy tasks.

What does that mean for us? Well, this change in youth culture (including early adolescent culture) means that our youth ministries can't be about entertaining kids anymore. We can't just provide a middle-school-appropriate "show" for them, with neat games and a young-teen-savvy sermon. Now more than ever, our ministries must be focused on helping young teens experience real belonging with each other, with adults who know them and care about them, and with the God who invented them and desires to be in relationship with them.

The Fabric of Culture

There are dozens of definitions for the word *culture*, as it's used by a variety of fields of knowledge. But for our purposes, this definition is helpful:

The sum total of ways of living
built up by a group of human beings
and transmitted from one generation to another.[86]

There are a few key words and phrases in that pithy little sentence:

- "Sum total": Culture is *all* the stuff we collectively do and think, the metanarrative that gives meaning and future direction to our collective story.

- "Ways of living": Culture is about how we think and live. In other words, it's not just esoteric and philosophical;

culture impacts our daily lives, moment by moment. It's about what we do and why we do what we do.

- "Built up": Culture is created. But it's not just created by *them*; we create it together. And since we all work together to make this thing—this "way of living"—it's constantly morphing and mutating, shifting and evolving.

- "By a group of human beings": Developing cultural norms is a human enterprise. We might like to point fingers at "the media" or "marketing" and blame them for the parts of culture we don't like. However, nothing becomes a part of culture without first gaining acceptance by the populace, which, to one extent or another, includes us.

- "Transmitted from one generation to another": Dude, that sounds almost biblical. While culture is evolving and shifting, it's also being handed down and cross-pollinated. Culture is transmitted along parent-teen lines, as well as via peers, social networks, and other arenas of human interaction and influence.

One more important framing idea: The aspects of middle school culture that we're going to unpack in the next section could be misunderstood as negative or as signs that humanity is on the decline. We don't write these with a "this is bad" mindset. Culture is neutral, at least in the sense that it is what it is, and youth workers are called to minister to middle schoolers in their real world. Sure there are aspects of culture that are unfortunate because they've caused kids to live in ways that aren't healthy or aren't best for their development. And there are times and reasons for us to introduce countercultural ideas and practices. But the argument over bad versus good isn't something we're going to spend time on. We will say that we find it interesting how some adults are so willing to adopt these technologies that shape our culture while they simultaneously dis the cultural impact of those "advances." It's time for us to own our part in the evolution of culture.

The Culture of Middle School

So how does all that shake down for today's middle schoolers? And what's unique or more intensified for young teens?

A CULTURE OF INFORMATION

We all live in a culture of information. So, in a sense, this isn't unique to middle schoolers. What *is* unique is that this reality is shaping them during their early adolescent development and in ways that weren't true prior to the last decade. What's also unique is that today's young teens have *always lived* in a culture of information.

Almost every bit of information needed (as well as excessive quantities of information that are *not* wanted) is available with the click of a mouse and in ways that shape our worldviews. This is both about access to information and the onslaught of information. The *access of information* shapes middle schoolers' culture of immediacy, their sense of entitlement, and their work ethic. On the other hand, the *onslaught of information* has a numbing effect.[87] Since everything middle schoolers need to know is readily available and since they're constantly bombarded with suggestions and data of every sort, they're less attentive to the stuff that passes by.

A CULTURE OF IMMEDIACY

Think for a minute about the things you had to wait for as a middle schooler that today's middle schoolers don't. They can take a picture on their cameras or cell phones and see the results instantly. They hear a song on the radio, and they can instantly download it to their computer or cell phone. Want to buy something? They can jump online in seconds, browse a customized and instantly generated list of sites, get others' input about an item via user comments, and then, if they want the item, make an instant purchase and wait a day or two at most for the item to arrive.

If you've ever been "stuck" somewhere without your cell phone and tried to find a pay phone to make a call, then you've been reminded of this shift.

Sure, you and I also have access to all this immediacy. But most of us didn't grow up with this being normative. Today's young teens have never known a world without instant everything. Doesn't it strike you as funny that their idea of "old skool hominess" includes making bread in a computer-enabled machine that does all the work?

Here's a great example of this shift: For us adults, email communication changed everything. We were able to send and receive written communication without writing it by hand and going through the "hassle" of using the postal system. Written communication became almost instantaneous. But no one predicted that teenagers would dispose of email as being too slow and clunky and then opt for the intensely more immediate communication pathway of text messaging. We adults saw text messaging as a utilitarian means of quick planning. Teenagers turned it into a social phenomenon.

Middle schoolers don't have a willingness (or even the capacity) to wait for anything. Our culture has trained them to expect everything instantly. Patience is a rough one; "delayed gratification" is a foreign concept; and slowness can have a deeply profound impact on them, since it's something they simply don't experience in their everyday lives.

A DISPOSABLE CULTURE

Along with everything being instantly accessible, we also live in an era of disposability. Some things, such as disposable contact lenses and printer ink cartridges, are *only* interacted with as throwaway items. Many more things have a sense of disposability to them, from cell phones to iPods to laptop computers. Even an MP3 file seems more disposable than a physical CD.

Just like other aspects of the middle school world, this "use it a bit, then toss it" mentality has been the norm for these kids their whole lives. So it naturally flows over into other realms of their thinking in ways that are new to this generation.

Relationships have a sense of disposability to them these days.

Knowledge has a sense of disposability to it these days.

Beliefs have a sense of disposability.

And affiliations.

And trust.

And truth.

The subconscious thinking is—*If something new is going to re-place this next week anyhow, why should I be attached to this now?*

A CULTURE OF CONSUMERISM

In the final sentence of the preceding section ("The Fabric of Culture"), we note that it's time for us to own our complicity in today's culture. Nowhere is this more true than with consumerism.

A significant portion of the still-forming identity of today's middle schooler is just that: "I am a consumer." They've learned this from the obvious places, such as advertisements everywhere. For example, do you remember when major sports arenas weren't "sponsored"? Or the era before ad revenue was the primary fuel of the Internet? Do you remember when *product placement* was a term you didn't know?

But schooling in how to be a consumer comes from much more than *those people* in the marketing world. Almost everything and everyone in the lives of young teens treats them as consumers.

And treating young teens as consumers—get ready for the "ouch"—is what most of our churches and youth ministries do also.

We recently heard British youth leader Mike Pilavachi speak at a Youth Specialties National Youth Workers Convention. He shared the narrative of his earliest days in youth ministry, when he worked hard to provide the best youth ministry show in town. A turning point came for him on the night he put together a fun movie party for his group. He arranged comfortable seating, provided fun movie snacks, prepared a bit of stand-up comedy beforehand, and showed a fun film. At the end of the night, the room was trashed and all the kids were walking out. The last girl looked at the state of the room, turned to Mike, and said, "Wow, this room is a real mess." He thought she might offer to help clean it up, but instead she said, "You're really going to have to clean this up!" And then she walked out.

Mike was furious as he went about the work of cleaning up. He thought about how unappreciative the kids were, and he even thought how they "didn't deserve him." But an intrusive thought (from God, Mike was sure) came to him: *Why are they this way?* The only honest answer Mike could give was, *I've made them this way.* Mike said, "When we treat them as consumers, they play their part very well."

This is one of those "less neutral" parts of middle school culture that we can work to undo. Or at least we can be intentional about not adding to it.

AN INTENSE BUT TEMPORARY CULTURE

In the chapter on middle school relational change (chapter 7), we wrote about young-teen girl friendships having an extremely high expectation of intensity, but that these relationships are often temporary. This is a thin slice of middle school culture in general.

Some of this is developmental. In their effort to sample and discover, middle schoolers often immerse themselves into their interests, affinity groups, or value systems. They try these on as if they're the last ones they'll ever try on, as if they're going to give their lives to this new direction.

My (Marko here) daughter, Liesl, who at 15 years old is just emerging from her young teen years, has always been an all-or-nothing kid. When she was into art (taking art classes and such), she was convinced she'd spend the rest of her life doing it. When she decided she wanted to be a skateboarder, she adopted everything of that subculture (including music, clothing, and many other seemingly unrelated variables) in a "this is who I am" manner. Liesl has gone through a dozen or more identity makeovers, and she's just now starting to settle into some less-temporary identity wrappings.

We adults tend to either try things on more tentatively or immerse ourselves in things we *will* stick with for a long time. Not so, usually, with middle schoolers. We titled this chapter "White-Hot Temporary" for this reason: Middle schoolers give themselves to the interest, relationship, choice, value system, or belief that's in their faces, but they also easily discard it for the next sampling exercise. This is a cultural issue, in addition to being a developmental issue, because it's what they observe all around them in other young teens. It's considered normal.

We adults might ask, "Why don't you ever stick with *anything* long enough to really know if it's you?" But their peers sure aren't saying that to them.

A NETWORKED CULTURE

Obviously, this is a huge shift in young teen culture. The fact that most young teens (sure, not all of them) have cell phones that instantly connect them with parents and friends is a whole new world of instant, networked connectivity. Text messages, MySpace, Facebook, Twitter, and other social networking tools have created a middle school culture that exists in bits and bytes.

This is a fascinating shift. While relationships are as important as ever, these relationships are more dependent than ever (seriously, *ever*—in all of history) on the written word. Friendships are no longer primarily dependent on physical proximity, audible vocalization, and listening. Friendships and social networks of middle schoolers are *more dependent* on networks played out over transmitted data.

As such, the "Who's in your network?" question of identity and affinity is more than a cell phone company marketing tag. Young teens consider online and text communications to be both the foundations and the buttresses of their relational cathedrals.

A quick example: Liesl (Marko's daughter) has a formerly very close friend who lives only about a mile away from us, but no longer attends her school. He has a cell phone, but it's almost always out of minutes (since he has a very limited prepaid plan). So she can rarely reach him by cell phone or text message. He doesn't use Facebook (which Liesl does). So even though he lives in reasonable proximity to Liesl, she's finding she has no real means of sustaining the friendship. She has other friends who also don't attend her school anymore (as a result of moving to high school elsewhere), but she still considers them to be very close friends because they constantly—daily—connect via text messaging and Facebook (and the occasional phone call).

A DRIVEN/SEDENTARY CULTURE

This is an interesting, paradoxical tension in today's middle school culture. On the one hand, the pressures on middle schoolers are greater now than they've ever been. Today's young teens are driven in ways that are almost scary. Some of this drivenness comes from their own choosing; but most of it is an external drive from parents and schools.

Not all kids play sports, of course; but for those who do, involvement in sports seems to be less about having fun and getting exercise. Instead, involvement in sports often carries with it a sense of the future: *What doors will this open?* Sports are seen in a utilitarian sense, as a means to get somewhere in life. In other words, the pursuit of the American dream (financial freedom and career success) is more competitive and fleeting than ever. And sports are seen as one of the many Lego pieces that will build an edge over others, increasing the likelihood of "success."

Yet sports are only one example. We see this driven reality play out in the lives of countless nonsporting middle schoolers, too. The message seems to be, *You must be the best at something if you hope to be successful in life.*

Of course, this plays out academically also. Not every kid is college-bound, but the pressure to succeed academically permeates much of teenage, including young teen, culture. We're pretty sure there was no such thing as SAT prep for middle schoolers when we were that age.[88]

But with all this pressure and drivenness, there's an odd tension at play in the lives of young teens: They are more sedentary than ever. They don't *move* as much. They watch more TV, sit at computers, sit in their rooms and text their friends, and sit in front of gaming systems for hours on end. The notion of a pick-up game of stickball in the street has little more than an old-timey Norman Rockwell vibe to it these days.[89]

When the young teen guys we know get together with friends, it's rarely for any kind of physical activity. Young teen guys typically get together to play video games.[90]

Our Role

So what's our role in middle schoolers' lives when it comes to culture? This is a challenging question, and it's easier to just blow it off. But youth workers who want to thoughtfully engage young teens must be proactive in two ways:

WE MUST BE STUDENTS OF CULTURE

It's close to impossible to be the life coach and spiritual journey guide that we hope to be for middle schoolers if we don't expend the effort to learn about the culture they live in. (This is similar to what we wrote earlier about how we need to learn about early adolescent developmental stuff.)

We believe this calls for a shift in youth workers' self-perception. Classically, youth workers have seen themselves (and churches have viewed us) as educators. This is both literal and metaphorical, by the way. In many churches, though, youth ministry was (and in some, it still is) part of the Christian education department.

The *currency* of any educational framework is *knowledge*. And while knowledge has its place and value in the development and spiritual growth of middle schoolers, we want to be (and must be) about much more than that.

We'd like to propose a couple of new metaphors: Cultural anthropologists and adventure guides. As anthropologists, we learn about the young-teen experience, we study the generalities of development and culture, and we get to know the real issues and stories of real-life young teens. Then we act as their adventure guides through the early adolescent experience, including—but not limited to—their spiritual journeys.

WE MUST ENGAGE IN CULTURAL EXEGESIS

Exegesis, if you're not familiar with the word, is a fancy synonym for *interpreting*. It's usually used in the church and in connection with the act of preaching from Scripture. A preacher engages in scriptural exegesis to dig into the original intention of the passage and bring about an interpretive explanation for our context. In the same sense, we need to dig into the values and forces that shape early adolescent culture and then work as interpreters for teens and parents alike.

But our response to culture shouldn't be passive. As people who care about young teens, we have an opportunity (even an obligation) to engage in both countercultural ministry and culture shaping. We might not be able to change all of early adolescent culture; but we can shape the cultural experience of the young teens in our midst.

This isn't about culture bashing. Helping young teens learn to see the good, bad, and neutral in their own culture is a huge part of good middle school ministry. And much of this can be accomplished by offering experiences that differ from what young teens experience in their everyday worlds. Two key words to think about in this area are *slow* and *quiet*.

The Dream of Culture Creation

A final idea as we're thinking about middle school culture and, specifically, the notions of culture shaping and being countercultural. Let's remember this: As followers of Jesus, we're living in the culture of the world but with a priority and allegiance to the culture of the kingdom of God.

We live for, long for, pray for, and dream of middle school ministries dripping with the values of kingdom culture: Love and grace, justice and mercy, selflessness and humility, gratitude and growth.

Wow. That's quite a dream, huh?

Recently, I (Marko) was asked during a magazine interview to provide "steps of discipleship" for teenagers. I'm not a big fan of a "steps" approach, which implies that the process of following Jesus is the same for everyone or every youth ministry in every context. I believe the process of discipleship has a cultural element to it. So I said that in my response, but then I went on to say that if I must provide "steps," they would be these:

- Get to know the middle schoolers in your ministry.

- Get to know Jesus.

- Live in the way of Jesus yourself so you become a living laboratory for your own reflection and for your students to observe.

- Exercise prayerful discernment *with* your middle schoolers about what an approach to discipleship should look like in your context.

- Try something. Live a life of faith in action together.

That, friends, is what it means for us to live into a dream of a kingdom of God culture for our middle school ministries.

CHAPTER 10

The Overlapping Transition

Do you remember the video game *Frogger*? To play it, you control a little frog that tries to cross a street or a river. You could move the frog to the left and right, forward and backward. On the street levels of the game, the goal was to jump off the safety of the starting curb and into the spaces between the cars and trucks driving by. And there was a median in the middle of the screen where the frog could rest before hopping through the traffic going the other direction. On the river levels, however, the goal was the opposite: You crossed over by jumping onto the moving turtles and lily pads before they sank.

In both cases, the overall objective was the same: Leave the safety of one curb or shore, navigate the potentially life-ending obstacles of the transitional space, and—hopefully—arrive at the safety of the far curb or shore.[91]

For many years we thought of the middle school experience this way. In our mind's eye, we pictured preteens ambling up to the shore of a turbulent river. Then at puberty, we pictured them wading into the swirling shallows and eventually moving out to depths beyond their ability to stand as they battled the currents, waves, and eddies of early adolescence.

childhood	middle school	high school/ young adult

Then as we handed them off to the middle teen or high school years, we pictured them safely arriving at some kind of distant shore. What, exactly, that far shore was didn't really factor into this metaphor too much. (Maybe it was just the median?)

But after many years spent working with thousands of middle schoolers, we've come to see this metaphor as flawed. The "Frogger Transition"—or any metaphor that portrays young teens leaving safety, moving into a transitionary space, and arriving at some kind of post-transitionary space—is *not* the experience of real middle school kids.

Instead, the shores (or curbs) of that metaphor need to trade places. In other words, early adolescence is an overlapping transition. The transitional space in the middle is both-and, rather than being "no longer-not yet."

	middle school	
childhood		high school/ young adult

In other words, young teens move into a transitional period in which they are *still* children in many ways—holding cautiously to childhood ideas and conclusions, finding safety and comfort in childhood toys and fantasies, retreating to spaces that are known. But at the same time, they're fully experimenting with the world of adolescence and adulthood: Trying on new behaviors and values like clothes on a rack, sampling attitudes and ideas, testing the waters of doubt and questioning.

We might think of this, in metaphorical terms, as the blending between colors.[92] Since this book is printed in black on white, we'll use a grayscale. But the metaphor works with any blending of two colors. Using this metaphor, middle school is gray. It's an overlapping or blending of the childhood and adolescent life stages.

Middle school is *not* this:

And middle school is *not* this:

Instead, middle school is this:

There's a sense of advance and retreat during this process, but it's not as clean as "two steps forward and one step back." Sometimes middle schoolers take one step forward and two steps back. But just as often, they'll take one step forward and then quickly take one step back. And once in a while they'll take two steps forward and no steps back. There's no predicting this at a micro level, and the whole process of moving from childhood to full-on teenagerhood can only be seen from a macro level, from a helicopter view.

Barbie Dolls and Punk Pokémons

Let's look at a couple of real examples to flesh this out a bit.

The first involved a girl I (Marko here) had in my middle school ministry a few years ago. We're sure you've had girls just like this, as we've seen lots of them in our ministries. Marcie was 12 years old and in 7th grade. She was ahead of the curve in her physical development. She could have easily passed for a 16-year-old girl. She was pretty, and she knew how to work that. Marcie had perfectly styled hair that wasn't one bit teenybopper, and she had fingernails that all the women in our ministry were jealous of. Marcie knew how to wear makeup tastefully (not like some young teen girls who look as though they're heading for careers in street walking or theater).

Marcie was also relationally mature, and she was comfortable and at ease in adult conversation. Adult leaders liked being around Marcie because she made them feel comfortable, almost as though they were chatting with a peer.

Pretty much everything about Marcie made her seem mature beyond her years—except Marcie was still totally into Barbie dolls. In a phase of life when almost every other girl had *long since* discarded her dolls or forgotten them in the back of a closet or sold them on eBay, Marcie loved her dolls.

And this wasn't the semi-acceptable Barbie affection of an adult collector. Marcie didn't value her Barbies for their monetary worth; Marcie loved her Barbie dolls as childhood playthings. She'd regularly bring a Barbie or two on overnight trips with the youth group, and they could be found resting on her pillow during nonsleeping hours. Some kids teased her about this, but Marcie wasn't emotionally perceptive enough to realize it was teasing. She believed the other kids thought her Barbies were fun. And she regularly mistook their play-along mocking as genuine interest in her dolls.

Marcie was in the midst of this overlapping transition. She was still a child in some ways, but she was already an emerging young woman in many other ways. Both-and.

Then there were the guys I (still Marko here) called "The Punk Pokémons." (I never called them that to their faces, of course.) You've had wolf packs of guys like this in your ministry, we're sure.

The Punk Pokémons were an affinity group of about five guys who were always present at our middle school ministry but never fully engaged. (Full engagement was contrary to the accepted norms of their group, after all.) They were in 8th grade, and they were all taller than I was. They wore all black, and they always slumped down in their chairs in the back row with their arms crossed and an "I dare you to try to engage me" look on their faces. Seriously, they were an intimidating lot with a constant façade of boredom and seething anger.

In the rare instances when they used words (they typically used grunts and other sounds more often than actual words), the PPs (ha!) would respond with one-word answers. They never initiated conversation unless it was to tell leaders that something was stupid. They all listened to old-skool punk music, and they were committed to a simplistic, childish concept of what anarchy might mean.

But they were all seriously into trading Pokémon cards. (This was a few years back, when Pokémon cards—those cute little Japanese anime trading cards—were the rage.) The PPs would huddle in a back corner of our middle school room, all brooding and quiet, and it looked as though they were in the midst of a drug trade, or plotting the overthrow of the world. But if one got close enough, one could just barely overhear a plea like, "I'll trade you two Pikachus for that Mewtwo!"

The Punk Pokémons were living large in the turbulent transitional waters of early adolescence. Certainly, within a year or two, most of them would leave behind their Pokémon card collections in favor of more fully teenage interests and pursuits. But, for now, they were blissfully unaware of the incongruency of this holdover from their childhoods with everything else in their carefully manicured affinity group norms.

WHAT'S OUR RESPONSE AND ROLE?

We've written this multiple times already, but it bears repeating in the context of this discussion of transition. We are grace-filled tour guides on the journey of early adolescence. This has a few practical applications:

1. We never try to rush kids or push them into adolescence. We show them grace by loving them in the midst of this weirdness. When you visit the home of a middle school guy and he shows you his room and you notice a stuffed animal on his bed, realize that you are on very thin ice. If you make a joke about it, you might "help" him discard this childhood holdover; but you're likely crushing one of the few safe zones he has in his otherwise upside-down and all-changing world. A little joke, no matter how unintentional, can completely destroy a kid—and destroy your influence on his life.

2. We protect kids from teasing. Sooner or later, Marcie will discover that the other kids were actually teasing her. And the realization that they've been teasing her all along will likely hit her like a tidal wave. She'll probably feel tiny and stupid, and she'll most likely experience betrayal. Be her ally in this, not tolerating any teasing when it happens and standing with Marcie if and when this realization does occur. Marcie will gradually move on from her Barbie dolls, and the PPs will lose interest in their trading cards. And hopefully this will occur naturally and without trauma and drama. There are enough opportunities for feeling stupid and outside the norm in middle school, so try to minimize those experiences in your ministry.

3. We walk alongside. Whatever metaphor you choose for the turbulent transition of middle school, it's messy. And good middle school youth workers will get some of this mess on them.

If we're using the river-crossing metaphor, we can't just stand on either shore (the "sending shore" or the "receiving shore") and shout out instructions and encouragement. We must get in and dog-paddle alongside our students. Hopefully, you've learned enough about the currents and obstacles that you can act as a river guide, providing some orientation, close-up encourage-ment, and the occasional lifeline. And if we're using the color blend metaphor, we become color consultants, palette guides, art coaches.

THAT HELICOPTER VIEW

In addition to being in the midst of things with middle schoolers, we have that helicopter view we referred to earlier. We have an understanding of what's going on in their lives; we have a sense of where they're headed; we have ideas about how their choices will impact them.

And, most importantly, we have a confidence about what God is doing in their lives.

We don't offer young teens our perspectives in condescend-ing ways. ("You need to grow up!" "Why would you make that choice? Can't you see where it will lead?") We don't offer our per-spective in a distant and removed way, shouting down on them from a metaphorical megaphone. And we don't pretend to know it all or to have all the answers or to have everything figured out in our own lives.

Instead, our perspective and involvement is that we *have seen* the situation from our helicopter viewpoint, but we're now jour-neying with and alongside middle schoolers. We have both un-derstanding and experience (our own and what we've observed in others) that are valuable, necessary, and helpful. But we bring that understanding and perspective just as Christ brought his to us: We live incarnationally among middle schoolers.

WHY I DO THIS

"Developmental crossroads" is why I choose to work with middle school kids. One degree of developmental influence to the left or right, extended over time, can have an impact that will affect a student for a lifetime. It could be a positive impact or a negative one. I want to set the stage for a positive impact.

There is a gigantic need to invest in kids at this crossroads. When I take the time to look into their eyes, their souls, I see how much every one of them has a need that will get filled with something. In my experience, the demographics or backgrounds of kids matter little as a predictor of which direction they'll choose. Sometimes it's a random meeting, a bored moment, or hanging with the wrong crowd that sends a teen in a certain direction.

All preteens or teenagers have transitional and crossroads needs that they'll fill with stuff. I want to help them make healthy choices—both spiritually and physically—to fill those needs. We cannot, and should not, force-feed these kids on what to do, say, or how to act. But we absolutely can assist them with self-discovery and the wonderment that God wants to expose them to. If they learn it, then it becomes part of their journey, part of who they are, part of their identity. If we cram it down their throats, chances are they'll reject it like bad food.

The idea of leading people to Christ is wonderful, but I like to take the approach of what space fillers they allow to take over their lives. If there's an opening and a quiet moment during which the Christ-teen connection can happen directly, then the result is powerful. That authentic connection can provide the one-degree shift in the right direction, the one that changes the trajectory of their lives.

That's why I work with middle schoolers. I want to "host" those connections with God that bring life-altering, story-shifting path diversions.

John Freese is a lighting engineer by trade and a middle school ministry volunteer by calling. He lives in Santee, California.

CHAPTER 11

See Jane Face New Issues

(Bonus Chapter by Kara Powell and Brad Griffin)

See Jane.[93]

See Jane thrive in elementary school.

See Jane enter middle school.

See Jane face new issues—different issues than Jane in the 1980s or the 1990s.

See Jane struggle.

See Jane grow.

While middle school has always been a time of developmental change, girls today face new issues, as well as new twists on not-so-new issues. As youth workers hustling to keep up with all that Jane (or Juanita or Janesha or Jin-Ha) faces, we're grateful for a recent batch of research that helps us understand all that our middle school girls navigate and walk alongside them as they tread new paths.

See Jane Cyber-Pioneer

ONLINE CREATIVITY

At age 14, Ashley Qualls built a million-dollar Web enterprise from her room.

Yes, at age 14.

And, yes, from her room.

By creating MySpace page designs and offering them via her site, whateverlife.com (which now draws 250,000 unique visitors—mostly teen girls—each day), Ashley quickly became the young-teen CEO of a booming online venture. The MySpace page designs are free; the money comes via advertisers who line up to buy a spot on Ashley's space.

Ashley is a prototype of the new tech-savvy teen girl. And Ashley's not alone—either in her success or her tech savvy. When she launched a magazine to get more girls interested in creating Web content, a thousand teens quickly volunteered to contribute.

TEXT FEST

Undoubtedly you've already observed that text messaging is vastly changing the way middle school girls (and of course guys) communicate and at a pace that's nothing less than breathtaking. Teen girls now report spending more time texting than actually talking on their cell phones—and the top reason for this is so they can multitask. Forty percent of teens would "die" if they couldn't text on their phone, and 45 percent agree that their cell phone is the key to their social life.[94]

Jane can be in touch with her friends anywhere, anytime, and in short bursts of gossip, affirmation, insult, or inspiration. Caught in a social setting where she feels unsafe, or stuck alone in her room or—*ugh*—with her family, today's Jane can find instant relational salvation via her trusty cell phone.

For the middle school girls in our ministries, an inbox with one new text sends Jane the message that someone cares. Our ministries have used texts as a way to ask for prayer, to send quick notes of affirmation to girls, and to invite girls to special small groups and ministry events. Kids have asked deep theological questions through texts, such as, "How is listening to the Holy Spirit different from just listening to our consciences?" Texts can also contribute to lighthearted fun, like the recent competition between classes to see who can send the weirdest text photo of a rubber chicken to their leaders. (And what middle schooler doesn't feel cared for by a picture of a rubber chicken?)

How We Can Respond

CROSSING THE LINE

In the midst of Jane's navigation of new technology, girls need us to help them think through what they should be sharing publicly and what they should consider keeping private (such as photos of themselves nude or in their underwear, to name one of the most rampant trends). Online boundaries are nebulous, and girls need caring adults to help them navigate the flood of possibilities that await them as they learn to express themselves digitally.

One middle school girl from our church received a text from a friend declaring her homosexuality for the first time. Interestingly, our middle schooler wasn't at all surprised that she'd learned this news through a text, but I'm so glad she shared the text with her small group leader who could help her explore the feelings this news generated.

CREATIVITY CHANNELED

We can actively tap into girls' creativity and knowledge of Web content creation and help them express that creativity in healthy ways. That may mean giving them outlets to use their Web skills in ministry, and it may mean giving them offline ways to nurture that creativity as well.

We're seeing a shift in terms of which students are most interested in being part of our church's middle school "tech team." In the past, it's been primarily boys. But now that the "tech team" has expanded beyond setting up the sound system to include PowerPoint slides, YouTube videos, and other Internet media venues—six of the seven kids involved are girls. To be honest, sometimes the "improvements" the girls make to the PowerPoint presentations that our middle school pastor has worked on all week actually make the presentation worse. But we love that their middle school fingerprints are all over them (even if they do leave smears and smudges).

MOM, CAN'T IT WAIT?

We also have the chance to directly address the issue of multitasking and the ways texting feeds into that practice. We can help middle school girls process the pros and cons of multitasking when it includes things such as talking to your parents (or God) and texting simultaneously and help them understand their parents' frustration with having to constantly ask them to put down their phones.

TO TEXT OR NOT TO TEXT?

Having said that, we also need to develop a healthy set of guidelines for ourselves when it comes to texting kids. One of our small group leaders had a two-hour conversation with a middle school girl earlier this year—entirely by text—about the girl's struggle with smoking pot. The medium provided a safe venue for the girl to express her turmoil, even her persistent desire to smoke and to engage in other self-destructive behaviors, in the midst of texting back and forth. The leader stayed engaged with her and respected her choice of texting as the mode of communication in which she felt safest. And ultimately, the girl decided to get on a journey toward becoming clean. (Recently they celebrated her 100th drug-free day—via text.)

That's a neat story, but we also have to step back and ask: Where do we draw our texting boundaries? How often will we participate in texting conversations that go on, and on, and on? When do we need to shut down the finger punching and choose either a vocal conversation or (dare we suggest) silence?

While students who text us may initially judge our care and concern for them by the immediacy of our replies, that can quickly lead to a life without boundaries. Talk with your ministry team (and your friends or spouse) about setting healthy boundaries for when you will and won't return texts and clearly communicate these guidelines to students in your ministry.

PHONES: AWAY OR NOT?

When we gather with middle school girls in worship, small groups, or other events, we should determine boundaries for if or when it's okay for them to text while in these settings. We've seen in our middle school ministry that texting is just as distracting for those who are watching and wondering what's being typed as it is for the girl doing the texting. To our chagrin, texting also brings attention to the economic disparity between the girls in our ministry who have a cell phone and the girls who don't. In the midst of their 24/7 use of cell phones outside of your ministry events, try involving students in developing a group covenant about texting and other mobile behavior as a way to help them own the decision, as well as consider their phone dependence.

See Jane Try to Be Sexy

THE DAMAGE DONE

Those of us who care about middle school girls have intuitively sensed that the pressure to be "sexy" damages the way they view themselves and others. A 2007 report by the American Psychological Association (APA) spells out the destruction more explicitly. Whether it's a five-year-old girl walking through a shopping mall in a short T-shirt that says JUICY or a magazine article that promises teenage girls that losing 10 pounds will get them the boyfriend of their dreams, sexualization is linked to impaired cognitive performance, eating disorders, low self-esteem, and even physical health problems.[95]

THE PARENT TRAP

More than 77,000 invasive cosmetic surgical procedures are performed on teens (middle and high school students) each year.[96] While that in and of itself is shocking, consider this: Minors cannot undergo these surgeries unless their parents consent. In most cases, since these procedures are not covered by medical insurance, parents pay for the surgery as well.

MOM-DAUGHTER COMPETITION

Much attention has been placed on the messages that the media sends to young girls about their bodies, and rightly so. But what about the messages from Mom? It seems that more and more moms are competing with their teenage daughters for the perfect body and wearing clothes that show off their efforts. Girls are struggling to keep up. With bodies that change faster than they can handle, and certainly more unpredictably than their mothers', middle school girls may find themselves in a losing race with their moms to be "sexier."

One girl in our ministry seemed to throw in the towel during such a competition. Like her incredibly thin mom, this girl had been an avid runner and healthy eater in 6th and 7th grade. All that changed in 8th grade when the girl got curves. Her mom still runs and wears spaghetti strap dresses, but the girl seems to be coping through potato chips and covering her body with baggy sweatshirts.

How We Can Respond

BOYS OUT

Schedule a girls-only series of small groups and invite moms or female mentors to attend. While you'll want to have the girls and women meet together much of the time, schedule a separate discussion with the moms and mentors about the messages they may be—often unknowingly—communicating to their girls when they make either negative or positive comments about their own bodies, as well as their daughters'.

MIRROR, MIRROR

Have a similar conversation with both male and female volunteers and small group leaders in your ministry, discussing the way our own pursuits of physical perfection shape the attitudes and behaviors of the girls we work with. Talk honestly about the ways we might be contributing to girls' confusion by gravitating either toward or away from girls who are wearing clothing that flaunts their bodies. With your female volunteers, role-play having a conversation with a girl who's trying to be "sexy" that sensitively asks her how she views her body, as well as why she wears the clothing she does.

DEAR DIARY...

Gather middle school girls who're ready to think more deeply. Give them notebooks and some art supplies so they can create their own journals to help them reflect on the pressure to be sexy. After a few weeks or months, have a check-in lunch and ask them to look back through their journals, identifying common words and themes that they can discuss together. By teaching middle school girls to journal and name forces like "pressure," "image management," and "sexualization," we're giving them lenses with which to interpret and process their experiences and feelings. Simply being able to identify and name their experiences can help young teenagers make sense out of what otherwise feels like chaos.

At our last middle school camp, we gave our girls a bunch of watercolor paints and pens and invited them to compare the media's view of who they are with who they really are. Girls insightfully wrote comments such as, GO GET PERFECT...AND THEN COME BACK and WHAT IF YOU DON'T HAVE THE RIGHT SHOES? One girl who seemed especially glad to express her feelings wrote the following anonymous poem:

Fame

Everybody wants fame.

Some use it just to look lame.

Fame or money can tear you up.

Stay in school

Keep your grades up.

Don't be foolish.

Look around.

See how Britney Spears turned upside down.

You can use Maybelline

But that can't show the inner queen.

Be who you are.

See Jane Play; See Jane Sit

THE COUCH POTATO-ETTE

There's mixed news about girls' sports these days. While more girls (middle school and high school) than ever are playing organized sports, overall they're becoming less active and less healthy. (Yes, even those who play a sport.) Outside of organized sports, girls seem to be sitting around (literally) a whole lot more than they used to. Girls lag behind boys in meeting age-appropriate healthy levels of physical activity, and they drop out of organized sports more often, especially as they transition from childhood to adolescence.[97]

How We Can Respond

NON-JOCKS WELCOME

Give Jane ways to appropriately express her physicality, even if she isn't a jock. What message are girls learning about their bodies by the sports or physical games involved in your youth ministry? Are these games targeted only to guys while girls sit on the sidelines and watch or cheer? How can you bring new twists to games so that differences in strength and athleticism are neutralized and the playing field is leveled? A girl who lacks confidence in her body or athletic prowess and who chooses to sit on the sidelines during volleyball might dive in and play a modified volleyball game in which everyone plays on their knees, or you play with a balloon instead of a real ball. Experiment with minimizing the competition focus of games and elevating the focus on fun and relationship building (which, of course, is good for guys, too).

WOMEN POWER

Jane will also be far more likely to get off the bleachers and into the game if adult volunteers understand the power of their own modeling. Every time your female leaders sit out, they're saying it's not only permissible, but also preferred for girls to sit on the sidelines. Instead, involve your female leaders in planning the games. And when it's time to play, hand over leadership to those same women so the girls see women not just playing, but also taking initiative and enjoying it.

See Jane Buy...and Feel Bad about Herself

I FEEL BAD...I WANT A NEW SHIRT

Okay, it's no shock that girls are a huge consumer market. But recent research shows another twist: Teen materialism has been linked directly to self-esteem—especially among younger teens, and especially among girls. When self-esteem drops (particularly in middle school), materialism skyrockets. When self-esteem rises, materialism drops—again, especially during early adolescence. Unfortunately, self-esteem usually doesn't begin to rise again until high school.[98]

FASHION BULLYING

Middle school girls who make the "wrong" fashion purchases are in a new kind of trouble. While fashion bullying (meaning picking on girls based on the clothing they wear) has been going on for decades, lately psychologists and school guidance counselors have noted a new level of intensity. The middle school hall has become a bloody corral for the fashion posse. One researcher studying teen behavior in more than 20 states says she's seen a stark increase in bullying related to clothes over the past few years, alongside an increase in high-end designers targeting early teen girls.[99]

How We Can Respond

MORE THAN KITCHEN AND KIDS

Give girls opportunities to increase their self-esteem by helping them identify and use their natural and spiritual gifts. Do girls experience themselves in your ministry and church as more than just a kitchen helper or a nursery worker? If not, brainstorm with your team until you develop a strategy for changing the perceptions and roles of young females across the spectrum of church ministry.

HELP JANE FIGURE OUT WHAT SHE ACTUALLY LIKES

One small group leader told us that she's on a mission to take middle school girls shopping and help them think about what they're drawn to and why. Most girls in her small group like a particular bathing suit or purse because of its label or the store it comes from, not because of what it actually looks like. So she takes girls to the mall and asks girls to explain why they like what they like. Some of them never get past "because it's cool," but other girls are starting to see that there's more to style than clothing labels.

TEACH GIRLS HOW TO ADVOCATE

A few years ago a group of 13-to-16-year-old girls was able to convince Abercrombie and Fitch to pull a line of T-shirts boasting slogans such as WHO NEEDS BRAINS WHEN YOU HAVE THESE? across the chest. Their "girlcott" is only one of a number of successful examples of girls advocating for the reduction of cultural sexualization of women.[100]

See Jane Soar

Are some of these research findings downright scary? You bet.

Should we fatalistically throw up our hands in surrender? Not a chance.

One of our colleagues at the Fuller Youth Institute, Dr. Desiree Segura April, has focused much of her research on studying girls around the world. Similar to the situation in the United States, girls across the globe face unique struggles including slavery, sex trafficking, and fewer opportunities to receive health care and education.

Yet girls around the world, especially if given a bit of nurture and support, are also often the most productive and engaged leaders. Some international leaders are advocating and ministering more to girls than boys because they see the influence that Jane has in India, Zimbabwe, and Brazil.

What does it take to see Jane reach her kingdom potential? It takes courageous youth workers who are willing to link arms with courageous young teen girls. As we strategically respond to these new realities that our middle school girls face, we can see Jane soar.

A GUY'S TAKE ON MIDDLE SCHOOL GIRLS

BRAD GRIFFIN

When most male youth workers are asked about working with middle school girls, they have a range of thoughts about what that experience might be like: *Disarming, intimidating, unnerving,* or *overwhelming* are frequently within that range. Other images don't pop up as readily (for example, *stable, quiet, safe, easy*). As a result, many men end up paralyzed. Too much drama. Too many tears.

And then there's the gender problem. We're afraid they'll either develop a crush on us or want us to be their substitute dads, and we have no idea what to do with either of those scenarios. Not to mention the fact that while 12-year-old boys remind us of our own awkwardness in middle school, 12-year-old girls remind us of the girls we awkwardly sought after in middle school (in our hearts, if not in reality), and probably of the first girls who caused us emotional pain. We instinctively want to run away from those memories.

Sadly for us, when we let ourselves give in to these paralysis-or-flight responses, we miss out on a world of discovery—of ourselves, others, and God—in which girls frankly *need* us to join them. Middle school girls (or MSGs—think of them as the *good* kind of MSG) need adult men who:

1. Genuinely care for them and treat them as daughters of God.

2. Consistently "show up" in their lives, giving them opportunities to develop stable, faithful relationships with guys within the body of Christ.

3. Don't objectify them, but instead provide a counter-narrative to what they experience every day through the media and at school.

4. Touch them in appropriate ways, keeping healthy physical boundaries that model healing and wholeness, rather than destruction and brokenness.[101]

As we work to move beyond our fears when it comes to MSGs, here are a few tips just for guys:

1. *Take MSGs—and their emotions—seriously.* A girl is likely to remember for the rest of her life (or at least the rest of this year)—when her thoughts or feelings are disregarded as laughable or stupid.

2. *Model appropriate behavior for middle school guys.* Show young teen boys how to treat MSGs (and all women) with respect and without objectifying them for their bodies.

3. *Know when to ask a woman for help.* You don't need to be the one to tell a girl she needs to wear a more modest bathing suit or not to hug boys so aggressively. Sensitive issues involving girls' appearance or their bodies in any way need to be handled by female adults, not us.

4 *Be safe and smart with boundaries.* Don't be alone behind closed doors with girls ever, and don't let girls ride in your car without a female adult present—these should be absolutes for all guys in your ministry.

5. *Never make fun of the way—or how much—they eat.* MSGs are balancing the voracious appetites of their growing bodies with constant pressure to eat less and look perfectly thin. Insensitive comments from significant men in their lives can be disastrous—even when we believe they know we're "just joking around."

6. *Have fun with them!* You're both likely to make and share significant memories.

Kara E. Powell, PhD, is a former middle school girl who now serves as a faculty member at Fuller Seminary and the executive director of the Fuller Youth Institute (www.fulleryouthinstitute.org).

Brad M. Griffin serves as the associate director of the Fuller Youth Institute (www.fulleryouthinstitute.org) and volunteers with middle school kids at his church. He was never a middle school girl, but he unsuccessfully pursued a lot of them as a middle school guy.

SECTION TWO
The Land of Freaks, Geeks, and Squirrels

CHAPTER 12

First Things First
(Remembering What It Was Like)

"My parents are COMPLETELY out of touch," said 13-year-old Kayla, as she popped her gum, twirled her hair, and rolled her eyes. The three friends huddled around her nodded in agreement and chorused, "Ohhhh yeah."

Encouraged, Kayla continued her rant, "My mom is so annoying—she doesn't get what it's like to be me. She just grounded me, but I can't be grounded this weekend—it's the biggest weekend of the year! She and Dad caught me texting Josh after bedtime last Saturday night. We weren't doing anything wrong. He was talking about stuff he wants to do with me, and I sent him a couple of pictures of myself. What's the big deal? But now I can't go anywhere except to school and church. And they took away my cell phone, too! How am I supposed to live when I can't call my friends? I know my parents don't want me talking on the phone all the time. But when I'm texting, I'm not making any noise. All I'm doing is trying to stay in touch with people and with everything that's going on. I *have* to know what's going on. Can't they get that? *They* get to choose what they want to do. It's not fair! They have no idea what it's like to be my age."

Minutes later, these 7th-grade girls are talking about a few of their teachers in the same way. Kayla said, "They're sooo old-fashioned! Even though they're, like, around us every day, they have no idea what it's like to BE us. My science teacher gave me a detention because I didn't get my paper done on time. Can I help it if my brother was hogging the computer all night? My teacher acted like I was dumb; he said I was irresponsible. Can you even imagine what our teachers were like in middle school?" That thought apparently causes one girl to laugh so hard that she chokes on her drink and it spews out of her nose. And this just sends the other three into exaggerated uncontrollable giggling.

Some parents and teachers may very well be "completely out of touch" with the lives of teenagers—at least in the eyes of a middle schooler. But could it be that many adults (and even young adults) haven't figured out how to do the hard work of connecting with the middle school world?

In the preceding chapters of this book, we've looked at the extraordinary development of a middle schooler in so many dimensions of their lives. It's an indisputable and significant fact: *They* are in middle school, and *you* are not. You've left that stage, and in some cases you've left it *far* behind. So that means, compared to middle schoolers, we're like citizens of different countries who speak different languages, wear different clothes, listen to different music, follow different customs and traditions, and all the rest. Maybe we need to look at middle school ministry in the same way that foreign missionaries perceive their work: These people from the land of Middle School are not like us.

Yet, in many ways they're very much like us.[102]

Two Truths about Then and Now

It's crucial to note two monumental truths that impact the way we view middle school students and our ministry to them.

TRUTH #1: BEING A MIDDLE SCHOOLER TODAY IS RIDICULOUSLY DIFFERENT THAN IT WAS FOR YOU

A quick glance around the airport newsstand or the scrolling CNN headlines gives a revealing, sobering picture of the accelerated world that middle schoolers are trying to grow up in today.

- The perpetual morphing of the online world (in both positive and destructive ways)

- New extremes in war and terrorism

- Inflation and economic crises of unprecedented proportions

- Unmatched extremes in poverty, environmental issues, and revolutionary advances against disease

- Cloning, genetic research, and all the associated ethics

And the list goes on.

Simply put, the world is not what it was even just a few short years ago. But these protruding boundaries aren't limited to headline news. The personal world and boundary decisions of middle schoolers are stretched to frontiers that would've been reserved for high school and college students of just a decade or two ago.

Oral sex, online porn, and homosexual relationships complicate the world of Boy Meets Girl. Students face increased pressure to perform academically, athletically, musically, or otherwise "extracurricularly" lest they risk future opportunities by underperforming in their pre-high school days. Suffocating peer pressure accosts them in school and increasingly in cyberspace as well. Electronic connections give them infinite chances to "plug in and tune out." Aggressive advertisers recognize the billions of dollars of purchasing power that middle schoolers control—they've increased marketing budgets accordingly (more than two-and-a-half times since the early 1990s), and they dangle carrots that have never looked sweeter, since adolescents now influence well over $600 billion in spending dollars.[103]

The challenges stalking this culture where middle school students roam are ridiculously different than in earlier eras. And in so many ways, they're infinitely larger than any average 13-year-old could—or should—be ready to handle. But whether or not to face those trials isn't a choice that young teens have. These ordeals stand before them, and they're forced to cope—ready or not. And yet...

TRUTH #2: BEING A MIDDLE SCHOOLER TODAY IS REMARKABLY SIMILAR TO WHAT IT WAS FOR YOU

- The discoveries (He used to want to pull her hair; now he wonders what it would be like to hold her hand.)

- The insecurities (*Everybody* is staring at this volcanic zit on my cheek!)

- The desire to belong

- The realization that you're not yet an adult, but you're no longer a little kid, either

- The thrill of new relationships

- The pain of friendships gone awry

- The realization that Mom and Dad aren't always right and you have the option to think in ways apart from their guidance

- The navigation of increased responsibilities, opportunities, and consequences

Growing up is still growing up. It's breathtaking and nerve-racking and confusing and sometimes upside down. You remember all the developmental growth and changes we've discussed during the last 10 chapters? We've all had to navigate that territory. And few of us are dying to relive those days.

Going Back in Time

I'm (Scott) a sucker for time travel movies—even the bad ones. There's *The Time Machine, The Butterfly Effect, Groundhog Day,* the *Back to the Future* trilogy, and even the *Terminator* movies. The thought of "seeing the future" thrills my mind! But as important as the future is in the life of a middle schooler, if we want to have a chance at understanding these young teenagers and their futures, then you and I have to jump into a mental time machine and roll back the calendar.

AMPLIFYING THE MUFFLED MEMORIES

When it comes to understanding middle school students, the best place to begin is looking at your own middle school career. You must be willing to do the hard work of really *remembering*—reliving those good ol' days of middle school. Here's the challenge: We don't run into many people who'd say, "If I could repeat *any* year of my life, it'd be 7th grade." And for good reason. We've blocked out some of those memories because our experiences were difficult, awkward, and not very fun. In fact, some are downright painful. And we're not just talking about extreme situations:

> Man, if only I could experience that first zit again—that was fantastic. The sense of utter humiliation I felt when I realized it was too gigantic to cover up, all red and swollen and oozing. And knowing for sure that every person in school was whispering about it whenever I turned my back. Now that was awesome!

> Wow, what a great feeling it was when I walked up to my "friends" at the lunch table, and they all got up and left at the same time. It was like a sign flashed the word LOSER above my head.

WHY I DO THIS

Why am I involved with middle schoolers? Good question! As with most classic youth ministry recruitment, it started because of a need to fill an empty space.

Our church hired a youth minister. She showed up on July 1, worked for two days, and then left for the Independence Day holiday. And never returned.

Suddenly, huge gaps of church staff coverage needed to be plugged up. Volunteers readily stepped in to assume many different responsibilities. Programming for my two senior high children was assured for the next school year. But my youngest daughter—just about to enter middle school and excited about the possibilities of youth group—seemed as if she might be disappointed unless someone stepped up.

The voice of God did not come in the flurry of recruitment phone calls. The Word of the Lord could not be discerned in an impassioned pitch from the pulpit by the pastor. Yet, when my daughter expressed her concern that there'd be no middle school youth ministry without some adult volunteering? Well, I heard that!

There is a faith that middle schoolers place in trusted adults that allows them to be able to still hear and imagine a simple story.

There is a hope that younger adolescents embrace in the possibilities of their teenage years, as well as their lives. There is a love and passion that these kids have that has not been dulled by hurt or boredom.

I've encountered the face of Christ many times. It's found with a little acne, maybe some stringy hair, and the scent of a sweaty middle school kid.

He or she is the younger adolescent who has breached the inner sanctums of the temple and has a few amazing things to share with the elders of the community. For me, theirs is the face of Christ.

D. Scott Miller is the coordinator for Adolescent Faith Formation for the (Catholic) Archdiocese of Baltimore, Maryland.

Just my luck that I was the last of my friends to hit puberty. My voice was higher than everyone else's in the locker room, and everyone who called our house thought I was my sister.

Researchers have shown that a biological mechanism in the human brain blocks unwanted memories.[104] And experiments have demonstrated that people are capable of repeatedly blocking a memory until they can no longer recall it.

Lucky you! You can suppress those painful middle school memories. But our students are currently living those kinds of awkward experiences.

REALIZING THAT TIME HAS...PASSED

Aside from the gift of painful memory suppression, adults just simply forget stuff. And as a result, we tend to overrate and under-remember what it feels like to be in middle school. We might tell ourselves that middle school challenges weren't that big a deal. We might even suppose that young teenagers are overreacting and they just need to "grow up."

In addition, our adult lives have plenty of drama, crises, busy-ness, and demands of their own. When we get caught up in our day-to-day challenges, we can sometimes rate our difficulties as being more "authentic" than what the average middle schooler faces.

PUBERTY? POPULARITY? PARENTS?

Almost unconsciously, we can find ourselves presuming, *You middle schoolers have no idea what real difficulty looks like. How about mortgages, marriage, and making a living?* But to a young teenager, their issues *are* big challenges. And they're every bit as significant and stressful and complicated to their middle school minds as your adult issues are to you.

Middle school ministry pioneer Wayne Rice discusses in his *Junior High Ministry* book a concept that's echoed in my head for many years: "Left to their own devices, young adolescents will gravitate toward the oldest person who will take them seriously..."[105]

What a phrase—"take them seriously."

Middle schoolers typically don't appear to take *much* very seriously, including themselves. But in reality, they're hoping that someone—anyone—will listen beyond the surface of what they're saying and give credence to their middle school life. Whether that older someone is a high school sibling, an uncle, a gang member, or a coach, there will be an invisible pull toward that person simply because the young teen is craving someone older to show authentic interest in them.

Here's an email that I (Scott) got from a student who was trying to make sense of her transition from child to teenager. It's forever preserved in her classic middle school grammatical style:

> Scott—hey wuts new I'm reely sorry for not really writing you during the summer. I've been really busy with soccer and junk i changed soccer teams!
>
> *(That exclamation point is the last punctuation mark in the email. Now I've been invited into her stream of consciousness.)*
>
> Its really weird i don't think I'm really fiting in not that I'm a geek or anything its just that I'm kinda a anti social kind of person I'm really shy and with school i haven't met anybody so far and when i think i made a friend they go on and ignore me and I'm kind of feeling distant from god and i don't know if he still loves me did you ever feel that way i kind of feel stupid though like i don't know what I'm doing in life and if i make a mistake it stands out to the whole world and since I'm the youngest in my family and my brother is not so excited about

halloween christmas easter new years thanksgiving or any other holiday and since my brother already went through that phase my parents kinda forgot about me and all those holidays so they forget that I'm still kinda a kid so that means I'm the only one to carve the pumpkin and the only one actualy getting up early for x-mas and it makes me wonder if we're eventually gunna forget bout x-mas and carving the pumpkin and be a family who doesn't really care PLEASE write back I'm really confused with my family and my relationship with god and i would like to start emailing each other again.

love always, lauren

Sounds like a middle schooler who's longing for someone to take her seriously, don't you think?

Reaching for a Genuine Understanding

Unless we've traveled back in time, we might not genuinely *understand* students to our fullest ability. Grasping a middle schooler's perspective of the significance, supposed implications, and perceived importance of the issues going on in their lives can be monumental. And these days, far too many students don't have an adult in their lives who's making the effort to really know them.

There's no replacement for a parent's listening ear in a kid's life. But the reality for so many middle schoolers is that there's *not* much time in their week when an adult is intentionally listening to them and seeking to look at life from their perspective. Statistics say that in the average American home, meaningful conversation between parents and kids happens only about 39 minutes each *week*.[106] That's a whopping six minutes a day!

Most of us have faced an extremely difficult situation and had a well-intentioned friend say, "I understand how you feel."

They mean well, but you know it's actually *impossible* for them to have the slightest idea of how you feel. I watched it happen several times when my wife's mom died recently. Good-hearted, well-meaning people said they knew how my wife felt; but most of these well-wishers had two living parents.

Likewise, it's possible for us to prematurely claim that we understand middle school life since, after all, "we've been there." This is exactly why we need to go back and reload our memories.

REMEMBER

So how *do* we remember? How do we wrap our brains around those glory days of our own middle school experience?

For some of you, this'll be easy. Your memories of middle school are pretty fresh. Maybe you still hang out with a bunch of people you knew in middle school. You're young, and it's pretty easy to recall images of middle school.

But for others, this is going to take some real effort. Maybe you're in your late twenties, or you have kids of your own, or maybe you're even a grandparent. You can barely remember the name of your middle school, much less who you hung out with and what you felt like. Maybe you can't even remember why you started reading this book. You're going to need to dust off your mental time machine and get ready for a ride.

(Okay, let's be honest. When you're reading a book and you get to a section that asks you to "interact," you sometimes skip over it, right? You probably almost *always* skip it. But this next section is crucial in order to go back in time and see life from the perspective of a middle schooler. Please don't blow past this!)

We want to give you some equipment to help you dig through the caverns of your memory. Take a few minutes and jot down some notes in the margins. Yep, go ahead and write in this book. You can use it as a reference when you're trying to "go back in time" to understand.

GET YOUR BRAIN THERE

So here's how to move toward that understanding. Jot down a few words in response to the following questions:

When you were in middle school, what was the world like?

- What was popular—the styles, trends, fashions?

- What shows were on TV?

- What was "cutting edge" in technology? Or what were the latest inventions?

- What stories were covered on the evening news? (Check out some history Web sites to jog your memory.)[107]

I (Scott) remember—

- Bell-bottom jeans, *The Six Million Dollar Man*, and Styx

- The 1980 U.S. Olympic hockey team beating the Russians and winning the gold medal

- Adults freaking out about a major nuclear accident at a place called Three Mile Island in Pennsylvania

- Hearing about a "Disco Demolition Night" getting out of control at a White Sox baseball game, with fans storming the field and tearing it up so much that the game had to be canceled

- A plane that crashed during takeoff from Chicago, killing more than 250 people

And even though I delivered the newspaper to 70 houses every day, I didn't pay a lot of attention to the current events described in it.

Now think about what your personal world was like.

- Who were your friends (think of specific names, faces, memories)?

- What was your family like? Who lived in your home with you?

- Did your parents work? What was their relationship like?

- Any family traditions? Vacations? Sibling relationships?

- What was your neighborhood like?

See if you can find your old yearbook or a shoebox filled with any middle school mementos. I actually keep an old middle school yearbook in my office so I can pull myself back to those days whenever I need to.

Now that you've transported yourself back in time, you can get more specific.

- What were your favorite things?

- What music did you listen to? (Come on, what did you sing when no one was listening?)

- Did you participate in any sports, clubs, or other extracurricular activities?

- What was summer like for you?

- Did you have any jobs or responsibilities in middle school?

- Did you have secret hangouts where you liked to go— maybe alone or to meet friends?

- Did you attend any school dances?

- What fantasies and dreams went through your head when you were 13?

GET YOUR HEART THERE

As you bring this thinking all the way to your heart, can you remember—

- A "highlight day"?

- A most embarrassing moment—one you could hardly talk about afterward?

- Anything that kept you up at night because it was so exciting...or scary?

- What did you worry about?

Bring It Right Here

Now you're ready to think about what it's like to be a young teen today. The good news is that your heart is ready to try. The bad news is that we probably can't fully understand what it's like to be a teen today. The pressures and challenges they face are likely far beyond the struggles we faced as 13-year-olds.

One recent study indicates that 70 percent of teens would appreciate their parents simply acknowledging that they don't fully understand all the changes but still affirming their love for their son or daughter and that they *want* to understand who their children are becoming.[108]

The bottom line is that kids don't need us to fully understand everything they're experiencing. But they do need to know that we care and we're willing to be in their corner as they figure out life. Young teens are changing so fast that they often don't even understand what's happening to them. So if an adult says, "I understand," the teen will quickly (and rightly) assume the adult is still in the dark.

You may be wondering, *So if all that is true, why did we do all this work to remember our middle school worlds if we can't even really understand middle schoolers today?* Simple: Because the process of reflecting and remembering prepares us to be better investigators of our students' identities—which is really what they're trying to figure out.

One More Thought

Are you a people watcher? People are funny creatures to observe. I (Scott) actually do it all the time, and I try to make up stories about where they're going or what they're doing.

I also like to watch people when they're around middle schoolers. Like this one time when I was in the grocery store with my wife and our three young sons. When our kids were little, Lynette liked to go to the store by herself—it was kind of a mini-vacation from us guys. But sometimes I'd convince her to let us come along. The only rule was that I had to entertain the guys while she got the shopping done. Once we were in the store, she'd send us off to get a few items—even though it'd be much quicker to get them herself. So we were on our way to the cereal aisle when Lynette swung past us and said she'd seen some of my middle school students come into the store.

There were four of them, and they were picking up something for one of their parents. They were elated to see me. So for a few minutes in the grocery store, we had a mini small group meeting. They were catching me up on life and school and jokes. One started a little game of tag with my five-year-old. My two-year-old was on my shoulders, so one of the guys wanted to show me that he could lift his short 7th-grade buddy onto *his* shoulders. (And reach the toilet paper on the top shelf next to him.)

I promise we were being respectful. But it was interesting to observe people's reactions as they turned into aisle four of the grocery store that day.

Some looked at us and kind of laughed...uneasily. Some assessed things more carefully and quietly tried to sneak by. Some looked annoyed, as if to say, "What in the world are *kids* doing in an adult grocery store?" (That sounds bad. It wasn't an "adult" grocery store; it was just a grocery store. You know what I mean.) Others quickly did a 180 and practically ran out of the aisle with their carts. *I'll get my cereal next week,* you could almost hear them thinking.

And one or two of them, like some of you, looked a little intrigued.

When some people look at young teens, they see people who

- Are hard to relate to

- Wear different clothes, listen to different music

- Don't "have their act together" yet

- Are too emotional when you don't want them to be

- Aren't emotionally engaged when you want them to be

But what does *God* see when he looks at middle schoolers? We believe God sees people he *treasures* and who just happen to be riding a roller coaster toward an adult body and mind.

Going back in time will remind us of what it was like when *we* traveled that road. And it will make us better able to lend our hands and hearts to middle schoolers as they continue on their own version of that journey.

CHAPTER 13

Dude! What's Up?

(Building Relationships with Middle Schoolers)

Some youth workers are great with names; the rest of us—not so much. I (Scott) can't count the number of times I've met someone and then 30 seconds after the introduction, I have no idea what the person's name is. I probably wasn't listening very well in the first place.

But with our students, there's an easy remedy, right?

"Hey, DUDE, what's up?"

"Hi, MY FRIEND, how's your week going?"

If we muster enough enthusiasm, maybe they won't realize we didn't call them by name. And they probably won't. At least not the first few times. But sooner or later, they're gonna catch on. One of the great things about young teens is their ability to be direct. Painfully direct sometimes.

"Hey! You don't remember my name, do you?" (This accusation is usually spoken in an exaggerated insulted tone.)

What's in a Name?

In *How to Win Friends and Influence People*, Dale Carnegie wrote, "The average person is more interested in his or her own name than in all the other names on earth put together."[109] And I believe middle schoolers' names are their most prized possessions.

If we frequently go the route of the generic "dude" or "my friend" monikers instead of deciding to commit people's names to memory, then we're saying to them that their names, their persons, aren't important. And it really does start with a decision. So many people are quick to say, "I'm just terrible with names." But the people who do the best with this are usually the ones who've simply *decided* that it's important enough to devote their energy to remembering people's names. And the payoff is big.

One of the most beloved middle school youth workers I know is a guy named Wes—he's funny and creative, he has a quick smile, and students pay attention when Wes speaks. But I'm convinced that he's popular with a great number of students (even in a large ministry) because *he can call so many people by name*. No photographic memory, no mysterious telepathic ability—he's just chosen to show middle schoolers that they matter to him by knowing their names. Scripture says God's people "listen to his voice. He calls his own sheep *by name* and leads them out" (John 10:3, emphasis added). Coincidence? Probably not.

Whatever you have to do to make it happen, start committing names to memory. Write 'em down, take photos, and quiz yourself. You could even ask the students to help you come up with ways to remember their names.

At the beginning of this school year, I (Scott) kept forgetting the name of a sweet little 6th-grade girl named Cassidy. She was charitable with my forgetfulness—even a little amused by it. But I told her it was important for me to remember her name, and I asked if she had any ideas to assist my recall.

She grinned and said, "Well, it kind of sounds like *quesa-dilla.*" (Huh?)

But since that moment, Cassidy beams every time I see her and say, "What's up, Quesadilla Cassidy?"

THE POWER OF YOUR INTEREST

One of the biggest benefits of remembering someone's name is that it proves you're *interested* in that person. It communicates value. "You're important enough to me that I want to know you individually." For middle schoolers, when someone who's not "required" to be interested in them (in other words, a parent, teacher, and so on) actually pays them some attention—it's a big deal. And they *notice!*

It's been said that in high school ministry, a student will look at a youth worker and ask herself, *Do I* like *this person? Is she interesting to me?* Yet through our reading, research, and personal experience, we'd suggest that a middle schooler is more likely to speculate: *Does this person* like me? *Is she interested in* me? It's one of the things we like best about middle school students. Very often, their main criterion for a friendship is simply finding someone who pays attention to them, and it's even better when the person seems genuinely curious about them.

In healthy adult relationships, we expect a certain level of mutuality in our interactions—some give-and-take. It might not always be 50-50, but if one person doesn't hold up his end of the relationship, then the other person usually feels less motivated to invest as much in the friendship.

- If she talks too much...

- If he's frequently selfish...

- If she tends to forget about your feelings...

- If his insecurity regularly gets the best of him, and he looks for a laugh at your expense...

But in the adult-to-student equation, the same relationship formula cannot be applied. The student is the not-yet-mature party in your association. So you can *expect* many of those things we just listed—and more. Remember, you're the adult; they're the students.

Middle School Conversations

What does it look like to have a "good" conversation with a middle schooler? Well, having realistic expectations is a great place to start.

I (Scott) remember working with my first middle school small group. I'd call the homes of the guys in my group—just to check in. It was a different kind of phone call than I was used to. And if you've ever experienced the exhilaration of a telephone conversation with a young teenage *boy*, then you know what I mean.

Talking with middle school boys on the phone is very different than talking with middle school girls. My wife leads a small group of 8th-grade girls. When she calls them to check in, she has to allow an average of 20 minutes for each call—sometimes longer. And with texting (as discussed in chapter 11), interactions can run all evening if appropriate limits aren't set. However, I can usually call all seven of my small group guys while my wife's still in the midst of the first conversation with one of her girls. Ahhh, it's good to be a guy.

This is roughly how one of my first phone calls went with one of the guys in my small group:

> Me: "Hi, this is Scott calling from church...is Trevor there?"
>
> Trevor: "This is me."
>
> Me: "Hey, man! How's it going...how's your week been?"
>
> Trevor: "Good."
>
> Me: "I know you had a test in math...how do you think it went?"
>
> Trevor: "Mmm...okay."
>
> Me: "Are you getting excited about the retreat we've got coming up?"
>
> Trevor: "Yep."
>
> Me: "Anything else interesting going on?"
>
> Trevor: "Not really."
>
> Me: "What're you going to do this weekend?"
>
> Trevor: "Probably nothing..."

I've gotta be honest—I felt victorious whenever I received more than a one-syllable response from a student. But for the most part, I felt like a big failure. I mean, I believe I interact with students pretty well. But talking to one of them on the phone—man, that's a challenge.

It got worse a few days later when I happened to see Trevor's mom. "Thanks for calling and talking to Trevor the other day," she said.

I paused and studied her face. Why would she *say* that? For crying out loud, I gave it my best shot. I couldn't help it if Trevor responded as if he were in some kind of a pseudo-coma. "Um... are you *mocking* me?" I finally said. She looked surprised and a little confused. Then she insisted she wasn't making fun of me.

"Did you *hear* our conversation?" I asked her. "It lasted all of about 90 seconds!"

I'll never forget her response—partially because since then I've heard many similar versions of parent reflections over the years. "Scott, I was right there while you were talking to him; he was standing in our kitchen. He'd had a really rough day at school, and he was in a terrible mood all afternoon—grouchy, grumpy, and actually kind of mean. Then *you* called. Even though he barely responded to you, when he hung up the phone, his mood had entirely changed. He actually finished his homework without complaining, and he was more civil to me than he'd been all week. Later that night he said to me, 'It was kinda cool that Scott called.'"

I looked at this mom for a few seconds, and then I said, "Okay, now you're just *lying* to me."

Even though Trevor didn't (or couldn't) find the words to say it out loud, what he experienced was the powerful feeling that someone thought of him. Not only that, but that someone was interested enough to call.

Just last week, my small group co-leader asked everyone, "What was a highlight of your week?"

One of the first guys to speak said, "Well...Scott called me this week."

Ha! Must've been a slow week for that kid. But later on my co-leader said to me, "Dude, I don't think he was kidding. It sounded like that was one of the best parts of his week."

Bottom line? Your interest *matters* to them—even if they act like it doesn't. (Or, maybe more accurately, even if they don't know how to express it.)

Let's get more practical. What are some big ideas to remember when making the most of middle school conversations?

THE POWER OF GOOD QUESTIONS

When someone's described as a "good conversationalist," they're undoubtedly a good question asker. Having a good conversation with a middle schooler means you have to be an ace at asking questions. And yet there's a fine line between "asking good questions" and "interrogation."

- Avoid asking yes-no questions because far too often you'll get a "yes" or a "no"—and nothing else.

- Comment on something about the student and invite a response. To break the ice, offer something such as, "That's a cool _____ (*scarf, hat, T-shirt, shoelace, cast, black eye, nose ring*). Where'd you get it?"

- Develop a mental list of *easy* conversation-starting questions. Nothing too deep—just a chance to get conversation rolling. (Check out the sidebar on page 212 for some ideas.)

- Listen for little clues as an invitation to probe deeper (maybe during that same conversation or maybe later). "You said your mom's sick...what's going on?" or "What do you mean you don't really hang out with anyone at school?"

CONVERSATION-STARTING QUESTIONS

- "What's the best or worst thing that's happened to you this week?"

- "What do you think you'll do for _____ (*Christmas, spring break, insert upcoming holiday here*)?"

- "How's school?" And then, "What's your favorite class this year?" and then "What do you like about it?"

- "Got any pets?" (Don't leave it at a "yes" or "no"—ask for more information about the pet(s).)

- "Do you play any sports?" "How's it going?" "What's your coach like?"

- "What school clubs are you involved with?"

- "What was your high point or low point for the week?"[110]

REMEMBER THEIR ANSWERS (AND THEIR NAMES!)

Asking good questions is a start, but the real value comes when students realize you actually listened to and remembered what they said. If you ask the same kid three weeks in a row whether or not he has any brothers or sisters, he'll sense that you didn't really care or weren't listening to him. But the reverse is true, too. When you see a student for the second time and you call her by name and ask how her sick cat is feeling this week, you've expressed great *value* to her. She mattered enough for you to remember.

If you're like me (Scott), that's easier said than done. But it's still crucial. So when I'm in a gathering of students, I usually keep a small notebook in my back pocket. I write down names, as well as other memory-jogging details that I can look at later: PETE— SHORT REDHEAD, PACKERS FAN, DAD JUST MOVED OUT. I don't write it down in front of them (duh). I'll usually take a few minutes at the end of the gathering and jot down reminders. Then I can quickly review a few notes before the next group gathering and almost instantly connect with Pete just by asking if the Packers won. I could even check the score or highlights beforehand, so our conversation could go a step further. And, if the situation is right, I can go a little deeper and ask Pete if he's seen his dad and how that's been.

Keep in mind that *remembering* communicates *value*, and students who feel valued are more open to relationship. More importantly, within a relationship is where growth happens best.

BE COMFORTABLE WITH AWKWARDNESS

Middle school life is fraught with awkwardness. Most young teens have an inner sense that people are becoming annoyed with them. Couple this with their increased sense of external awkwardness, and as a result, they'll make regular social blunders that can damage their relationships. Not that they'd ever admit it—or are even consciously aware of it—but middle schoolers are learning a lot about social interaction in the midst of this tension.

There's no doubt that it's much easier to spend time with a young teen with well-developed social skills and the ability to take part in a conversation. But when a student feels grace in a relationship with his youth leader, it adds a dimension of safety, which often leads to increased openness to learn. This grace resembles patience. It means not being easily annoyed by their habits, which allows them to work through their awkwardness. Our students typically don't even know this process is happening; they just feel that safety. So if a kid says something embarrassing or commits a social blunder, we can help him avoid humiliation by how we react.

While we should try to be comfortable with the awkwardness, it's best for adults to avoid adding more. Here are some don'ts to keep in mind if you want to reduce the number of awkward moments with your middle schoolers:

- *Don't* extend your hand for a good old-fashioned handshake when you introduce yourself. Middle schoolers don't do that—it's for "older people." A high five or the trust fist bump are still okay, though. Just be casual and you'll be fine.

- *Don't* guess their year in school. ("Good to meet you, Tyler. Are you in 6th grade?") The short 8th-grade boy you've just mistaken for a 6th grader will feel even shorter and think, *WHY did you have to point out how short I am?* And the tall, gangly 6th-grade girl you mistook for an 8th grader definitely won't feel any shorter. But she'll probably think, I *must* look like a GIANT.

- *Don't* be nervous. The students are nervous, too. One frequent sign of our own nervousness is when we spend most of our time talking to other leaders at a middle school gathering instead of engaging with students. Check your body language and relax. Trust us, they usually aren't paying attention to whether or not *you're* nervous.

- *Don't* be surprised if a student's response seems stiffer or more curt than the last time you talked to her. She could be unwilling to share more because of other listeners. Most middle schoolers will answer questions differently when someone else might hear their responses. But if it's just a one-on-one conversation with you, then a student doesn't have to worry about how a peer might interpret her answer. Maintaining cool—or at least minimizing embarrassment—is high on the list of social values when you're 13.

- *Don't* feel impaired if you don't know much about your students' favorite video games or TV shows or bands or other interests. In fact, if they sense you're interested, most middle schoolers are more than willing to teach you something about the stuff they like. To take it to another level, go home and Google a topic they love. Imagine their surprise when you can ask an intelligent question about it the next time you see them.

STUDENTS WON'T EXPRESS A TON OF GRATITUDE, IF ANY

Realistically, gratefulness is often a slow-developing character quality for most middle schoolers. "Wow, Mom! I just want you to know how much I've appreciated all the car-pooling you've done for my soccer team this season, not to mention the huge financial investment you made so I could play on this team." That's not the kind of comment that parents will (ever?) hear from a middle schooler.

In the same way, a student in your youth group isn't likely to say, "Hey, *thanks* for volunteering your time with us. I can't believe you'd willingly give up your free time to try to help me understand God—that's amazing!" Your students *are* thankful for you, yet they usually have no concept that it'd be cool for you to hear them say it out loud. Years later, though, they may remember the contribution you made to their lives.

Just this week, I (Scott) was at a National Youth Workers Convention. A college sophomore named Phil walked up to me; he'd been in my middle school ministry six years before, but I hadn't seen him in a few years. I had no idea he was attending the convention or preparing to be a youth pastor. We chatted for a while, and then before we parted ways, he said, "I just want to say thanks. Your influence on me when I was in middle school is still one of the things that's affected my life the most."

As he walked away, I thought, *Now that's cool. I guess God wanted to give me another little reminder of what he's up to in the trenches of youth ministry.*

An Often-Overlooked Ingredient

Because we've (Marko and Scott) been doing this kind of ministry for so long, we've seen literally hundreds of small groups of middle schoolers. (We're old, okay?) And these groups have had all kinds of leaders, all kinds of settings, and all kinds of students. As you can imagine, some small groups have been spectacular, some very "middle-of-the-road," and some very forgettable. And that's led us to ask a question, which we've asked many times over: What makes some groups seriously great, while others aren't?

Is the key having a small group leader with seminary-level Bible knowledge? We don't believe so.

Why I Do This

I remember middle school. I remember feeling awkward, alone, embarrassed, annoyed, excited, full of energy, angry, happy, and aloof. I remember feeling as though I had to be perfect and come from a perfect home—hiding the fact that our cars barely ran and our bills were hard to pay. I remember feeling as though it was my responsibility to make everyone happy and stop the tension, to always smile and pretend things were fine.

When I spend time with my students, I'm reminded of the myriad of emotions, reactions, and feelings I had in middle school.

Every Monday I attend a school lunch. One particular day I saw two of my students, who I always thought were fabulous and full of life, eating at a lunch table with just one other friend. When I sat down, the two boys looked at me as though I were doing something extremely out of the ordinary. One of the boys stopped me mid-sentence and asked why I chose to sit at their table. He went on to inform me that there were much cooler students than him and that he didn't deserve my time.

A few years ago, I was at a girls' retreat when three of my students pulled me aside and asked if we could talk. One of the girls broke down and told us she didn't believe she fit in her family and was convinced her family didn't love her. She was the youngest of three beautiful, smart sisters who always had boyfriends, got As in class, and looked like models. This girl did not see her own beauty; instead, she saw her differences that set her apart from a family that she believed would have been picture-perfect without her. This girl was so convinced that her family wanted nothing to do with her that she began cutting to hide from the pain she felt at home every day.

I'm afraid that all middle school students feel trapped in a world that expects them to be perfect and makes them feel as though they're never good enough. My heart breaks for the students who don't recognize the image of God that dwells inside of them. I get angry when I hear others talk to or about middle school students in ways that suggest they're too young, a burden, annoying, useless, or exhausting to be around. Middle school students are at such a transitional age; they're adults, children, and everything in between—all at the same time. They need caring adults around them who respect them and aren't afraid to call them to their full potential, to a life that God is inviting them to live, a life they were created to live. Middle school students have the imagination, creativity, excitement, and faith to bring heaven to earth.

I choose to work directly with this age group because I believe in middle school students and desire to help them believe in the person God created them to be. I hear their stories, I'm inspired by their hearts, and I'm moved by their actions to love God, others, and the world. I believe God created every person at every age to bring his kingdom to earth now—and I want to be one of the people who gets to share this great God-given power with young teens.

Middle school students deserve to hear that they're loved, needed, respected, and uniquely designed by God. They must understand their thoughts, questions, and actions are needed by others to understand God more fully. I'm drawn to this age group because I hear the voices of many who tell them, "Not yet." I see the opinions, ideas, and dreams of middle school students get thrown out the window by those who don't dare to believe in someone younger. I feel the weight of disappointment, sadness, and destruction that's placed on this age group over and over again because these students are hearing and believing they're not good enough.

In this beautifully difficult age that I adore, I'll give everything I have to go into a lunchroom, sit next to any group of students, engage in great conversation, and have them never question why I chose to sit with them. Knowing the reality of this world's cruel voices and the ever-changing emotional status of a middle school student, I'll continue to work with this age group because they'll always need someone to fight for them and to repeatedly remind them that they're amazing, important, created by God, and needed in this world.

Corrie Boyle is the associate pastor of student ministries and the director of the element at Mars Hill Bible Church in Grandville, Michigan.

Is it crucial to have students who are all alike? Not in our experience.

Is it the curriculum that pushes the small group to the top of the heap? Nope.

Ding! Ding! Ding! The envelope, please…

It's one thing to build relationships with students when they come to your church or youth group. And that's cool. But a huge difference between an okay small group and a *fantastic* small group has a lot to do with *interacting with students outside of youth group.*

Please hear us out here. We realize you might be thinking, *Hey, when the church needed help with the youth ministry, I felt pretty valiant for faithfully showing up for this crazy middle school Sunday school class.* And you were!

But think about it: Isn't your goal to do more than just keep the middle schoolers in line for an hour or two each week? Didn't God call you to help young teens—

- Wrestle through the issues they're facing in life?

- Point their lives in God's direction—even when the popular crowd is going another way?

- See God's power unleashed in their souls—even if their home situations make it more challenging?

- Begin a lifetime of following God—even when much of the world is not?

Helping with a middle school group is a fantastic start. But at some point, we need to decide if we're just helping a group at church or if God is inviting us into the *lives* of a few students.

> Be sure you know the condition of your flocks, give careful attention to your herds. (Proverbs 27:23)

> But encourage one another daily, as long as it is called 'Today,' so that none of you may be hardened by sin's deceitfulness. (Hebrews 3:13)

We're not talking about adopting middle schoolers into your family. But if we see our students only once a week—and even then we may not get to really talk to each one—then we probably won't see the progress we long for in their spiritual lives.

HOW TO CONNECT

When we suggest that you stay in touch with your students throughout the week, you might instantly imagine the phone call we described earlier in this chapter. A phone call can be good, but there are so many other ways that we can touch base with young teens today.

- Send students a piece of old-fashioned snail mail. Receiving a postcard or short note in the mail can make a student's day.

- Stop by their next sporting event or fine arts performance and say hi to them afterward.

- Organize a fun small group activity: Bowling, miniature golfing, even a trip to the donut shop.

- Meet up with them before your regularly scheduled weekend event and have a smoothie together. Or grab some food together after your event.

- Send them a text. Text messaging is the current national pastime of middle schoolers. (Just be sure they've got a texting plan on their cell phones first. If not, parents may share their cell phone bill with you.)

- Email. Sure, most middle schoolers, if they have a cell phone, prefer to communicate via text messages. But when a student writes you an email, it gives them a chance to process their own thoughts in writing. They may surprise you. (And as an added bonus, you might get to read the world's longest punctuation-free sentence!)

- Leave them a message on Facebook or MySpace (if your students have hit the age of 13, that is—those sites state that users must be 13 to have accounts).

BUT THERE ISN'T ENOUGH TIME!

Tell us about it. Like anything else of value, unless you *plan* for some time to touch base with your students, it'll probably never happen. So what's the best time for *you*?

- We know leaders who pick a day of the week and make calls during their commute home from work.

- We know leaders who write a card to one or two students in their group and mail them on Mondays.

- We know leaders who've set up Web pages to connect with their students.

- We know leaders who meet with a rotating list of students at a coffee shop after church.

It's all in the *planning*. If you wait until you have nothing else to do, then you'll wait forever.

CONSISTENCY PAYS

If you have 8 or 10 or 12 students under your care, it may seem impossible to keep up with that many young teens outside of youth group. And we'd agree. But what if you could connect in some form with three or four students each week? Consistently. Regularly.

When you look at the life of Jesus, it was no secret that he had a unique relationship with Peter, James, and John. Jesus invested in them at a deeper level—in a different way. Even though Jesus still invested time with the rest of the Twelve, he was more consistent, more regular, more intentional with the three. Don't be afraid to focus and be especially consistent with those students you sense God laying on your heart.

There can be other students in your group whom you don't talk to every single week, but they hear from you once a month. The key is regularity. Not every conversation will be earth-shattering or groundbreaking—in fact, some may not seem to have much substance at all. But with consistent connection—in addition to the regular ministry meetings—your relationship with students will slowly grow. And God will build into a student's heart in ways you're not even aware of.

Simply put, the difference between good and *great* small groups is *outside contact*.

"GOING DEEPER" QUESTIONS

When you've moved beyond the initial stage of just getting to know a student, you can (and should) take your questions to a deeper level—sometimes. If you pummel a student with deep questions too often, their brain may quickly hit overload and they might start avoiding you. So proceed cautiously, yet at the same time, don't underestimate a student's ability to talk about the stuff that really matters.

Here are some of the kinds of questions that might move you to a place of more substantial conversation (at least for a few minutes).

- "How are you doing...*really*? I'm not looking for the 'everyday answer'—I've got time to hear how things are really going." (And make sure you *do* have time before you say this.)

- "Is there anything stressful going on in your life? What's the most stressful?"

- "If you could change one thing about your life these days, what would it be?"

- "Is there anything really challenging going on in your world?"

- "What's life like at home these days? How well are things going with your mom or your dad?" (If they're "less than perfect," ask, "Why do you think that is?")

- "Is there anything you think God's been trying to teach you recently?"

- "Is there anything you've wondered about God—you know, something that you really don't understand but maybe it seems like you're supposed to just believe it?"

- "What's the most fantastic thing and the most frustrating thing in your life right now?"

- "How connected do you feel to God? You know, like sometimes you feel more connected to your good friends than at other times. Got any ideas about how you could move closer to God?"

- "Do you ever make time to talk to and listen to God when you're not at church? How's that been? Easy? Tough? Why do you think that is?"

- "If you could ask God one question about life—and you knew God would answer—what would you ask?"

- "In what areas are you the most or least satisfied in your life right now? Why?"

The "Expectation Continuum"

Okay, so you've read this chapter, and maybe you've considered some new thoughts. You might even feel ready to apply some strategies to move into deeper relationships with middle schoolers. Way to go! But as you lead and get more comfortable with students, we have a caution for you.

During our ministry years, we've observed a kind of "continuum of expectations" as people get involved in middle school ministry. Let us explain. Many leaders begin their middle school ministry journeys on the left side of the spectrum. Their aspirations may sound like, "I'm going to see God rock students' worlds every week," or "We're going to continually have conversations that dig deep, maybe bring a few tears, and definitely revolutionize students' thinking!"

The Expectation Continuum

Soul-level, spiritually charged
conversations every week,
seeing middle schoolers move
toward Jesus in profound and
astounding ways!

We don't want to diminish that target at all. But after a while, the middle school ministry rookie may not experience the "depth" of interaction they'd first anticipated. In fact, a newer leader may have a conversation with a more experienced leader who says something like, "Oh, that doesn't happen every time. You're not doing anything wrong if students don't well up with emotion at the end of every conversation. Or even if they look like they don't understand what you're talking about."

So the new leader (appropriately at first) begins to alleviate the self-imposed pressure of trying to turn punks into saints at *every* youth group meeting. A subtle slide starts to happen, and before long, the leader can't remember the last time she asked one of her students a probing question.

It's not that "nothing" is going on in this small group—far from it. The leader may still be keeping up with what's happening in her students' lives—at school, at home, and in their other activities. They're still working through a small group curriculum together, and maybe they're even having some decent discussion time about God's Word. But the truth is, this leader hasn't been looking for opportunities to ask "The Bold Questions" that might (or might not) lead to a deeper connection with a student.

And so, unconsciously, our once-fired-up leader has slid all the way to the far right side of The Expectation Continuum, and a "successful gathering" of middle schoolers now means that nothing caught on fire, no major fights broke out, and nobody had to call 911. In some ways, the middle school ministry has become little more than glorified baby-sitting.

The Expectation Continuum

Soul-level, spiritually charged conversations every week, seeing middle schoolers move toward Jesus in profound and astounding ways!	Just hang out together and make sure nobody loses an eyeball or goes to the ER or bleeds on the carpet of the youth room.

You and I signed up for *way* more than that.

So how do we avoid "The Right Side Slide"? Although *every* youth group or small group meeting can't be a life-changing event, we've found a helpful strategy to keep leaders tuned in to the work of the Holy Spirit: Come to your middle school ministry gathering prayed-up—*every single time*. Even if that means staying in your car for five minutes after you arrive and asking God to use you. Then, after you walk in the room, keep inviting God to show you the right opportunity to ask even *one student* the deeper question that might lead toward a conversation of great (or medium or any) substance. In this way, you can keep yourself "leaning left" in your expectations.

Healthy Boundaries

Although this chapter is about the whys and hows of building relationships with students, we really must include some thoughts about setting appropriate boundaries in our interactions with students. The regrettable truth is that a simple error in judgment, an inappropriate step across the line, or a simple foolish decision can spell disaster. And while we wish we could assume that the only people drawn to volunteer in youth ministry are those who have the students' best interests in mind, we have to be ever watchful for those who're attracted to young teens with harmful intent.

Like many other churches, the church where I (Scott) serve has developed a Child Protection Plan that we use to screen, interview, background check, and train any applicants who desire to work with students. We really encourage you to work with your church to develop these important guidelines, if they're not already in place. Not only is it important for the protection of students, but it's also a safeguard for youth workers and for your church. (And if you want more wisdom on all sorts of ministry-related safety issues, check out the YS book *Better Safe Than Sued* by Jack Crabtree.)

We intentionally train our volunteer leaders with specific guidelines for working with middle school students, and we establish clear rules that everyone must follow. We'd encourage you to ask some questions, such as the ones below, when developing your own ministry guidelines.

- When a leader meets with a student outside of normal youth group or small group time, what parameters should be in place for these interactions? (For example, should they meet only in public places? For what amount of time? Should there be permission forms? Should other leaders be present?)

- How do you help leaders form healthy emotional boundaries with students? (In other words, how do we make sure that neither students nor leaders become inappropriately attached to one another?)

- What behaviors are off-limits and which are permissible for leaders as they represent Christ in adult-student inter-actions?

- What physical boundaries should be in place for the kinds of interactions that many middle school students love to participate in? (For example, wrestling, roughhousing, and sitting close.)

Even though it seems there's always a need for more volun-teer help in our middle school ministries, we can never fall into the trap of believing that "any warm body will suffice." We must take steps to ensure that the people stepping forward to serve are emotionally healthy so they won't damage students' fragile hearts and lives.

Plan to Laugh

I've got a confession to make. From time to time, I (Scott) start to take myself too seriously. (I could feel the seriousness in my heart as I thought about all the implications of that last section on boundaries.) The pressures of work life, family life, and ministry life start to close in, and it can feel weighty and solemn.

Fortunately, middle school ministry provides a built-in rem-edy for that. A middle schooler's appetite for fun, silliness, laugh-ing, practical jokes, and goofiness is just too much for some overly serious-minded adults. We all know there are some people who just can't deal with the "immaturity" of middle schoolers. But we believe it's an immaturity that needs to be embraced some-times. So although there are times where we need to look for that "deeper question," there are other times when we simply need to be ready to *laugh*. Even if that means laughing at ourselves.

In my very first year of leading middle school ministry, I was in that vulnerable place of meeting students for the first time. There was one energetic 7th-grade boy, whom I'll call Nathan, who seemed to want to hang around me all the time. (This tends to make you feel a little more confident, especially when you're first starting out.)

One night we were finishing some crazy competition thing, and Nathan and I were laughing and talking. *Good stuff,* I remember thinking, *he's letting me get to know him.* As we were talking, though, he lowered his voice and said, "Dude...do you want a *mint?*"

I didn't really want one, so I said, "No, thanks."

But Nathan was insistent. "Dude...seriously...have a mint."

Wait a minute. Was he trying to tell me something? "What?" I said, "Do I *need* a mint?"

"Yeah...I'm sorry, man...your breath kinda stinks," he whispered so no one else could hear.

Later that day I asked my wife, "Have you ever noticed me having bad breath?" She insisted that she'd never thought so. But the next week when I was talking to Nathan again, he stopped and offered me another mint.

"Sorry, dude. Breath's still not so fresh, man."

So then I got self-conscious. I bought myself a whole roll of mints to carry around. Still, I was feeling pretty good that Nathan had been kind enough to point this out to me, without announcing it to the whole group. Trust building.

That is, until the next weekend when I watched as Nathan quietly told no fewer than *three* of our adult leaders that they had bad breath and then offered them a mint. Apparently, this was some form of entertainment for him. Accusing leaders of halitosis and making them squirm. My first thought was, *That little brat!*

But my next thought was, *Actually...that's really pretty funny. Even if the joke's on me.*

As we're building relationships with middle schoolers—remembering their names, asking good questions, keeping expectations high, and being ready to laugh at ourselves when the situation calls for it—there's no telling how much of an impact God can make on our students' lives as we invest ourselves and get to know them, one at a time.

If you ever see me when you know you need a breath mint, feel free to ask me for one. Ever since that week with Nathan, I always carry a roll of 'em in my pocket.

CHAPTER 14

You Can't Always Wing It
(A Few Thoughts about Ministry Structure)

A few months ago I (Scott) decided to switch the location of our annual small groups fall weekend retreat. We found a spectacular location at a ministry site with a great facility—we were set up for an amazing weekend. The only catch was that instead of our usual 90-minute drive, it would take us more than five hours—in good conditions. *No problem*, we thought. With very careful preparations, we'd still get there by 10:30 or 11 p.m., even if we encountered any minor delays. (Can you smell the snag coming?)

Anyway, after *three* separate flat tires, each one complete with lengthy holdups that had our volunteer leaders ready to poke their own eyes out, we finally got everyone safely into their cabins by *3:30 a.m.* Then I spent the next few hours thinking through schedule adjustments that might salvage the weekend. (And by God's grace, much good still came out of the retreat.) Without team members who could rework things on the fly, we'd have been in deeper weeds.

Adaptability...or Else

Let's admit it up front. If you're going to thrive in middle school ministry, you're going to have to figure out how to adapt, flex, rearrange, revise, rework, and adjust—all while you're traveling about 100 miles an hour. Even when you're living the healthiest life you can, staying close to God, and anticipating as much as possible—you need to be as bendable as Gumby if you have any hope to stay sane. That's true for all ministry, really. Sometimes— maybe due to an incident in your community or a prompting from the Holy Spirit—a change in what you had planned for your middle school ministry gathering needs to happen. On short no- tice, you may have to replace your plan with something relevant that would help your students respond to a crisis or maybe ad- dress an issue God has laid on your heart for your ministry.

But we all know a crisis or a prompting aren't the only things that can catalyze the complete rearrangement of the best-laid plans. How about when you're at summer camp and half of your middle schoolers get food poisoning from the infamous catfish casserole, and they spend the night vomiting? Or what about when an issue comes up in your ministry that you know you need to teach biblical insights on *right now*—not when the calendar "opens up."

Lots of us in middle school ministry take great pride in our ability to shoot from the hip. And anyone who's served young teens for more than a few years knows they'd be out of the game without that ability. But too often, winging it can become a way of life. We're not talking about the occasional time when you find yourself thinking *What are we going to do with those middle schoolers?* the night before youth group (or even during the drive to church), but when this has become a regular pattern for you. And although you may tell yourself, *It's just the way I'm wired,* inside you know you haven't committed yourself to the planning that's necessary to make your ministry all that it can be—and everything your students deserve.

Before we go any further, take a deep breath and be honest with yourself. On a scale of 1 to 10 (with 1 being "I plan out every possible detail" and 10 being "I minister by the seat of my pants"), how do you rate as a wing-it type? Look up at the ceiling, give it five seconds of consideration, and come up with a number. If you want to make it more interesting, ask someone who knows you well. The goal isn't to beat yourself up but to see how you can take a step toward improvement.

Structural Questions to Consider

This was a challenging chapter to write and that's because of the *context* factor. There are so many different kinds of middle school ministries. Structure in a very large church is going to look much different than that of a very small church. Urban ministries, suburban ministries, and rural ministries will all look different from each other; but even within those distinctions, there will also be key variables. Denominational context, church-parachurch context, ethnicity context—these are factors we all need to consider when it comes to how to structure our ministry.

WHAT, EXACTLY, ARE YOU TRYING TO DO?

It's important to think through your ministry's *mission*. And if it's been a while since you've considered it, to perhaps *re*think it. Is everyone involved in your ministry clear on what you're trying to do? Without clarity as to why your ministry exists, it's difficult for everyone to pull in the same direction. If someone were to ask the leaders in your middle school ministry what the group's mission statement is, would they hear the same answer? (If you're the only one serving in your middle school ministry—assuming you don't have multiple personalities—here's one place where you have an advantage.)

The mission statement of our middle school ministry at Willow Creek is "To Help Junior High Students Follow Jesus." We've actually shortened it down to that over the years, but it really has become our central measuring stick. When we consider any event, activity, or opportunity we could engage in, we just ask whether it will help our students follow Jesus better, and we've got our answer.

What about you? Why does your ministry exist? Could the people involved articulate it?

HOW WILL YOU GO ABOUT GETTING IT DONE?

Once your mission is clear, there's a great advantage to being clearer about the greatest values that your ministry will live out. They'll serve as the guiding principles for how your team will accomplish the mission ahead. It's also a fascinating team-building exercise.

Every team needs to figure out their own unique values, but here are the ones we've been using in our middle school ministry at Willow Creek:

We believe **All Students Matter to God** and also to us!

We believe in **Being Led by God and Partnering with Parents and our Church** as we prepare students for a lifelong relationship as the bride of Christ.

We believe **God's Word** is complete, knowable, and intended for everyday use.

We believe God delights in **Life and Ministry Characterized by Worship and Prayer.**

We believe students are developed best through **Trained Volunteers Who Serve in Community.**

We believe **Authentic Relationships** create an atmosphere where students can be known, taught, and challenged.

We believe **Being Relevant to a Student's World** is crucial to reaching and leading this generation.

WHO MAKES UP THE TEAM TO GET IT DONE?

Once you have an idea of the ministry structure that you're inviting people into, you can provide clear ministry opportunities for people to use their gifts. Without diving into a deep theological lesson, think about Paul's words concerning spiritual gifts: "There are different kinds of gifts, but the same Spirit distributes them. There are different kinds of service, but the same Lord" (1 Corinthians 12:4-5). How well are you discerning the range of spiritual gifts needed to run your thriving ministry that points middle schoolers to Jesus? And are you communicating those needs to others? (See chapter 17 for more specific ideas on building a team.)

It's easy for people to assume they could *never* make a difference with students because they don't see an opportunity for their gifts to come into play. It's obvious that people with counseling gifts are needed to help young teens wrestle with how they apply their faith. However, at first glance it might be less evident that people with administrative gifts are just as crucial in middle school ministry.

A great starting place for the point person of a middle school ministry is to get very clear on what your *own* spiritual gift mix includes—and what it doesn't include. One of your first moves should be to invite people who have the gifts you lack to join your team. Is your ministry weakest where *you're* weak? Look for someone with the giftedness you don't have and give them a vision for where your ministry is heading.

IS THERE SUCH A THING AS A "TYPICAL YEAR"?

Of course not! But practically speaking, we all have to make decisions about what stuff we'll do (and won't do) in each ministry season. What does your annual calendar look like? What experiences, events, and gatherings will be a part of your ministry year?

Yet another reason why we hesitate to be overly "prescriptive" stems from thoughts that Marko has written in his book *Youth Ministry 3.0*. (At this point, I should tell you that this is Scott writing now, lest you believe that Marko is using this book to brag about his other book. But since I'm not him, I can brag about it and tell you that it's a very thought-provoking book, and it's worth reading as soon as you've finished reading this one. Um, I mean, after that middle school event you're about to do!)

Anyway, Marko addresses how *programs* have been the driver of youth ministry for the last couple of decades. And he makes the case that as we move into the future, to be "driven" by anything other than being *present* with students is a dangerous place to be.

So as we take a look at what kinds of things your ministry might "do" during the year, consider Marko's words: "The road forward must first go through the valley of doing less....Strip down your programming so you have space to spend time with teenagers, spend time with God, and consider rebuilding something new and fresh."[111]

Learning

Now that you have some idea of where you're going, how you're going to get there, and who's going with you, it's important to take a look at how to serve the students through what they'll be *learning*. We've been asked many times about "a scope and sequence" for middle school ministry, or a strategic two- or three-year teaching plan. You may find a good template somewhere in another ministry or resource, but we strongly believe determining the long-term agenda for your students is very ministry-specific.[112] You must devote time to thinking through a plan for your own ministry setting.

WHY I DO THIS

Sweet innocence. That's the heart of a middle schooler. When I first began in youth ministry, I wasn't really sure I wanted to work with middle school youth. After all, everyone always talked about how great it was to be able to sit down and have an actual conversation with the high school teens. But it didn't take me very long to figure out that with patience, TLC, and a lot of corny jokes, middle school youth ministry is where the amazement begins.

Middle school youth are trying so hard to break out of their shells—to discover who they are in relation to their friends and families. Without the support of mentors, teachers, youth ministers, priests, core team members, ministers, and other adults, they'll become the lost children of the church. I don't want to wait for them to become "old enough" to sit down and have a high school conversation with them; I want to teach them how to have the conversations now. I don't want them to be afraid to explore deeper theological questions; I want to teach them how to ask questions and where to find the answers. For me, it's not about their potential; it's about who they are today. I don't want to pacify middle schoolers and hope they'll return when they're in high school. I want to show them that right now, at this time, the church loves them, needs them, prays for them, and is there for them.

I love the sweet innocence of middle schoolers' hearts. I love sitting down to listen to them ramble about 10 different topics in 30 seconds. I love their childlike faith. I love that once I've gained their trust, they become open to hear the truth. And I love that when I reach out to a middle school youth—I have a friend for life.

What a joy it is to help young adolescents understand their goodness and see them develop a love for the church and Jesus Christ. It's an amazing gift to watch them grow and mature into amazing young adults. The middle school youth I've been blessed to work with have taught me about the simplicity of faith and the complexity of life. I don't want to miss a single handshake, high-five, or hug!

Kevin Hickey is the director of Youth Faith Formation at St. Elizabeth Ann Seton Catholic Church in Houston, Texas.

Of course, that's easier said than done, isn't it? Because when it comes to middle school ministries, staying in the same role for a student's three-year middle school run is part of the challenge. (Unfortunately for middle school students, youth leaders come and go way too often.) Not only that, but when you're beginning a new role in a ministry, it takes at least a year to figure out the environment. It would be presumptuous to believe that a middle school ministry leader could walk into a new situation and immediately impose a teaching plan that would be right on target for that group of students. And yet, this is a great conversation for a team to have.

We know it might seem "easier" to just provide a bulletproof, three-year, middle school ministry teaching plan. But we don't believe one exists. Part of the challenge is getting to know your setting well enough to figure out what needs to be covered.

Here are some suggestions:

- Pull together a few people in your church who understand middle schoolers well.

- Talk about what five (or seven or nine) main things you want students to end the year having "owned" in their walk with God.

- Do some research into what other ministries similar to yours have done, and then decide what will work best in *your* setting.

- Structure your teaching calendar around those things.

- Think through the topical subjects you want to tackle, as well as the Scripture passages you want students to learn.

We'll offer some more thoughts about teaching a little later (chapter 16), including the reality that even topical subjects must have a clear scriptural foundation. But thinking in terms of topical subjects and biblical subjects can be helpful.

TOPICAL SERIES

What things does a middle school ministry need to teach each year? Some of the topic areas that we visit on a regular basis include friendships, family, relationships, sex and dating (or "guys and girls," as we often call it since the range of middle school experience with sex and dating is so broad), and wise decision-making.

BIBLICAL SERIES

Yes, every series should be "biblical." But the difference is letting the flow of the section of Scripture guide the topics you cover. Lessons from the life of Joshua. The Sermon on the Mount. The apostle Peter. Teaching through a section of Scripture helps familiarize a student with the life-changing words of the Bible. But it must provide more than just "information." Helping students draw relevant personal applications from God's Word is a skill that will serve them the rest of their lives.

Gatherings

Even as you remember that your ministry should be about so much more than programs, it's crucial that you be strategic about scheduling gatherings that provide the space for relationships to start, get nurtured, and grow. There are countless ways to pull that off. We must resist the notion that there's a "right kind of schedule." You may be tired of reading this by now, but here's another area that will take *your* discerning mind (and the minds of those around you) to determine the best path for your ministry to take.

THINKING WEEKLY (NOT "WEAKLY")

What are your ministry's primary gathering times each week?

Large Group Gatherings Most middle school ministries have at least one weekly large group program, but some have more. When's the last time you thought through *why* your schedule is set up the way it is? Many middle school ministries have a weekend connection—whether it's a Sunday school setting, a youth class, or just the middle school group—*as well as* a midweek gathering.

Often a youth pastor simply inherits a format when she accepts the new ministry role. But here's a hint: Even if you're not sure you like the format, it's wise not to change everything (or even a lot) in your first few weeks (or months) on the job.

Before changes take place, you need to be a student of your environment and ask a *lot* of questions about why it's done the way it is. However, if you do some scouting around and find repetition in the schedule, it's possible that having two gatherings a week (oftentimes without distinct differences) isn't the most strategic setup. Consider the objectives of every weekly ministry event. Most middle schoolers have a full schedule, and "more programs" can actually get in the way of being *with* students.

When I (Scott) stepped into the ministry that I lead now, there were two weekly gatherings. One was intended to "go deeper" than our main weekend program, but there were two small problems with that. First, despite our best efforts, it tended to receive less attention than our primary gathering. We couldn't find time to do both programs at an acceptable level of quality. The other difficulty was that even though our target audience was "a kid who wants to go deeper," many of the students simply came because their parents were attending an adult program at the church during that same time period, and the parents needed their kids to be somewhere.

I knew better than to make a change right away, but I began to gather a *lot* of information about why we were doing it that way. Ultimately, we made the potentially risky move of discontinuing that program, but it freed up our energy to be able to focus on a bunch of other things that could accomplish our mission.

One note on making changes: If your ministry isn't new, then you probably have a few people who like doing things "the way they've always been done." Generally speaking, you'll want to move cautiously and generate conversation about the idea of change before you make any announcements about something new. If you can get a few individuals on board with your ideas, then you'll have momentum for any change that's presented to the group.

Small Group Gatherings Our very next chapter (chapter 15) is devoted to this topic, so we won't go into much detail here. But as far as your *structure* goes, when do students have the chance to interact about the teaching? This is at least as important as any large group program you do. Some ministries plan for small group conversations on the same day as their large group gatherings; some do it on a different day. What works best for your church and the middle school students in *your* context?

THINKING YEARLY

What does the annual calendar look like in your ministry? Aside from a weekly program and some kind of regular smaller group conversations, there are all kinds of things that need your consideration.

- Ministry Year Kickoff for Students—Is there a "starting line" for your ministry year? There's such momentum that can come from a fall launch, but it takes planning.

- Ministry Year Kickoff for Volunteers—Before you can launch into a new year with students, your leaders need to be prepared for a new season. There are many ways to do this, but there's as much of a need to catalyze energy in your leaders at the start of the year as there is to build momentum for the students.

- Weekend Retreat—Will you do one? What should the purpose be—outreach, individual spiritual growth, community building? What time of year is best?

- Summer Camp—We've all seen the power of a summer camp experience. But what's the best setup for your students? Camp is another great place for leaders to get some space to be with students and away from some of the distractions of everyday life.

- Compassion Opportunities—Not only mission trips (although that's another great opportunity to look into), but what about local compassion partners? What time commitment makes the most sense? This is a great place for students to grow while they serve.

- Outreach Events—Are there any special times during the year when you want to do a special gathering that's an "easy invite" for middle schoolers to bring their friends? All our ministries should be ready to welcome first-timers, but our students often respond well to a special event where we specifically encourage them to bring a friend. It could be as simple as a pool party or a dodgeball tournament.

- Parent Events—How and when do you acclimate new parents who are coming in from a kids' ministry context? (Or those parents whose kids haven't been involved in the past?) What about events for moms and their kids, or dads and their kids? We've done some of those on an annual basis, and it's a great way to partner with parents (see chapter 18).

- Links to "Big Church"—While we're on the subject of parents and families, when do your students get to be a part of an "all-church" service or ministry throughout the year? How often does that happen?

- Leadership Training and Team Building—This is a crucial element that's covered more in chapter 17, but where do you put it on your annual calendar? Consider both in-house training as well as taking volunteers to a training event near you.[113]

- Student Leadership Strategy—Do you have a student leadership team? How does it work? Where does it fit into the schedule?

- Volunteer Celebrations—When will you recognize the contributions of your volunteers? We (Scott) do a year-end celebration recognizing the heroic investments of our volunteers, as well as a Christmas party just for the leaders, where we celebrate Jesus, give out awards, and enjoy some hilarity without any middle schoolers present. Our people love it!

What else? This isn't meant to be an exhaustive list. There are sure to be more opportunities and ideas in your ministry setting. What else is crucial to your ministry year?

It's easy to see how a calendar can quickly become packed with all kinds of great ministry initiatives, isn't it? You must think *strategically* (in other words, think with your context in mind) about what structure will serve your students best, not what will "keep everyone busy." All those options above (and more) can have a place in reinforcing godly teaching and the mission of your ministry—helping middle schoolers follow Jesus.

And still, when it's all said and done, they're just events. It's the life-on-life experiences that will reach a student's heart.

I (Scott) remember the first "event" I was involved with as a leader. It was a good event (a camp), but it was apparent that it was just a mechanism for young teens to be with Jesus-following leaders who cared about them. All the formal structures, the program, and the sessions were subservient to the ultimate goal of Christian adults having a space to hang out with middle schoolers.

Keep in mind that I was a middle school ministry rookie at this point, so I asked some naive questions. For instance, one night while I was doing cabin checks (making sure everyone was accounted for before lights out), I walked into a cabin full of middle school boys and a couple of leaders, and I decided to ask one final question to end the evening: "Does anyone in this cabin have any special talents they'd like to show off before we go to sleep?" (Remember, I was *new*. I didn't know any better.)

One boy waved his hand wildly. It seems like every youth group has a double-jointed kid who can make his limbs bend in ways that seem humanly impossible, doesn't it? Well, that was his trick, and everyone was suitably impressed. There were a few more random demonstrations of talent, and then one guy said, "Check this out: I can pick my nose *with my tongue!*" My first thought blurted out of my mouth, "Come on, nobody can do that!" (And who would *want* to even if they could?) But sure enough, this guy stuck his tongue out, and it wasn't just that he could *touch* his nose with his tongue, but he could actually jam it about half an inch inside his nostril. Amazing! I believe I said something like, "That must be really…helpful?"

One guy was kind of sitting back and watching everyone else share their remarkable (?) skills. It was almost as if he knew he had a trump card, but he was waiting for the right moment to play it. When I finally called for lights out, he yelled, "Wait, wait! I've got the best one." Against my better judgment, I agreed to one more. He proudly proclaimed, "I can fart *whenever I want to!*" Once again, I was a doubter. "No *way.*" So he proceeded to grab onto the end of the bunk bed (apparently there's a necessary position for best results) and started to crank them out, one after another. I've got to tell you—it was impressive. After about a dozen or more, I begged him to stop. I was envisioning an accident that might take some cleaning up.

"Just out of curiosity," I asked him, "What's your all-time *record?*" (I was sure he'd counted before, and I was right.)

"Sixty-three in a row."

The guy in the bunk below him said "Ooooh! Oooh! I can vouch for that, cuz the last half of those *he did on my head!*"

I looked at the leaders in the cabin (thankful I was staying somewhere else) and thought about how even though ministry structure is important, it must be carried out by leaders who are willing to flex—with almost anything.

CHAPTER 15

Get Small
(Small Groups)

"How's your ministry going?"

You've been asked that question before, haven't you? When someone discovers that you work with middle school students, it's a reasonable question for them to ask, right? When you hear that question and you know the person's really interested (not just making small talk), what comes to mind? How *do* you assess how your ministry is going?

Can you measure it by how many students are showing up? Sure—that's probably one indicator. And when you look to the early church, you see repeatedly that God "added to their number" (Acts 2:41, Acts 2:47, Acts 5:14). But you don't have to be around student ministry for very long to see that attendance is so often overemphasized.

"How was (*insert the name of your*

ministry here) last week?"

"Great...we had (*insert large number here*) students show up. It was *awesome!*"

Does having a large number of students make a ministry great? We just don't believe that.

Still, there can be what seems like a magnetic pull toward using attendance as the measure of success in our ministries. As Francis Chan said to a gathering of youth workers recently:

> Let's say I've got a little salt...it has flavor...it's just a little bit, but it's the real salt. Now let's suppose I have a container of flavorless salt—salt with no flavor. (It is of no value—there's nothing you can do with it.)
>
> What would be the point of taking this good salt and going like this (pouring all the bad salt all over it into my hand). Do you see any reason in doing that? I do. So I can walk around and say, "Look how big my pile is!" I like doing that. "How big is your pile? Look how big my pile is." I go around telling everyone, "Look what a big pile I've got." We like this. Let's be honest. We like this. I like big crowds. Isn't it true? We like it. We like this thought of bragging about this and that and everything else.[114]

Can you measure success by how full the calendar is? Probably not. Sure, activities are a great springboard to ministry and a rallying place to gather students. But it's also pretty easy to get caught up in planning events to entertain and occupy students and still not see their hearts touched by the loving God.

Can you measure it by how your ministry is being perceived by parents or your senior pastor? Again—these are possible indicators but probably not the real thing. Don't get us wrong—what parents and senior pastors think of your middle school ministry should matter to you. But they're not necessarily the definitive authorities on how your ministry is accomplishing its purpose.

For us (Marko and Scott), we can only answer the question "How's your ministry going?" in one way: Small group, by small group, by small group.

I (Scott) have the privilege of leading a large middle school ministry. (Leading *any* ministry is a privilege.) But the question of how my ministry is going—really—is what keeps me up at night. And an honest assessment of our ministry is that it's—amazing! (Before you write me off as an arrogant knucklehead, please read the next few paragraphs.)

Students' souls are being touched by the gospel, and they're deciding to follow Jesus. Students' hearts are being softened to where it's becoming *less* about me, me, me, and more about other people. Students are talking about what it's like to live and love as Jesus does. Not perfectly, for sure—but the trajectory is exciting. And that's what my ministry is like.

But in another very honest assessment of our middle school ministry, I'd have to say that it's simply okay. Students are making some progress toward Christ-likeness, but it's sporadic, semi-focused, and sometimes off track. Follow up isn't always what it could be, but it's still going pretty well. And it has almost everything to do with the kind of small group those 6 or 8 or 10 students have.

And in some places (the defensive part of me says "just a few"), an honest assessment says that our middle school ministry stinks. Students aren't *known* by a leader. Students aren't missed when they don't show up. Nobody knows them well enough to talk with them about their thoughts or to understand what they're facing in life. Sure, the ministry has a lot of people coming to it. But these kids feel more like a part of the crowd than a treasured child of the Father.

That's painful to write. But it's true. How my ministry is going is directly tied to how small groups of students are experiencing it.

So What's the Big Deal about Small Groups?

Dr. Urie Bronfenbrenner, now retired from Cornell University, identified early adolescence as the most destructive period of life.

Bronfenbrenner recalls being asked during a U.S. Senate hearing to indicate the most critical years in a child's development. He knew the senators expected him to emphasize the importance of preschool experience, reflecting the popular notion that all significant learning takes place during the first six years of life. However, Bronfenbrenner said he'd never been able to validate that assumption. He agreed that the preschool years are vital, but so is every other phase of childhood. In fact, he told the Senate committee that the middle school years are probably the most critical to the development of a child's mental health. It's during this period of self-doubt that the personality is often assaulted and damaged beyond repair.

Consequently, said Bronfenbrenner, it's not unusual for students to enter junior high as happy, healthy children and emerge two years later as broken, discouraged teenagers.[115]

When you read that statement, you may have nodded your head in agreement. Now more than ever, the middle school years are so formational for our students. But it may surprise you to know that Dr. Bronfenbrenner made this statement way back in the early 1970s.

We don't believe things have gotten easier for students. Not at all. They truly need a safe, inviting place to figure out life, to talk and ask and wonder, and to be encouraged to lean into knowing God and following his plan. Middle school ministry matters—now more than ever.

At its core, middle school ministry is about relationship. First and foremost, a relationship with God. But in addition, relationships with caring adults and a few other middle schoolers provide the atmosphere in which students can best thrive in our ministries.

Our friend Mike King puts it this way:

> Youth ministry is about being with youth, not just as a role model or friend but also as a spiritual guide and traveling companion. They need someone who will enter a sacramental relationship with them and someone who will listen to them. They want compassionate listening, which is desperately needed in our churches."[116]

Everyone knows that the content of what's taught (and how it's taught) in a middle school ministry is crucial. (We'll talk about that in the next chapter.) But middle schoolers need to do much more than simply "hear truth." They need to *interact* with truth.

What Does It Mean to Interact with Truth?

Because allowing students to play with their ideas is key to its life application, let's think about student interaction in three ways.

ASKING DANGEROUS QUESTIONS

- Middle school students need to feel *safe* enough to ask questions—even if the question seems risky to them.

- They need to know their questions won't be laughed at or mocked.

- They need to know their questions will be taken seriously.

- They need to know they won't be told "just have more faith."

As we mentioned in chapter 4, young teens' cognitive development has come a long way since they navigated earlier childhood. But at some point, the elementary Sunday school answers

WHY I DO THIS

I love rooting for the underdog, and middle school students are the underdogs of the church. In most churches, middle school students are mostly ignored and misunderstood by pretty much everyone. They're seen as a bunch of "not yet's" and "will be's" that no one understands or wants to deal with. They definitely aren't cute anymore, they aren't socially responsible or mature—and what about the smell?

The middle school years are a turbulent time. And in this chaotic existence, students need their families, friends, and significant adults in their lives as never before. We need to help them understand that they will make it, they will survive. We need to help them understand that what they're experiencing is totally normal and that God created them to be just the way they are.

I love the *place* of middle school ministry. The middle school years are the most turbulent years of a person's life, involving some of the most drastic change. Mentally, students are changing from concrete to abstract thinking. Physically, students are growing by the day and developing muscles, fat, and hair in places they never thought possible. Socially, their network of friends is expanding to include members of the opposite sex (from cooties to cool). Spiritually, their relationship with God is starting to be personalized, and they're beginning to understand God in a new way. I believe the middle school years are the most influential years in a person's life. It's a privilege to help lead middle school students through the maze and confusion of early adolescence.

I love the *pace* of middle school ministry as it clips along at such an amazing rate. I'm not sure if I'm a little ADHD myself, but I like the randomness of what the ministry calls me to. It seems there's always something new around the corner, calling a middle school leader to wear many hats and respond appropriately to many different challenging situations. Middle schoolers are like the Energizer Bunny on caffeine, with energy to burn. And if I can focus that energy, then I can help them tap an unlimited resource. It's the pace that keeps me young at heart and feeling alive, challenging me and keeping me coming back.

I love the *peace* that middle school ministry brings me. In my heart, gift mix, and ministry life, I've found my niche. Just as the apostle Paul was called to the Gentiles, I feel called to minister to middle school students with the love only Jesus can offer. Please don't misunderstand me: Saying middle school ministry brings me peace doesn't mean it's safe or easy. Middle school ministry is anything but safe or easy. In the midst of all the craziness and roller coaster of emotions, I find a peace that I'm in the right place at the right time doing the very thing that God created me for. (Okay, cue *Chariots of Fire* theme music.)

You can probably tell by now that I love what I do. I've worked many different jobs from the time I was in high school and college until I entered ministry, but I've never worked a job that's as challenging and rewarding as working with middle school students. Go underdogs! I'm your biggest fan.

> *Even when I am old and gray,*
> *do not forsake me, O God,*
> *till I declare your power to the next generation,*
> *your might to all who are to come. — Psalm 71:18*

Mark Janzen is the student ministries team leader and Riptide pastor at Willingdon Church, BC, Canada.

aren't going to cut it anymore. And let's be honest, sometimes they ask questions that many adults aren't sure how to answer. Questions such as, "If God created the world and then created Adam and Eve on the sixth day, then what about the dinosaurs?" If we stammer and stutter or mumble something about them "just needing to believe," then they'll think to themselves, *Huh. You don't know either!* And they'll wonder why you don't have the courage to go looking for an answer.

Other dangerous questions are even more difficult to answer: "Why didn't God answer me when I prayed that my parents wouldn't get divorced?" It's not a simple question, and a simple answer doesn't hold water. (In reality, God did answer. And the answer was no.) But middle schoolers need Jesus-following adults who are willing to help them live in the question and unpack the issue.

Recall for a moment Acts 8, when Philip speaks to the Ethiopian eunuch. (If you study this passage with your students, tell them their parents can answer the question "What's a *eunuch*?")

> Then Philip ran up to the chariot and heard the man reading Isaiah the prophet. "Do you understand what you are reading?" Philip asked.
>
> "How can I," he said, "unless someone explains it to me?" So he invited Philip to come up and sit with him. (Acts 8:30-31)

So many middle schoolers have significant questions weighing on their hearts and minds, and they're looking for explanations. We need to "sit with them," even if that means looking for the answers together. Hearing an adult say, "I'm not sure...let's find out," can be powerful to a young teen. And it doesn't matter if we have the answers right now; it only matters that we let them ask their questions.

We must help students understand that "dangerous questions" are actually far better than "safe ignorance." By asking leading questions of our own, we can help young teens exercise their inquiring skills.

- "Did you *agree* with what was taught today, or does it seem easier said than done?"

- "What difficulties might happen if you tried to live the way this passage teaches?"

- "Can anybody follow that Scripture completely? Why or why not?"

- "What would be the big loss if we ignored this teaching? Would there be any?"

All of the above are meant to be thought-inducing questions. We often tell our middle schoolers that we're trying to help them learn to *think*, not robotically go through the motions or clean up their act. After all, we're not trying to help them *act* like Jesus followers, right? Our goal is to *be* people who follow Jesus.

EXPRESSING HONEST DOUBTS

Sometimes questions produce answers; sometimes they unveil doubts. But what better place for our students to wrestle with their doubts than under the watchful eyes and the encouraging and prayerful heart of a small group leader? It's tough for us to overstate the value of this.

One of the most common questions we hear from middle schoolers is, "How do we know that our God is the *right* God?" I (Scott) recently had a middle schooler say to me, "Did you know that there are *other* gods out there? And other people believe they're *really real.*" I think he kind of expected me to say "What? You're kidding me! This is terrible news!"

Some people get scared when students verbalize their doubts about God. But in reality, it's part of a healthy process as they move toward owning their faith. If students can't have *doubts* about their faith and *test* it, then can they ever really own it?

One of my favorite theologians of our time, John Ortberg, has written a book called *Faith and Doubt.* In it, he more than validates the process of working through our doubts as adults. Check this out—

> Every question I had led to more questions, but they also led to more faith....To be able to think and poke and doubt and ask made faith a living, breathing thing to me...doubt could make me a better believer.[117]

When we adults wrestle with our own questions about God, it's easier for us to invite and encourage students to do the same. If we choose to engage the students in our small groups, then they can do their own poking and asking and testing so they, too, can become stronger believers. "Examine yourselves to see whether you are in the faith; test yourselves" (2 Corinthians 13:5).

INTEGRATING TRUTH INTO EVERYDAY LIFE

The "So what?" question is a great one, isn't it?

Consider this: Peter stepped out of the boat when Jesus called to him from the water (Matthew 14:22-31). And many adults can see the correlation between that episode in Scripture and a current situation in their own lives for which they need courage. They can often draw an application for how to focus on Jesus and take a bold step. (Notice we say "many adults," not all.)

For students, this biblical application process often needs a little jump-start. What better place than a small group to provide students with the catalyzing conversation that can help them make the connection between Scripture and their day-to-day actions? Because, simply put, the goal of a small group is this: *To help individual students take individual steps closer to Jesus.*

It's where the mission statement of your ministry really plays out.

The Key Ingredients

If small groups are such a crucial dimension of middle school spiritual formation, then what can we do to help them be as effective as possible? It's all about making room. We want to suggest these fundamental elements for making a small group the best it can be.

MAKE ROOM FOR STUDENTS BECOMING KNOWN

One of the most significant things that can happen in a small group—that simply can't happen the same way in a large group setting—is people becoming known. But this crucial element of a small group doesn't happen overnight. When an adult invests his time to help students connect with each other—breaking down walls and sharing things about themselves—a real community begins to form. Bill Hybels often talks about how community is a place of "knowing... and being known" and that's a great way to say it.

MAKE ROOM FOR FUN

Are you surprised to see this value so high on the list? "Fun" is a crucial part of middle school life. And in some ways, it serves as the "oil in the engine" of young teen relationships. When a middle schooler gets invited somewhere (church or otherwise), one of the first questions she'll ask is, "Will it be *fun*?" And that's a legitimate question. "Want to come to my family reunion with me?" or "Want to come to my church with me?" Hmm...initially neither invitation sounds very appealing to a young teen. But what happens when we add the potential for fun into the equation? ("The reunion's at my uncle's lake house. He's got jet skis!" or "My church is awesome—we play hilarious games, my leader laughs a lot, and there's always a ton of food!") Wait! That sounds more interesting now. Some of us grew up believing that church is a place of seriousness and that God's expression had a consistently furrowed brow. Yet God created all dimensions of our experience—fun included. A leader has a key role in making small group a highly anticipated place of fun (and learning, too).

MAKE ROOM FOR CELEBRATION

Birthdays, accomplishments, bold faith moves—young teens need a place to be celebrated. (Ideally it happens at home, too, although there's no guarantee.) Hearing people—especially an adult—say, "Way to go!" and "You are so valuable to me" really matters.

MAKE ROOM FOR QUESTIONS AND
LISTEN TO ANSWERS

This is waaay more than just "going through a curriculum." Most people want to feel as though their opinions matter, but *listening* is a learned skill (as opposed to an innate ability) for most people. A leader must not only ask great questions, but also model attentive listening and help students learn to really listen to each other. There's a deeper dimension to this than simply getting through the curriculum and checking off all the questions. Small group leaders can't be afraid of the tangent. Sometimes what seems like a rabbit trail can actually be a divine agenda—something more important than what we'd originally planned.

MAKE ROOM FOR SEARCHING SCRIPTURE AND EXAMINING TRUTH

The middle school years are an ideal window of time for students to move beyond simply "hearing" God's Word (often read to them by someone else) to investigating Scripture for themselves. Certainly, there's a great diversity when it comes to students' appetites for reading. But even students who aren't library hounds can come to understand that the words of the Bible are a light for their path and become drawn in by the transformational power of God's written words (Psalm 119:105). If some students in the small group don't have a Bible—or if the ones they have are more of a kid's version—encourage them to purchase one. There are lots of good student Bibles available. Do some homework to find one that your students will connect with the best. Then encourage them to underline in it, write questions in the margins, sketch out their thoughts—anything to help them really own it.

MAKE ROOM FOR HONORING VULNERABILITY (BUILD AUTHENTICITY)

In a young teen culture where sarcastic humor is often esteemed and letting one's guard down is often met with ridicule, vulnerability doesn't come easily or quickly. The case could be made that this is especially true for guys. So when a leader declares safe space and affirms openness and sincere questioning in the small group, authenticity can start to take root. Masks can be lowered—even if it's only for a few minutes at a time. And students get a look at each other's true thoughts and emotions. Imagine a world with less jockeying for position but more empathy and hearts coming together. These seeds can be planted in the souls of middle schoolers, through what a leader values in the small group setting.

MAKE ROOM FOR NEW LEVELS OF CONVERSATION

As mentioned in chapter 4, middle schoolers' brains are growing like crazy. That means they're capable of whole new dimensions of critical thinking. But what does that mean for a small group? Discussions can and should move into territory that their younger brains weren't ready for. And that's huge when you consider the new situations that young teens will encounter in middle school—and beyond. If you haven't already caught our message, it's worth repeating: Small groups should be a safe place in which teenagers can talk about the situations they're facing head-on and process how to handle them with a leader listening and guiding them with God's wisdom.

MAKE ROOM FOR CONNECTIONS TO REAL LIFE

The prime objective in following Jesus isn't conversational ability. The goal is to live life the way Jesus instructs. John 10:10 talks about living life to the fullest. Small groups are prime places for students to wrestle with *how* they can really live the way Jesus describes. After all, *talking about* Scripture is a world away from *living out* Scripture, isn't it? It's far easier for middle schoolers to verbally analyze "loving the outcast" than it is for them to sit down at a lunch table with the kid in their class whom no one talks to. (Come to think of it, that's true for adults, too.) Small groups should provide a challenge for students to connect Jesus to their lives.

MAKE ROOM FOR TALKING TO GOD

Simply put, small groups are a place to learn prayer. Many middle schoolers have never spoken to God out loud in the presence of anyone else. (And some may not have been around people who pray aloud, either.) Small groups provide an opportunity to help students learn the power of corporate prayer. The beauty of hearing a young teen speak honestly to God—in praise, in hardship, in confusion—is one of the highlights of middle school ministry. Don't worry if the words don't come out smoothly. A leader should be sure to encourage *any* participation by any student in the prayer category—from sharing requests, to doing the praying.

MAKE ROOM FOR STRANGE SOUNDS

In other words, farting, belching, and other bodily noises—even if you lead a girls' group. (We've gotta tell the whole truth here, right?) Often these noises will come at the most inopportune time. Jimmy's starting to open up about a difficult time he's having at school, and then Austin lets loose with one that he sincerely insists he "just couldn't hold in." Then it takes a few minutes to settle the group (and let the odor dissipate). It requires great skill, patience, and perseverance for a leader to put that train back on the tracks—but it can be done. Sometimes.

MAKE ROOM FOR THEIR FRIENDS

It can be challenging to have new people visit your established small group, as embracing new people can often be awkward for a group that's growing closer. Yet, we need to watch out for the danger of our small groups becoming holy huddles of exclusivity. While a group with *constantly* changing membership will have trouble growing deeper, students who invite friends into their small group can extend God's community to people who desperately need it. At a recent retreat that I (Scott) was on, a group of 13 eighth-grade girls and their two leaders were discussing what it would be like to talk about God with anyone outside the small group. Initially there was a sense of resistance from this tight group. But then they recalled how two years earlier, their group had only been six girls and one leader. One at a time, the girls in this group—by remaining open to including new friends—had invited people who needed what this circle could provide. And each new person had been welcomed in.

MAKE ROOM FOR NURTURING YOUNG LEADERS

As middle schoolers gain experience in being a part of a safe, healthy small group, they can experiment with what it means to take a more active leadership role within the group. If a small group seems to be getting stale with adult-only leadership—or if you just want to shake things up a bit—see what happens when you invite a young leader to help prepare and lead discussion in the group. Not only is it amazing to see what students can do when they're challenged, but a group often responds with even greater interest when "one of their own" takes the wheel. And, in the process, a leader can help students try out their spiritual gifts. How cool is that?

How to Get Started

Okay, let's get practical. As you process the following elements (and observations from us), remember that *you* must be a student of your own context and environment, pray for the guidance you need to choose well and be able to adjust as you learn. These questions can help you get the ball rolling.

THE "WHERE AND WHEN" QUESTION

Do middle school small groups work best meeting in a church building, in homes, or somewhere else? Are they most effective when meeting during a Sunday school hour, after a youth program, or at a separate time during the week? Great questions! But there's no single, definitive answer. It depends on your situation. And the best way to answer these questions is—by asking more questions. We're aware of many different times and settings for successful middle school small groups. There are obviously pros and cons to each arrangement. But if your ministry has attempted to use small groups before, ask people a whole bunch of questions about what worked and what didn't work regarding where and when those small groups met.

If small groups have never been a part of your middle school ministry, ask students, parents, and other youth workers—inside and outside your church—a whole bunch of questions. But be cautious about listening to one loud voice over all the rest. In Scott's ministry, small groups meet at the church on weekends, immediately following the large group gathering. And it works fabulously—most of the time. In the ministry where Marko serves, small groups meet in homes on a different day during the week. And it works fabulously—most of the time.

THE GENDER QUESTION

We'll offer a stronger opinion on this one. In some smaller ministries, when there are only a few students, it can be tempting to say, "We've only got a few guys and a few girls. Why not just have a small group all together?" It can be done, but the guy-girl dynamic in middle school is definitely a hindrance to personal sharing. In an era of life when students are discovering the wonder of how the mind of the opposite sex works, mixed-gender conversations add a level of complexity that can be a barrier to deep discussions. She's thinking, *If I say that...what's he going to think?* He's thinking, *Maybe I can impress her if I say this.* Our take? Do whatever you can to have separate gender groups; same-gender small groups will remove one barrier to authentic conversation.

THE AGE QUESTION

This is pretty intuitive; but whenever possible, keeping students in same-grade groups is a wise idea. Not only will it help the group focus on the most pertinent age-related issues and experiences, but when an 8th grader transitions to high school, she won't have to leave her small group support system back in the land of middle school. This middle school to high school transition is already challenging. So we don't want to add another element that will make the "being known and feeling safe" equation any more difficult for students.

THE GROUP SIZE QUESTION

How many middle schoolers does it take to make a good small group? (It almost sounds like the start of a bad joke, doesn't it?) We're not ready to proclaim an "optimum number," but we'd definitely wave a caution flag about groups that get too big. Anything more than seven or eight middle schoolers makes it hard to ensure that everyone gets a chance to share their perspective. (This is especially true when you consider how you can usually count on at least one person in the group having I-love-to-hear-myself-talk syndrome.)

One issue we've seen pop up more than once is when students have such a positive experience in the small group that they want to invite their friends to come. And then they want to invite *more* friends. It's a good problem to have, but it's a problem, nonetheless. As a group starts to grow, one great strategy is to add a second small group leader to the mix. Not only does that make it possible for the group to morph into two groups at some point, but it also makes it possible for the group to occasionally subdivide for discussion. When a group hits double figures, it's also more difficult for one leader to check in with students outside of the regular meeting time (see chapter 13).

Another philosophy is to "close" the group for a specific season of time, in order to build trust and intimacy within the small group. This can add to the sense of safety and invite the kind of healthy vulnerability we want to see happening in these groups. Still, be cautious not to slam the doors on others looking in from the outside. Not only could they receive a terrific benefit from being in your small group, but they could also be great contributors, too.

What Do I Have 'Em Talk About? (The Curriculum Conundrum)

So you've gathered them together, the cell phones have been quieted, and now's the big moment for you to launch into—what?

Small group curriculum can be a fantastic tool to guide conversations. Yet even though the publisher of this book offers some mighty fine curriculum options, there's no perfect product that's going to turn your group into the heavyweight champion of discussions. (We do believe there are some poor choices out there also, which can make good conversation even more difficult.) If you do use a published curriculum, though, make sure it's one that really helps students delve into God's Word. We want to continue to remind students that Scripture is the place to look to gain perspective on what a Jesus-following life looks like.

My (Scott) strong opinion is that when a small group can link their discussion to what the ministry is teaching in the large group settings, it allows students to personalize the concepts to their own lives. Many youth ministries operate with a twice-a-week gathering schedule—once for large group teaching on one topic, and then another time for small group meetings on an entirely separate topic. It just doesn't seem wise. Why not let your students look more deeply into the subject matter you're tackling, by dissecting it together in a small group setting? If you don't know of a curriculum that mirrors what you're teaching, realize that sometimes all you need is about 10 good questions (thought-provoking, open-ended questions) to get conversation rolling. Uniting your large group teaching with small group conversations can significantly multiply the learning that happens.

LEADER POINTERS

Leading a middle school small group, though, is far more of an art than a science. The best plan can unravel quickly, leaving a small group leader thoroughly frustrated. If it's ever happened to you, then be assured that you're not the first, nor will you be the last. This endeavor is a slippery uphill climb, but with occasional vista points that can blow your mind. Here are a few cautions.

Manage the rabbit trail. Discussions in middle school small groups can jump the track faster than a box of donuts can disappear from the youth room. A single word can launch a 13-year-old brain into a new orbit.

> Leader: "So why do you think Jesus asked Peter to step out onto the...?"
>
> Student (*interrupting*): "Hey! Steps? Oh, oh, there are 33 steps at my school, and the other day my friend Connor and I raced up and down them 14 times. I beat him almost every time, except for when this teacher walked by, and she..."

Ever been there? We have! You listen patiently and wait for the student to take a breath so you can jump in, politely, and say, "Um, that was entirely unhelpful to anything we're talking about." Just kidding!

Believe it or not, occasional rabbit trails can lead to a discussion that's more important than whatever you *thought* the agenda of the day needed to be. One of our leaders recently turned a tangent about a troubled NFL football star into a conversation about character.

We must be on alert so we can sense when the Holy Spirit is whispering, *Now* that's *a trail worth following for a little bit.* Sometimes we can get so focused on getting through the material that we end up missing the material God had for us to share. We've both been guilty of that one before. Keep your radar sensitive for a "God-inspired rabbit trail" and don't be afraid to put the curriculum plan on hold so you can chase a conversation like that.

Follow the 80-20 Rule. A far too common mistake in middle school small groups is when the adult leader talks way too much. Maybe she's uncomfortable with silence, or perhaps she has a desire to cram students full of more "instruction and wisdom." But if students don't get a chance to voice their opinions, questions, and doubts, then we run the risk of missing the whole reason for the small group. A good target to shoot for is that *students* speak *80 percent* of the time, and *leaders* talk only *20 percent.* Easier said than done. The next time you're leading a small group, estimate the ratio of your words to theirs and decide whether you're allowing students an adequate amount of space to think out loud. (Hint: If you see their eyes glazing over and they look somewhat zombie-esque, you might be slightly over your 20 percent.)

Share personal experiences appropriately. In adult small groups, the person leading the group is often a "co-learner" and "co-sharer" of experiences. Not so when you're leading middle schoolers. While it's necessary for students to understand that you're not claiming perfection and that you've compiled your share of mistakes, the *details* of those mistakes are often not helpful (or even appropriate) for the group. Remember, this is *their* place to process life; you're there to assist and facilitate. That wrong turn you took in high school might intrigue them and make for a good story, but will it ultimately be *helpful* for them? If you're ever in doubt about whether something from your past would be constructive, then err on the side of withholding that information (at least until you've been able to run it past another adult you trust).

WHAT I WISH I'D KNOWN...

We asked a handful of middle school small group leaders to finish this sentence: *What I wish I'd known about middle school small groups....* Here are some of the responses we received.

I wish I'd known that in the midst of being funny, they were revealing the seriousness of what they were dealing with. —Chris

I wish I'd known that any contact with them is a form of worship and impact. Relationships are messy and middle school students embrace messy more than any social group I know. —Tim

I wish I'd known that it's the little things you don't even try to do or re-member doing that count the most. That they'll come the next week so much more open and comfortable and you won't know why. That God is always faithful in helping those connections along, even when you don't know it. —Amykay

I wish I'd known sooner how much more fun leading middle school kids was compared to pastoring the whole church. —Larry

I wish I'd known beforehand that feeding a dozen junior high boys 50 bean burritos before bed would be a disaster! —Matthew

I wish I'd known that the games, random talk times, stories, and running around crazy while screaming is vitally important to building a commu-nity. If we're meeting them where they are and doing what they want to be doing, then they're much more willing to try what I consider to be important. —Hannah

I wish I'd known how much a part of my life those guys would become. It would have made me more patient with them. —Lars

I wish I'd known how open, honest, and random middle schoolers can be. —Kevin

I wish I'd known that "I don't know" is a perfectly acceptable answer and "Let's figure it out together" is an even better answer! —Erik

I wish I'd known that connecting with students outside the walls during the rest of the week is more important than the time I spend with them "officially." —Joel

I wish I'd known I had no cash on me before offering $20 to the first kid to try the dog food. —Tim

I wish I'd known that middle schoolers get it and then don't get it and then get it and then don't get it and then get it.... —Mark

I wish I'd known that some junior high kids aren't really interested in knowing God better when they're in junior high—even though they come faithfully to church. Having faith in the fact that God is still at work in their lives, even when I don't see it, is hard for me. —Kathy

I wish I'd known that middle school culture changes so much all the time—change is the constant. —Amanda

I wish I'd known that this was so much fun—I would have joined in sooner! —Bruce

I wish I'd known how big of an impact that spending just one hour with a group of middle school boys would make on their lives. —Jon

I wish I'd known just how much these junior high kids would affect my life and my own spiritual growth! —Heather

I wish I'd known that every lesson we teach, or try to teach, to the junior high kids is directly applicable to my life as well and that I learn as much from them as they do from me. —Lane

I wish I'd known that if a 6th-grade boy pulls your chair out from under you when you sit down, it's not an insult but a sign of friendship. —Adam

I wish I'd known about the special attention and encouragement kids need as they open up and communicate the challenges they face at school and home. Most kids just want someone to believe in them and recognize the good they accomplish (but it often gets overlooked in this hectic world we live in). —Chris

I wish I'd known that junior high students won't usually express their appreciation for you as their leader. —Carolyn

I wish I'd known that under that restless, hyper exterior is a sponge that wants to learn and a child that wants to be heard—really heard. —Brien

I wish I'd known that I didn't have to be perfect and have great discussions with my group in order to be effective. —Jen

I wish I'd known that when I walked into a room full of junior highers, they'd yell my name and get excited about me! I came in expecting to give, but God showed me his love through these kids. —Kim

I wish I'd known that building into 6th graders' lives early and often, even when it didn't seem like they were paying attention, can pay huge dividends come 8th-grade year. Do whatever you can to get them involved with each other and build cohesiveness early. —Kermit

I wish I'd known that kids need someone other than their parents to listen to them—*really* listen and not jump in and judge them. The kids *need* us. —Angie

I wish I'd known that being a small group leader has very little to do with relating to them on a cultural level (sports, video games), but has everything to do with showing a genuine interest in them. —Christian

I wish I'd known that if I just *stay*, it speaks volumes. To them actions really, really do speak louder than words. —Tammy

I wish I'd known how important it is to connect with the parents and allow them to help you, and you *support* the guidance of their children. —Jo

I wish I'd known that three years go by so fast. —Bob

I wish I'd known that they're paying attention even when you think they're not, that they avoid the questions but are disappointed if they're not asked, and that they love to talk—but they often need to choose the topic. —Susan

I wish I'd known how spiritually hungry and engaged 6th-grade boys could be. —Joe

Keep expectations high and persevere. As The Expectation Continuum of chapter 13 illustrates, we have to keep our hopes and optimism high, especially on days when it seems like the small group doesn't go anywhere or it even quickly spirals out of control. Trying to figure out what's going on in the mind of a single middle schooler can be a monumental challenge, let alone attempting to make sense of the thoughts of several. (And they said herding cats would be challenging.) We must take a long-term view, remind ourselves of prior victories, and anticipate that the next small group could be the one with the breakthrough we've been praying for. And, ultimately, God is in control of what happens in each student's heart. God's just asking you to come prayed-up and prepared.

Last, But Definitely Not Least—The Most Important Volunteer in Your Church Is...

...A middle school small group leader!

All church volunteers are important, but volunteer middle school small group leaders are ridiculously important—to your students and to you. They have the opportunity to be the link between a middle school student and a life of Jesus-following.

Volunteer small group leaders can function as "adult guides" for students as they explore the landscape of middle school. This doesn't diminish the role and influence of parents even an ounce (more about that in chapter 18), but a trusted small group leader in relationship with a student has the ability to say things that will be heard differently, simply because they're *not* the student's mom or dad. If we had a burrito for every time we've heard parents say something like, "My kid came home and told me what you said to them—as if it was the first time they'd ever run across that thought. But I've been repeating that very same thing to them, in every different way I can think of. What's up with that?"

As we mentioned in chapter 12, middle school students will gravitate toward the oldest person who takes them seriously.[118] And that's often true regardless of who that person is. It could be a coach who encourages them, a teacher who calls out potential in them, a gang member who gives them attention, an older relative who invests time in them—you get the picture. So where do you *find* great small group leaders, and how do you equip them? Check out chapter 17 where we'll talk about building a team.

Recently I (Scott) went back to visit the town where I lived when I was in middle school. Ironically, the small church that my family attended during those years was right across the street from the public school where I went to 6th, 7th, and 8th grades. I was in town on a holiday, so both the church and the school buildings were closed. But as I stood and looked back and forth between those two places where I'd spent so much time as a young teenager, I felt a profound sadness for what could have been. Including me, there were only three regular kids in my middle school Sunday school class, and we often felt as though the "teacher of the week" was the adult who drew the shortest straw. Our church was too small for a paid youth pastor, but I can imagine the difference that a motivated volunteer could have made for us. Instead of feeling as though we were "extras" at the church, maybe we would've felt as though God actually wanted to speak to us or wanted to hear from us or even wanted to use us to make a difference.

It wasn't until the summer before my senior year in high school that I realized the saving grace that Jesus was offering, and I invited him to lead my life. It was like a whole new world opened up to me. As a freshly redeemed 17-year-old, another student and I went to talk with the leaders of the church to express the concerns we had for how our church might be missing some opportunities with younger students. Honestly, I don't believe they understood what we were saying. (We probably weren't articulating it too well.) But I do remember them looking at each other and saying, "Why can't more teenagers be like these two?" It was so frustrating! I wasn't some "good kid" (they didn't know me very well), but I *was* a new Christian.

If I could live that day over again, I'd make sure those church leaders understood. Because there's an exceedingly high need for *intentional, focused adult volunteers* who get to know and love students and help them discover their next steps of spiritual growth in becoming Jesus-followers. It was worth my feeble efforts to try to get their attention—even though they didn't respond.

Today, more than ever, it's worth *your* highest attention.

CHAPTER 16

Hitting the Bull's-Eye
(Effective and Creative Teaching)

I (Scott) remember getting ready for my very first talk to middle schoolers. Honestly, I was pretty nervous. I'd taught adults before, but this was different. I was sure I could *lead* a ministry but could I *teach* middle schoolers?

I recall my boss trying to give me some kind of well-intentioned encouragement that sounded something like this: "Don't worry about it— it'll be fine!" *Easy for him to say,* I thought. *He won't be the one standing up in front of all those 11-to-14-year-olds.*

And if that wasn't bad enough, right around that time I was reading through the book of James, and I came across verse 3:1. Remember what it says?

> Not many of you should presume to be teachers, my brothers, because you know that we who teach will be judged more strictly.

Oh great, I remember thinking, *What if I'm horrible at this? Not only could I have kids hating me, but God will judge me more strictly, too. Awesome.*

I believe that for most of us who teach, going back and sitting through some of our early attempts at teaching middle schoolers might be somewhat painful. And even now, after quite a few years of combined teaching experience, Marko and I still aren't claiming we're the world's foremost experts at it. But we *have* learned some things along the way—after many tries. And through our learning, we hope this chapter will help you improve your own teaching, too.

Values for Teachers to Consider

Before we get into the nitty-gritty of preparing messages, it's worth recognizing some values that we believe are absolutely pivotal for a teacher to consider—long before you begin delivering a talk—because teaching students is *way more* than just delivering a message. In reality, everything we do around students is "teaching" them something.

1. THE "HIDDEN CURRICULUM"

Whether or not we're super-organized in our teaching plan, most of us would agree that it's important to have a curriculum: "What We're Planning to Teach Students." Maybe you map it out a year ahead, maybe you sketch it month to month, or maybe you're flipping through your Bible on the way to youth group. But we need to know what we're going to teach. A series on prayer, a camp theme about friendships, a series on the book of Habakkuk—it comes together to form our planned curriculum.

The term *hidden curriculum* has been around for a while, but it was probably first coined by a guy named Philip Jackson in the '60s.[119] I believe the concept of a hidden curriculum (the stuff that's learned that wasn't overtly taught) is fascinating and very significant to take into account. And if you hang around any group long enough (youth ministry or not), you'll pick up on *their* hidden curriculum.

The hidden curriculum is more about *how* we do stuff than what we say—the unwritten rules and unspoken expectations. It's less about what we *teach*, and more about what we *do* (and don't do). It's definitely not limited to church, either. Almost all parents tell their kids to be honest, right? That could be called the "curriculum." But the hidden curriculum is what gets communicated when two parents and a kid are sitting at home and the phone rings. The mom answers the phone and looks at the dad who shakes his head "no." She then tells the caller Dad's not there. What's *actually* being taught (the hidden curriculum) is that honesty is a really good value—except for the times when lying is more convenient.

The hidden curriculum in our ministries can range from the feel of the room to how an adult treats a student to the body language of those "on stage" for any program element. We can post a message on our youth group's Web site that says: NEW STUDENTS ARE WELCOME HERE! But when no one speaks to the newcomers after they arrive, the hidden curriculum says, "We don't care enough to talk to you."

But when we pay attention to the hidden curriculum, great things can happen.

- When a leader confronts a student with discipline, you're teaching that there are *boundaries* to be honored.

- When a leader admits he was wrong and apologizes, you're teaching *humility*.

- When you play a game, you're teaching that *fun* is okay in church; God actually designed it.

- When a student gets another chance after screwing up, you're teaching him that *grace* is real.

- When a leader husband and leader wife hold hands at a retreat, you're teaching that *marriage* can last.

- When you involve students in leadership, programs, and event planning, you're teaching that they're not too young to *serve* (1 Timothy 4:12).

Think about it: This short list represents lessons on boundaries, humility, fun, grace, marriage, and serving—each one taught without a sermon.

(Note: As discussed in chapter 3, there's another type of curriculum called the "null curriculum." [Elliot Eisner has written much on this concept as it relates to the educational system.[120]] You might recall that the null curriculum is what we *don't* teach, thereby giving the impression that it's not important for students to experience in our ministries.)

2. HOW YOU INTERACT WITH STUDENTS... PERSONALLY

Your conversations with students—before *and* after your teaching—absolutely affect how your message is received. They'll have an impact on how students hear what you have to say.

Of course there's no doubt that good preparation for teaching really matters. (Later in this chapter we'll talk about how you can prepare well for a middle school lesson.) But when you're getting ready to speak publicly in most any setting, it can be tempting (some might even say strategic) to continue reviewing your notes right up until the moment you deliver a talk.

However, when students have begun showing up and you still have 15 (or 30 or 60) minutes to invest in either reviewing the lesson one more time or connecting with students—we urge you to choose connecting with students. Because your interaction with them, your *relationship* with them, will affect how they hear your message. A middle schooler probably isn't going to say to you afterward, "I really appreciated the way you explained the nuances of that particular verse; your exegesis of that passage inspired me." But you can bet that your pre-message interaction can make a student feel like, "This person seems to really care about me, which makes me care about what he wants to tell me."

Recently I (Scott) was teaching at a student ministry event out of town, and a whole bunch of youth groups had come together for a retreat weekend. There's a different dynamic at events like this because (especially at the beginning) students don't know you. You're just "the speaker dude."

As I drove into town, my stomach growled, so I pulled into Arby's. (Hey, it was a small town; I had limited choices.) Church vans had begun to descend upon this town, and the diners at this fast-food restaurant were about 80 percent teenagers. I was almost stampeded by a group of middle schoolers who were debating whether to enjoy the fine cuisine of this restaurant or run to the McDonald's next door. (Like I said, limited choices.) There were about six of them in this group, and five decided to go visit Mickey Ds. The remaining guy looked really disappointed, but he was determined to stay at Arby's. So they all bailed on him and said they'd be back in a while.

Since no students from my own church were there, I decided to strike up a conversation with this kid. I asked him if he was going to the same event I was, and he sheepishly said yes. I told him I was going to be there, too. His unimpressed expression said he couldn't imagine why some crazy old dude would be going to the middle school event. So I told him I was the speaker. Now his look turned skeptical. I chatted with him for only a few more minutes, as he seemed fairly uninterested (or maybe just worried that I was one of those people his parents had warned him about). But I asked him his name (Cody), and I told him I'd say "Hi" to him over at the event. His countenance clearly communicated one thought, "Whatever, dude."

Fast-forward a few hours. I'm introducing myself to the crowd of students, and I ask if there's a group there from Ft. Wayne, Indiana. Of course their group went crazy cheering. Then I mentioned Cody—and I told the audience he was a new friend of mine. His buddies who ditched him to go to McDonald's spun their heads toward him and looked at him with wide eyes. *YOU know the speaker?* He grinned, enjoying his spotlight moment. Afterward I heard his friends say, "Cody! Introduce us to him!" So Cody and his friends came up and talked to me for a while. He was the last one to leave our conversation, and he quietly said to me, "That was cool what you taught tonight."

I said, "You mean when I told everyone your name?"

He said, "No...I liked what you *taught* about. I learned stuff."

Now maybe he was just saying that to make me feel good, but I don't believe so. I believe he really raised his level of attentiveness because of our personal interaction. And because he felt like I was interested in him.

3. YOUR PERSONAL GROWTH QUOTIENT

When you're communicating God's Word to any audience, the Bible is your central tool. But here's where it can get tricky. We've got to be careful *not* to reduce the Bible to being just a textbook. This same Bible that serves as an instruction manual and that we're using to teach kids is also the primary source of God's personal communication and connection to *each of us.*

When I'm under pressure because I know I've got to teach something—or I'm behind schedule—it's tempting for me to skip the connecting-to-God part and just pray, "God, help me out. I need something to *teach* out of here. Please give me a talk." Or perhaps when you're spending time alone with God and you sense him speaking to you, you find yourself a bit *too* quick to think, *Oh, I could teach that truth*, when what you really need to do is lean into and live with that truth personally.

Sometimes when I'm reading Scripture, I make an outright promise to God, saying, *Right now my mind is open to* learn, *not prep a talk.*

The Best Teacher Is an Unquenchable Learner

Now that we've taken a look at some crucial values for setting up a healthy teaching environment for middle school ministry, let's turn the corner and tackle the elements that make for great teaching—the nuts and bolts of message-giving.

WHY I DO THIS

For my first four years in ministry, I worked with primarily senior high students. I liked it. When I heard about an opening working with middle school students at another church, I thought it would be a good chance to round out my experience and determine which age group I'd like to focus on. That was 12 years ago, and I haven't left the beautiful chaos of middle school ministry.

I enjoy being a part of their lives when, developmentally, middle schoolers are discovering so much about themselves, life, their families, and God. It's exciting to see their eyes light up when they understand something for the first time. It's inspiring to hear them ask so many questions about ideas or truths we often take for granted.

Early adolescence is a time of struggle for many kids. I like walking alongside them as they wade through issues with parents, friends, school, sports, and loss. As an objective outsider, I can offer validation, insight, challenge, and encouragement that wouldn't be heard the same if it came from a parent. It's great to be someone they can run things by or even emotionally vomit on, if needed.

Frankly, I find it difficult to understand how any youth worker can't see what I see. I believe this is the most effective time to touch the lives of students for spiritual change. Middle school students have incredible value right now—not just when they become senior high students. I am here to stay!

Here's a quick list of what I love about middle school students:

- I love their enthusiasm for life. Most haven't reached the "too cool" status and enjoy nearly anything you put out in front of them. I love hearing things like: "I am *so* excited for the retreat this weekend!" "I invited 17 friends to the All-Night Blitz!" "When are we going to play that game with the nylons and eggs again? I *love* that game!"

- They genuinely like adults and desperately want to be liked by adults.

- Their emotions are challenging, but fun. There's never a dull moment when you strap yourself into the roller coaster of emotion with a 13-year-old. I thrive on their honesty. It's a refreshing contrast to the often-masked world of adults. They are resilient. If I need to reprimand them, they often love me more after the reprimand than before.

- Two words: Mountain Dew.

Heather Flies is the junior high pastor at Wooddale Church, in Eden Prairie, Minnesota.

IN THE BEGINNING...

One of the biggest challenges a teacher faces is The Beginning. The Blank Page. Whether you're staring at an actual piece of empty paper or a completely white computer screen, getting started can feel like a mind-numbing obstacle when it comes to writing messages for middle schoolers. To address that, I (Scott) have developed a little habit to eliminate the blank page and get the ideas rolling. I begin by listing a few things at the top of my page every time I write a message.

WHAT'S THE BIG IDEA? (OR, WHAT'S THE ONE THING?)

This big idea is more specific than your topic. (Examples of a topic would be prayer or popularity or courage or community.) It focuses your topic into one clear statement. For example, if you were teaching on courage, your big idea could be "God will meet you in the tough challenges, but you need to take the first step."

When I write WHAT'S THE BIG IDEA? at the top of the page, I think about the answer this way: Imagine a student getting into the car with his mom or dad after your middle school meeting. The parent asks, "So what'd you guys talk about today?"

Have you ever been there when a parent asks that question? (Ha!) The answer can be pretty depressing. Typical answers such as, "Uh...nothing" or "I don't remember" aren't very inspiring, are they? Truth be told, sometimes responses like that are more accurately translated to, "Mom—you're *embarrassing* me! Cut it out!" But sometimes students can't answer the question clearly because they're just not sure. Your "One Thing" wasn't obvious.

Think about the most recent message you taught and the big idea. Can you say it in a sentence? If *you* can't say it in a sentence (after you *wrote* the talk), then your middle schoolers won't be able to, either.

One common mistake in preparing a middle school message is trying to cover too much. Because we're so excited about what students can learn, we may try to include too many things. And as a result, we don't get much of anything across. When listening to the classic three-point sermon, most middle schoolers will wander off the trail somewhere around point one-and-a-half. So instead of trying to throw too much at them and just hoping some of it sticks, pick *one* really important thing and do everything you can to get that point across.

We're not sure who said it first, but if you're going to stick with a three-point sermon, here's the best outline to use for middle schoolers:

1. Tell students what you're about to teach them.

2. Teach it to them.

3. Tell them what you just taught them.

WHAT'S THE ANCHOR SCRIPTURE?

When I (Scott) first started to put together middle school lessons every week, I felt the *pressure*. Not only had James 3:1 appropriately scared me, but I was looking out at my students each week and realizing that lots of them were actually *listening*. And I remember clearly thinking, *Man, I hope what I'm saying is on target.*

Maybe you've felt that same stress. After all, we're trying to help students understand the *Bible*—God's Word. Our goal isn't to try to get middle schoolers to fly a little straighter or behave a little better or keep their noses a little cleaner. Our desire is that God's Truth will *grip their hearts* and *transform their lives.* But my anxiety level plummeted when I realized this: I have the God of the Universe as my Chief Advisor. I'm not just teaching from "my best thoughts and strategies." That definitely takes some of the pressure off.

Along with James 3:1, there's another section of Scripture that's really made an impression on me when it comes to teaching. I think of it almost every time I prepare a message:

> Not until halfway through the Festival did Jesus
> go up to the temple courts and begin to teach.

> The Jews there were amazed and asked, "How did this man get such learning without having been taught?"
>
> Jesus answered, "My teaching is not my own. It comes from the one who sent me. Anyone who chooses to do the will of God will find out whether my teaching comes from God or whether I speak on my own. Whoever speaks on their own does so to gain personal glory, but he who seeks the glory of the one who sent him is a man of truth; there is nothing false about him." (John 7:14-18)

Our teaching isn't our own. We hope you find as much comfort in that thought as we do. When there's one big idea for a middle school message, you can usually pin down one "anchor Scripture"—straight from the mouth of God—that can serve as the mooring to secure the point you want to get across. Use this Scripture to not only keep you on track, but also keep God's Word as a reference in your message to remind students where the ultimate truth comes from.

WHAT'S THE TAKEAWAY?

My (Scott here) sons and I like to play darts together, but I often have to remind them to think clearly about *what they're aiming at.* Sometimes their strategy is just to heave the dart as hard as they can. It makes a convincing sound as it slams into the dartboard, yet they didn't give any thought to the dart's desired destination. This also explains all those tiny holes in my wall. (Even so, that's one step better than playing darts with my long-time junior high pastor friend Phil, who once threw a dart toward the target that ended up in my shin.)

Think for a minute about what you ultimately want a student to *walk away with* after you've slaved and sweated over the preparation of a middle school message. We need to shoot higher than hoping they'll be entertained and laugh a lot, or at least stay engaged the whole time and don't doze off. And our goal also needs to be higher than impressing them because we're such Bible wizards, and we have mental powers they can only hope to have one day.

In thinking through the "takeaway value," Bill Hybels put it this way:

> If you want to improve your communication, strive for clarity. When I coach our teachers around here I always ask them two questions. "What do you want them to know? What do you want them to do?" If they can't answer those two questions immediately, I say, "You're ill prepared. Don't inflict that message on our people."[121]

I (Scott) recently gave a talk on the changing emotions that a student can expect to feel in middle school. I taught from 1 John 3:20 and Luke 12:25. And at the top of my page in my "What's the Takeaway?" section, I wrote what I wanted students to know and what I wanted them to *do*.

KNOW: EMOTIONAL INTENSITY IS PART OF GOING FROM BEING A KID TO BEING AN ADULT.

DO: *UNDERSTANDING* YOUR EMOTIONS IS EVEN MORE IMPORTANT THAN SIMPLY *CONTROLLING* YOUR EMOTIONS.

Defining the takeaway *before you begin writing a talk* is crucial. We must be crystal-clear on what the bull's-eye of the target is so we can take aim and hit it.

WHAT WILL BRING IT TO LIFE?

Let's do a little mental exercise together. Imagine yourself giving a talk to a room full of adults. When you teach grown-ups (even if you're *really* boring), what are most people in the audience going to do? It's pretty easy to predict, right?

- They'll maintain eye contact.

- They'll nod their heads from time to time.

- And most of the time, they'll attempt to be subtle if they're dozing off, just so they don't hurt your feelings.

But when we teach *middle schoolers* (we can see you smirking already), it's a different story. If you're even *marginally* boring when you teach a room full of students, what do they do? Let's see…

- They start talking (not whispering, but *talking*) to the person next to them.

- They make airplanes, origami animals, or spit wads out of any available paper.

- They recline and count ceiling tiles or stare out the window.

- They turn completely around to see if the person behind them is doing anything more interesting than you are.

- They draw intricate tattoos on their arm, or their neighbor's arm, or the chair, or…

- They ask you, loudly, how much time is left until it's done.

- They lie down on the chair next to them and try to get a nap in.

- They start texting the person two seats down, or maybe they text you—even though you're still teaching.

- The girls giggle at the guys nearby.

- The guys throw things at the girls nearby. (On second thought, the guys may throw things at the girls even if your talk *is* interesting.)

You know what we mean, don't you? Almost every middle school communicator has seen it happen. And at first glance, it might seem frustrating. But when you think about it, we middle school teachers have a built-in *advantage*, don't we? It's nearly instant feedback. Many speakers who teach adults can *bore* them and not even realize they're not connecting. The grown-up audience is usually so polite that the speaker doesn't get as many signals that it's not going well. Our students don't usually leave us wondering.

You've probably heard it said that middle schoolers have a very short attention span. But how long can the average 7th-grade boy stay tuned in to his favorite video game? Yep—until you pry the controller out of his sweaty fingers. Our friend Kurt Johnston (middle school pastor at Saddleback Church) says we really need to consider the "interest span" even more than we're considering their attention span.[122] Video games, movies, the Web—they all keep students' interest. And with a little work, *we* can design messages that can bring God's truth to life and hold their interest, too.

To help you consider holding the interest of middle schoolers and bringing your message to life, let's take a look at some helpful elements. You won't use every one of these areas every time you communicate to students. (But if you do give a message without using *any* of these strategies, you may want to remove sharp objects from the room.)

Consider giving yourself a rating of 1 to 4 in the margin of the following pages to indicate how well you take advantage of each of these strategies to keep you focused on the bull's-eye.

BEING CREATIVE—EVEN IF YOU'RE NOT

Creativity seems to come far more easily to some people than others. But even if you wouldn't describe yourself as imaginative, inventive, or original, you're still not off the hook. Creativity is, by nature, somewhat experimental. So take some risks. If it bombs, you'll know not to try it again. But if it works, you may have creatively permeated a student's memory with a piece of God's truth. Remember, we're not being creative just for fun; it's all about finding innovative ways to help our students know, learn from, and follow the Creator of creation—*and* creativity.

As you exercise your creativity, keep in mind these two things:

- *It's tough to be creative in a hurry.* So plan ahead. Driving in your car on the way to youth group isn't the time to be thinking, *Hmm...how can I bring this teaching to life?*

- *It's tough to be creative alone.* Sometimes really strange or seemingly dumb ideas will spur a conversation that turns into a really great idea. Collaboration is a huge key to creative communication. Whether it's a monthly "creativity" meeting or talking through a message outline with one other person, invite others to join you in the quest for creativity.

USING OBJECTS

The object lesson still works. In some churches we've heard adults say, "I get more out of the children's sermon than I do the main preaching," and often that's because of the item the pastor uses to illustrate the point. There are resources available to give you ideas.[123] But with a little creativity, you can develop great illustrations that are tailored to your specific point.

Here are some simple examples:

- I (Scott) recently taught about Genesis 28, when Jacob dreamed about the stairway to heaven. As I did, I slowly climbed a giant ladder as I made each point. Students' eyes were fixed on the ladder the whole time.

- Another time, we were teaching on relative truth and how simply saying you don't believe something doesn't change whether or not it's true. We compared God's moral law to the law of gravity, and then we dropped stuff (an old cell phone, a watermelon, a broken TV) from the rafters of the gym to see what would happen. We also recorded a video of us throwing an old toilet off the church building. Not only did the students *love* it, but they remembered the point.

- During the last session of a weekend retreat, we talked about how even though the retreat was ending, God wanted to "launch" us back into our schools and homes to tell and show people what Jesus was all about. I gave my entire talk while bouncing on a trampoline in the middle of the room. Not only did students pay attention, but it was also hilarious for me to see everyone's heads bobbing up and down the whole time.

MOVING AROUND

This one is simple, but it can make a big difference. A speaker who stands cemented to one particular spot loses an advantage. Purposeful movement can draw a listener into what you're talking about. Random, aimless meandering, on the other hand, can just be distracting. Have you ever seen someone walking rapidly back and forth while they teach? The speaker looks like a leopard pacing their cage at the zoo.

Picture what happens when you're listening to someone teach and that speaker steps out into the audience. Eyes follow her, and the audience wonders what she's up to. Try using this tool to select a "human prop" for an illustration, or maybe ask a student a question related to what you're teaching. And when you have a few students in one section of the room who are goofing off, just taking a few steps toward them can draw them back in and help them refocus.

It's easy to get into a "regular teaching routine" though, so this takes some forethought. To sharpen this skill, ask yourself, *Do I use the whole room when I teach?*

TELLING STORIES

We adults love a good story, don't we? Middle schoolers are no exception. But storytelling is an *art*, and it takes practice. Not only is Jesus the Son of God, but he's also a master storyteller. That's one reason why people were (and still are) drawn into his teaching.

Here are a few storytelling tips.

- **Make sure the story *fits* what you're trying to teach.** Have you ever heard a *great* story or had something crazy happen to you and one of your first thoughts was, *I've gotta put that in a talk. That was* awesome! The trouble is, it doesn't really fit into your next talk, but you *know* it'll make people laugh. As a general rule, save the story. If it's strong enough, a lesson will eventually come along where it'll get the reaction you're hoping for *and* drive home a point.

- **The "payoff" of the story must be equal to the time it takes to tell it.** A good friend of ours is a terrific storyteller. He's fantastically animated, can make great sound effects and facial expressions—the whole deal. But we joke with him now because we knew him when he used to spend 16 minutes of a 20-minute talk telling a hilarious story about a white gorilla and making students double up with laughter, but then only barely connecting it to the point he was making. (But man, the story was *funny!*) These days, he can take a few minutes to tell a great story—sound effects and all—and then masterfully link it to a scriptural truth. Jackpot!

- **Look for stories in your own life.** We've heard people say, "My life's just not that interesting, so I get my stories from other places." We beg to differ. Just look around you. Your life probably has more stories than you realize. Not only that, but your students want to *know* you. Personal stories feel more authentic and build relationships. Keep a file—start a list. The next time something crazy or just out of the ordinary happens to you, write it down. Then tell *your* story.

- **Tell vulnerable stories.** Be vulnerable in your stories. Remember, now that you're an adult, it's easy for middle schoolers to believe you've got it all together and that you can't relate to them when they feel awkward or fail or get embarrassed. But everyone stumbles. So help normalize their experiences by sharing yours. And it *almost* goes without saying that you need to apply great wisdom as to the specifics of your failures. Too many details won't be helpful to them.

- **Practice.** Take the time to get it right. Even though you know the story, write it out instead of relying solely on your memory. Then practice it (and your whole talk) in front of someone you trust, so that person can help you think about what needs to be more clear. Practice is vital to making your message all it can be.

INVOLVING STUDENTS

When teaching middle school students, it seems *everyone* pays more attention when there's a student standing up front. Maybe it's because they're all thinking, *Hey, that's one of us up there!* Or maybe it's because it's an underutilized strength in most middle school ministry settings. Regardless, whether you're inviting a student to read Scripture, demonstrate something, be interviewed, tell a story, or be used as a human prop, bringing a student to the front of the room almost always draws others in.

It's important, however, to give students time to *prepare*—especially if you're asking them to do something serious. It's our responsibility to make sure they're not going to stand in front of their friends and embarrass themselves. On our 8th-grade graduation day, I (Scott) have a few students cover the "teaching" part of our program, but we spend a few weeks ahead of time helping them think through everything from their topic to their delivery. And every year, all the rest of the students are riveted to the words they speak.

GIVING SYMBOLIC MEMENTOS

When your objective is to help students remember God's truth and take it further than the church parking lot, giving them a memento is a great strategy. And, if done well, there's even potential for the students to be able to explain what they learned if their parents ask, "Why do you have that _____?"

Symbolic mementos don't have to be expensive, either. During a message on how your life affects other people, we talked about the ripple effect—like what a stone makes when it lands in a pond—and we gave away little rocks. When we taught about the salvation Jesus brings, we used the phrase "Everyone's betting their life on *some*thing" and we gave away dice to every student. (That one might not go over quite so well in some denominations, we realize. "Hey! Who's teaching gambling to the middle schoolers?" Use your discretion.) When we taught the Luke 11 passage about putting your light on a stand, we gave out glow sticks. The possibilities are endless. And having a trinket like that at home can help students recall the message for longer and increase the odds that they'll live it out.

CHANGING UP THE ROOM

Consistency can be comforting to middle schoolers; but at the same time, predictability can be boring. When's the last time students walked into your meeting space and saw something *different*? Recently, I (Scott) was teaching on community, and we set up the room "in the round," instead of having everything happen from the front. It was a great feel! Another week we were teaching on simplicity, and we unplugged everything that used electricity in the room—only acoustic music, no gaming systems, videos, or microphones. It was a very memorable weekend. During a teaching on Communion, we had every group recline at tables and eat a meal together as we talked about the Last Supper. (The meal was only cereal, but it was still a great effect.)

How can you use your meeting room in a fresh new way?

INVITING A SPECIFIC RESPONSE

This really helps bring into focus the takeaway value of the teaching. Adults are more capable of discerning what next steps they should take after hearing a message. (Although it could be debated how many adults actually *do* anything as a result of the sermons they hear.) For middle schoolers, even when they're convinced that God wants them to do *something* in response to the teaching, they often need an assist in deciding what exactly that action step could be. We've found that middle schoolers respond remarkably well when a specific challenge is given.

Here are just a few examples:

- When teaching about relationships with parents, give them a card with three bond-building questions to ask their mom or dad.

- When teaching about sharing their faith, challenge them to *ask* one person (who's not a Christian) what he or she thinks about God and then simply *listen* to the answer.

- When teaching about Scripture reading, throw down the gauntlet with a specific reading target—and then follow up on it.

Speaking of challenges, look back at the topics we just unpacked and do a little self-assessment. Are there any that stand out as ones you're doing pretty well? Be encouraged! It's making a difference in helping students *get the message*. Consider picking one that you believe could be improved on and do something about it—*this month.*

SOME FINAL THOUGHTS

Once teaching preparation, practice, and delivery are complete, you're still not quite finished. There are just a few more steps you need to take to ensure that the impact of your teaching will continue to increase.

After You Speak...

MAKE SURE STUDENTS GET A CHANCE TO TALK, TOO

Since our goal is *way* more than just downloading information into middle school brains, it's important for students to have a chance to "verbally digest" what's been taught. We talked at length about this in the last chapter on small groups. But whether or not your ministry has "official small groups," it's crucial for middle schoolers to have a safe place to ask questions, express doubts, and think through how truth applies to their lives.

DEBRIEF

After you prepare and deliver teaching for students, from whom do you seek feedback? Not only do we teachers need someone to help us improve, but we also need confirmation and encouragement about the dimensions of our teaching that really connected with middle schoolers. We (Marko and Scott) invite feedback nearly every time we teach students, and it helps us grow and improve at sharing God's truth with students.

When you're seeking feedback, here are a few suggestions about the type of person to ask.

- Someone who loves you. It feels vulnerable to seek the critique. Make sure you're getting it from a person you trust.

- Someone who really knows middle schoolers. Your senior pastor may believe your message was brilliant, but your students may be scratching their heads.

- Someone who knows you sincerely want the truth. Your goal is to continue to get better. If you never hear any suggestions for improvement, you may be asking the wrong person.

One related debriefing question: Do you know your most

persistent, annoying teaching habit? Our goal as teachers is to minimize distractions when we're sharing God's truth, so we need to be aware of anything we do that can take the focus off the message.

I (Scott) recently saw a nationally known speaker teach middle schoolers, and I was surprised to see him continually raise and lower the music stand holding his notes—the entire time he spoke. You've probably heard a middle schooler tell a speaker, "You said 'ya know' (*or 'um' or 'I mean'*) 63 times!" Do you think that kid was doing more learning or counting?

I (still Scott) have a habit that shows itself sometimes when I really want to make a point. For some reason I'll put my hands on top of my head. It looks kind of silly, and it doesn't help me communicate anything—but without feedback, I'm not even sure I'd realize I do it.

KEEP LEARNING ABOUT TEACHING

Good teachers know they need to keep learning how to teach better. And there are numerous ways to approach this goal.

Read about teaching. We're limited in what we're able to cover in one short chapter, but there are some great books available that will help you teach better.[124]

Listen to great teaching. What great teachers do you listen to? There's a steady stream of free teaching available online.[125] Not only can you learn from the content, but when you pay attention to *how* they teach, you'll also learn to communicate better.

Find a teaching mentor. If you have the good fortune to know some great communicators, take lessons from them. Ask them to review your messages. Request input on ways they grow in their message-giving skills.

There is a danger in constantly thinking about teaching and how to do it better. Have you ever felt like it's difficult to just "listen and learn" from a sermon? The Acts 2 church devoted themselves to the apostles' teaching so they could live more like

Jesus, not so they could teach more like him.

This past summer I (Scott) was on vacation with my family, and we were visiting the church of a fantastic teacher. I loved just listening—and learning. This guy made God's words come to life. My family was sitting on one side of me, and on the other side was a guy I didn't know. About halfway through the message, I glanced at him because he'd started to *snore*. As it got louder and louder, I looked over at the seat on this man's other side to catch a glimpse of the guy he came with. But he was asleep, too! In a strange kind of way, I was actually encouraged. If these two guys could sleep through a message *that* good, I was reminded that it's not always the speaker's fault.

"My teaching is not my own. It comes from the one who sent me" (John 7:16). And God has sent us to his middle schoolers. So let's give it our best!

CHAPTER 17

Do or Die
(Building a Team)

Most of us have volunteered for something (or been volunteered for it), but we had no idea what we were getting ourselves into. (For some of you, that's the whole reason you find yourself reading this book.)

When my oldest son was seven years old, I (Scott) found myself serving as the soccer coach of his community rec. team. I played soccer as a kid, but that experience sure didn't qualify me as a coach. I'm honestly not sure how it happened. But I do remember the first practice.

There were seven kids there, plus my own son. Two of them were first-generation Japanese boys, which was very cool, and their skills showed that they'd clearly played a lot of soccer already. However, one of them spoke only about three words of English, and I speak *no* Japanese. Luckily, his buddy was a ready translator. (Although I often thought his translation wasn't exactly what I'd asked him to say. By the amused expression on his friend's face, I believe my "translator" might have been saying something like, "Hey, our coach is *crazy!*")

One kid's mom pulled me aside and said, "Coach, I just wanted you to know something about my son. He won't look you in the eye, and when you explain something, it's pretty certain he won't get it the first time." Hmm…that sounded like most seven-year-olds to me. But she was right; it usually took six or eight explanations just to get that kid pointed toward the right goal. And then there was an adorable-but-stocky little guy who came up to me partway through that first practice and said, "Uh, Coach? I don't know if this is my sport. Nobody told me there'd be this much *running.*"

Luckily for me, I wasn't alone. I'd somehow conned another dad into coaching with me. I knew Steve didn't know much about soccer, either, but he was good with kids and enthusiastic about pitching in. Plus, he was a hockey player, which is a lot like soccer on ice, right? (Well, wrong. But that's another story.)

Now community recreation department sports are great. But we'd unapologetically say that the stakes in middle school ministry are *much* higher. Still, some of us insist on doing ministry alone or at least with far less people power than our ministry calls for and deserves.

But WHY Do I Need a Team?

OVERCOMING OBSTACLES

If you're going to get any traction from this chapter about building a team, you must first be convinced why you *need* a team. When God tapped you on the shoulder and challenged you to step into the crazy world of middle school ministry, maybe you didn't consider whether or not there'd be anyone else who'd answer that same call to action. But even in the smallest of ministry settings, going solo simply isn't the best way to go. None of us has a complete array of gifts and skills capable of spanning all dimensions of middle school ministry. None of us has firsthand experience of middle school from both a guy's *and* a girl's perspective. None of us has limitless relational capacity, capable of expanding infinitely as students bring more friends into the community.

But let's be honest. Sometimes it's *fear* that stops us from building a team.

- What if other people don't share my vision for what this ministry should be?

- What if additional leaders make things messier or more complicated?

- And even more directly, what if some students seem to like the other leader more than me?

- Or, being brutally honest, what if I just don't feel very capable of leading other adults?

If one of the hallmarks of following Jesus is really about giving up control, then this is the perfect opportunity. There's no doubt that complexities increase with more people on a team. But at the end of the day, our whole objective is to help students understand the crazy love of God, right? And *with the right people* (more on that in a minute), a team will be able to serve that mission better than any one person can.

But there's another obstacle preventing many people from building a team—and many of us have fallen victim to it at one time or another. We know the emotional investment it takes to serve middle schoolers is huge. We know monumental patience is required to serve middle schoolers. We know the time expenditure can be enormous. And even though we've decided it's an investment absolutely worth *our* attention, somehow we just can't bring ourselves to put the challenge out there to someone else.

Care to guess the main reason church people give for not volunteering in a ministry? *Nobody invited them to volunteer.*[126] When we think of those with all the tools to help lead our middle school ministries, our minds somehow come up with a dozen reasons why they probably wouldn't want to do it. But Bill Hybels has a mantra that's difficult to argue with: "Never Say Someone's No For Them."[127] When you know of a specific need and you think of a person who'd be *great* at making that contribution, pray. Ask. Invite. Sure, it might end up being a short conversation. "Um… no, thanks." But if you don't ask, you'll never know. And *what if…* what if that person says *yes*? What if that person is willing to get quiet and ask God if this is an opportunity she should take seriously, and God says, "Do it!" Both of us (Marko and Scott) can immediately think of many invitations we've floated in front of people, wondering if they'd just chuckle and walk away. But instead, they turned into fantastic middle school ministry teammates.

It takes a shift in perspective to move from believing that you're out there "asking for favors," as you challenge people with the thought of serving middle schoolers. But we challenge *you* to adjust your thinking. Don't think of it as "selling" them on something; think of it as painting a vision that they can partner in. We have to realize that we hold the *power* to invite them into a life-changing assignment.

I (Scott) experienced the exhilaration of it again just recently. There's this really capable guy in our church named Paul. I've known him for a little more than a year; and as the new school year approached, I told him we could really use a guy like him to lead a middle school boys small group. Even though I described what a crucial role it is, I wasn't sure if he'd go for it. He's a commercial airline pilot flying 777s on a transatlantic schedule—not the first "profile" you might think of when imagining a middle school ministry volunteer.[128] But it thrilled me when he said he'd give it a shot.

About a month after he'd joined the team, I got up on a Sunday morning to find an email he'd sent me at 2:15 a.m.—from Moscow. "I'll see you tonight at Elevate, but I'm probably going to be a few minutes late. I'll be there in time to lead my small group, though." (I figured if anybody could influence an on-time arrival, it'd be the guy steering the aircraft, right?) So that evening during our program, I saw him sneak into the room just after we'd started. That was cool enough, to see his dedication to these guys he's only known a few weeks.

But then after our small group time was done, Paul hustled over to me and said, "Man, this middle school ministry thing really *works*!" When I asked what he meant, he said, "One of my guys brought along one of his buddies tonight. He was asking a lot of questions, so we just spent this small group time helping him understand what it means to be a Christian—and he decided to become one tonight! I had a feeling when I woke up today (and I'm thinking, *Yeah—in Russia!*) that the most important thing I might do today is come to my middle school small group tonight. Looks like I was right!"

When Paul walked out of our church that night, he had a spring in his step even though he hadn't slept in more than 24 hours. God had *used* Paul to impact a life. And by following God's prompting, I had the thrill of being the one who'd invited him onto the team.

A PROCESS

Teams really do need to be *built*, and that's a process. Most of us like to see things happen *fast*. We hate waiting in lines, we believe email is too slow, we record our TV shows so we can watch them on "our time." And when it comes to building teams, many of us wish we could just click on a few icons at www.SpecialOrderMiddleSchoolTeam.com and—*pow!*—there's our dream team! Ah, if only it were that easy.

The people on your team—whether there are two or twenty or dozens of them—really do make the biggest difference. Middle school ministry is all about a team of individuals that God brings together to serve students. It's way more than clever programs, good facilities, and creative events. It's even more than having a cool logo and ministry name, if you can possibly imagine that. An unstoppable middle school ministry team starts with a few key people, and someone's got to *lead* that charge.

Maybe it's easy for you to see yourself as a leader, and the thought of assembling some fired-up people to tackle this challenge simply *thrills* you. But maybe you feel like you're already in deeper waters than you ever imagined, and the thought of leading students *and* adult leaders is a bit overwhelming. Regardless of your mindset, there's no doubt that God can use you to pull together a team (be it large or small) of people in your ministry to radically impact the spiritual life of middle schoolers around you. Don't do it alone.

Three Dimensions of Team Building

We're not suggesting that building a team is simple, and it's definitely not as easy as 1-2-3. But consider these three dimensions of banding together a squad of fired-up people who can see the vision of helping middle schoolers follow Jesus.

DIMENSION 1: INVITE

We must consistently invite quality people to consider serving middle schoolers.

We're not wild about the term *recruiting*. Maybe that's because it sounds a little too military-like. (Although, on second thought, sometimes it might feel like bearing arms could be a helpful thing to keep students in line.) But whether you call it recruiting, inviting, envisioning, enrolling, or drafting, don't fall into the trap of viewing it as a seasonal activity that needs to happen only as the ministry year is starting up. To be most effective, we need to be prayerfully prepared and have our eyes peeled constantly, looking for the next potentially great volunteer. *Inviting* should be happening all the time.

WHY I DO THIS

At last count, I've held more than 28 jobs in my life: Waiter, barista, corn detasseler, nanny, wrestling coach, delivery boy, custodian, video store clerk, limo driver, and pizza maker, to name just a few of the job titles that fill my resume. Some jobs have lasted a few years, and some have lasted a couple of days. I went into each job with a romantic idea of what it would be like to do a certain task. In college, I really wanted to work as a barista at a bohemian coffee house. However, instead of hanging out with young post-modern philosophers, I faced snobby suburbanites who were incensed that I couldn't remember their drink orders.

I'm ashamed to admit my disenchantment led to my unceremoniously rendering my resignation—not even bothering to return my apron and hat. I wanted so desperately to be excited about what I did, but I never found a job that gave me life. I'd rather go broke than do something I don't feel passionate about. I just couldn't find the right fit.

When I took my first job in youth ministry, I wasn't looking to be a middle school pastor; it was just an opportunity to get my foot in the door of youth ministry. The kids were fun, but I didn't sense a call to minister to young teens. Then I attended my first National Youth Workers Convention and sat in Mark Oestreicher's middle school ministry Critical Concerns Course. His passion for middle school ministry was overwhelming. He advocated for middle schoolers, instead of dismissing it as a phase. He described middle school ministry as uncharted territory that needed pioneers to join in the expedition.

I went home from that conference with a sense of calling to full-time middle school ministry.

There will always be an ebb and flow to a calling like middle school ministry. It can be difficult for people who want to see results. Because middle schoolers are constantly in process, we never get to see immediate results of our ministry. It takes a few years before we see the fruits of our labor.

There is no greater reminder of the importance of what I do than when a former middle schooler returns, having successfully made it through adolescence, and wants to give back to the next generation and keep rolling, searching for their identity in Christ and obeying God's calling on their lives. I'm comfortable with the messiness of my life because it serves as a constant reminder of what I do as a middle school pastor. I pray I get to keep on rolling alongside middle schoolers.

Andy Jack is the middle school pastor at Christ Church of Oak Brook, Illinois.

Okay, so we're ready to hand out some invitations. As we scan the horizon (or the pews, or the fellowship hall, or the unsuspecting new members list), just *what* are we looking for? It's not "just anybody," right? But without thinking, we can inaccurately stereotype what a great middle school ministry worker looks like. Our friend and fellow middle school pastor Heather Flies says, "We often think of a 20-something male, muscular, who sports a goatee, drives a jeep, wears the latest fashions, plays the guitar, (insert the rest of your own stereotype here)..."[129] Simply not true! Sure, that person might be a great middle school ministry volunteer, but not necessarily.

Our friend Kurt Johnston agrees that we need to throw out the conventional formula. He says students need "spiritually mature adults who love God, like middle schoolers, and want to be part of their life."[130]

In the ministry where I (Scott) serve, we have lots of "stereotype-breakers."

- A 29-year-old information systems guy named Brett who is decidedly more techy than hip.

- A high school senior named Jonathan who helps one of our autistic students every week.

- An empty-nester named Nick who owns his own company, plays classical piano, and hunts bears.

- A 39-year-old salesman named Coop who's a dad of preschool girls and can also start a conversation with any middle school boy.

- A fantastic middle school mom named Pam whose daughter cautiously allows her to volunteer as long as she doesn't embarrass her (too much).

- A hard-driving businessman named Paul who's 69 but still remembers his own kids' journey through middle school.

- A sweet-hearted newlywed named Jenni who grew up at our church and now serves where she once learned.

If we had to boil it down to what to look for in every middle school ministry teammate, I (Scott) love the concept of the "3 Cs" that we use around Willow: Character, Competency, and Chemistry.[131]

Character. This is really the starting place. We need people in middle school ministry who love Jesus and are growing in their relationship with him. Perfect? Of course not. But you've got to be able to rely on someone's character in all situations. It affects how they'll deal with conflict, how they'll view students, how reliable, honest, humble, and teachable they'll be. When you see someone with a fantastic skill set ("Man, that person's *really* creative"), but you get a little queasy when you think about their character, think twice about inviting them into middle school ministry.

Competency. The gifts and abilities that someone brings are really important. You need the person in charge of your budget to be great with numbers and strategy. You need people leading small groups who are discerning, able to lead conversations well, and can shepherd their group members. The "warm-body approach" just doesn't work. No matter how strong someone's skill set is, we need people who are competent in a *student* environment. For some people, middle school ministry may simply drive them crazy. In those cases, we feel no shame in letting people know that there's sure to be a perfect fit somewhere in "Big Church" for them.

Chemistry. How does the person fit relationally with you and the other team members? The middle school ministry environment is heavily influenced by the relational tone of the adult leaders. It's important to realize that affinity and connection really matter when it comes to your middle school team. When you're thinking of who you want to serve with, first think of the people you love to be around—and feel no guilt about that. (More on that in a minute...)

So where do we start to look when we're ready to begin handing out invitations? As we've talked to middle school ministry peeps far and wide, that's one of those *million dollar questions*. As you're looking for the right people to add to your middle school ministry team, consider these observations that we've had over the years.

- There's no "silver bullet source" when it comes to finding new volunteers. You may get one or two from each place you look.

- The personal invite can't be overestimated. Personally asking someone to pray about this opportunity—and specifically telling that person why you believe *he'd* uniquely bless middle schoolers—is powerful.

- Our best source for more middle school volunteers has been our current middle school volunteers. If you're crazy enough to work with young adolescents, then you probably hang out with other people who have what it takes.

- Help "tire kickers" get a one-time look. Many people hesitate before committing to serve when they sense they'd have to sign up for a weekly commitment "indefinitely" (which to them sounds a lot like "forever"). Think of some ways that you can expose potential teammates to one-time service opportunities—just to give them a chance to check things out. Let them see what God is up to in your ministry.

- Be a storyteller. When good things happen in your middle school ministry, find ways to let people know about it—your senior pastor, the adult congregation, everyone. In other words, be like Garrett (Marko's Mexico trip evangelism kid from chapter 4). Help people know that middle schoolers do more than just break things.

- Pray, pray, pray. Ask God to show you the person you haven't thought of yet. They might be right under your nose—or next door.

DIMENSION 2: EQUIP

It's the rare middle school ministry worker who comes trained. In almost all cases, we need to specifically equip people to prepare them for leading young teens. From time to time, we've been lucky enough to have someone move into town who was part of a great middle school ministry somewhere else—and then we do cartwheels. (I believe it's happened to me [Scott] about twice in the last 10 years.)

But even the most fired-up volunteer needs to be equipped to serve with middle schoolers. We need to provide them with a clear picture of what we're asking them to do. Remember, just because someone has served in a similar role in another church, or another area of your church, it won't necessarily translate on all dimensions when they enter the middle school realm. (For example, the guy who has experience driving the van full of senior adults to their social activities is in for an all-new experience when he pilots the van on middle school activity night!)

The second-worst serving experience is showing up to volunteer somewhere but not feeling properly equipped and trained for how to do it well. (The worst, of course, is when you show up to serve and there's *nothing* for you to do. But that's a story for another time.)

Walking volunteers through sections of a book like this one will help them better understand middle schoolers. Write out a list of the key skills needed for a particular role in your ministry. Here's a sampling of the kinds of things you might include in small group leader training:

- Understanding the basics of early adolescent development

- Facilitating a conversation with young teens

- Building relationships with parents

- Listening skills

- Dealing with discipline issues

- Having a one-on-one conversation with a student about what it means to be a Christian

- How to prepare for the middle school retreat weekend

- Responding to tough questions middle schoolers might ask

- Strategies (and even procedures) for dealing with complex situations that could come up (for example, depression, abuse, cutting, eating disorders, and so on)

- And on, and on, and on

You need a plan. Since leaders likely won't arrive already trained, and since there are so many issues worth discussing, you must develop a strategy to equip your team. This is one of many places where there's no "right answer." (Although the *wrong* answer would be to just shrug your shoulders, do nothing, and hope that somehow things will work out.) We know of ministries that start out the school year with an all-day training, and others who actually go on middle school retreats—with no middle schoolers—for the purpose of getting leaders equipped and ready to serve.

I (Scott) like an approach that spreads training throughout the school year, since it's tough to cram everything in once or twice a year and hope people will not only be able to arrange their schedules for these large time commitments, but also remember all the training they received. Our strategy is to ask our leaders to show up 45 minutes before the students do, every other week, so we can tackle a training issue.

Once we have the training on the calendar, though, *we must make it worth people's time*. Their minutes are precious; therefore we can't afford to waste them. In my first ministry experience, my then-girlfriend-now-wife, Lynette, and I were volunteer leaders of high school students. We regularly cut short our Sunday afternoons to attend a one-hour mandatory volunteers' training. But too often our leaders didn't seem well prepared for it. On those weeks we volunteers would say to each other, "They wanted me to come early for *this*?" And it made us much less motivated to show up for future weeks.

In order to equip people well and communicate that you value their time, we've identified three criteria to make our training "F.I.T." The training must be:

Focused—We tackle one specific issue in the brief amount of time allocated. It doesn't have to be long to be worthwhile—*if* it's focused and targeted.

Interactive—People learn more when they can personally engage in the learning. Sometimes that means role-playing (for example, you're the leader, I'm the student). Sometimes it's talking through a sample situation. Sometimes it's Q&A with an experienced panel of volunteer leaders. But what it's usually *not* is a talking head droning on and on and on.

Timely—This one has to do with "scratching where it itches." Sometimes people will ask, "How do you get people to come to training?" The best answer we know is make it *so* worthwhile that no one will want to miss it. Promise leaders you'll help them address the issues that are most vexing to them as they serve—and then deliver on it. If volunteers have a vision for what God can do in the life of a middle schooler, and if you're talking about an applicable, timely topic that will make them more effective in accomplishing that vision in practical ways right now—they'll show up. Not only that, but they'll feel more prepared and informed and valued. If they're not showing up, then instead of asking what's wrong with them, consider asking if something's wrong with your training.

DIMENSION 3: ENCOURAGE

We believe that students' spiritual growth happens best in small groups led by adult leaders who serve in community—and who find encouragement there. Many churches have mission statements that say they're "building a community to reach a community," which rings true. Henri Nouwen's thoughts about community are relevant here:

> By community, I don't mean formal communities. I mean families, friends, parishes, 12-step programs, prayer groups. Community is not an organization; community is a way of living: you gather around you people with whom you want to proclaim the truth that we are the beloved sons and daughters of God.[132]

This idea jumps back to the Chemistry point of the "3 Cs" we mentioned earlier. Middle school ministry is *not* a solo sport; this is a team game. Be cautious of the person who says, "I don't really want to know the other adults in this ministry. I just came here to work with students." Even if they don't realize it at first, the community *will* be of value to them, usually on those days when the middle school boys are more interested in who could drink the most "shots" of coffee creamer than they are in the lesson, or when the flatulence factor is so far through the roof that it's just not funny anymore (to you), or when the middle school girls are embroiled in a petty relational standoff (the week after you taught on love and acceptance).

Volunteers need someone to remind them it's worth it. Really, we *all* need someone to remind us it's worth it. We need someone to slap us on the back and jog our memories about the places we *have* seen God at work in those middle schoolers' lives.

And that person's probably going to need a slap on the back in return a few weeks later. The encouragement we receive in community isn't a side note of serving—it should be part of our serving foundation.

Encouragement is more than just expressing appreciation every time someone invests in students, although that's a part of it. Encouragement is also the "sweet revenge" of the *fun* that leaders can have together. Honestly, there's a part of the middle school ministry shenanigans that's just plain enjoyable. How many other church ministries ask you to get messy in ways you'd never imagined (maybe with some combination of chocolate sauce, vegetable oil, shaving cream, or lipstick), dress in ways you swore you never would, and laugh at things you'd never guessed could be funny? If you're not letting the silliness of your middle schoolers leak into your adult community, then you're missing something crucial.

Take a minute and honestly assess the level of adult community in your ministry on a scale of 1 to 10 (where 1 is no adult community, and 10 is off-the-charts adult community). Is this a place that needs some attention? Think of the person in your ministry—or even in your church—who's just *great* at building community, and then schedule a cup of coffee with that person. If you can build the level of community among the volunteers in your ministry, your students will be able to sense that. An environment that has a solid, supportive community is magnetic to them.

Identify the amount of time that you can realistically devote to building the adult community. Is it a monthly gathering? Is it time to schedule an overnight retreat? I (Scott) mentioned that in our ministry we ask leaders to come 45 minutes early every other week for training. On the "other" weeks, we *still* ask them to come 45 minutes early, but for the purpose of building relationships with other leaders. We ask how each other's small groups are going and how each other's *lives* are going. We pray for each other, celebrate each other, and get to know each other better. We tell stories about what's happened in our small groups, and we share frustrations about students (or small group "stuff") who make us nutty. The crazy thing is, these leaders are busy people—but they still value the time to come together with like-minded servants. We've heard people say many times, "I came to serve students; I stayed for the adult friendships that came with it. I had no idea how much fun I'd have with these people and how much I'd grow."

Note: Because not all adults feel the need to invest the extra time in adult-friendship building, it's wise to think through what the bottom-line expectations are for those serving in your ministry. Perhaps it's not a deal-breaker for them to miss the "adult community" element, as long as they're involved in a healthy adult community elsewhere.

Concluding Thoughts

Our ministries have been blessed to have some leaders who've served middle school students for a long time—some more than 10 or 15 *years*. Even though these leaders have a deep love for middle school students, a deep tolerance for middle school student behavior, and found a place to use their gifts, I'm convinced they wouldn't still be serving if they hadn't experienced a place that cares about their time, their commitment, and their experience.

As you reflect on the ideas presented in this chapter, we pray you'll be encouraged to take a step forward in "not going it alone." And if you're already building a team, we pray you'll embrace the three dimensions of Inviting, Equipping, and Encouraging to further bless your team—and keep them coming back. Not only will those leaders feel used by God in their various roles, but they'll also be partnering with a team that cares for them and shares the same vision and love for middle school students.

Imagine what God can do with such an unstoppable team…

CHAPTER 18

From Enemy to Advocate

(Working with Parents)

Have you heard the sarcastic adage that says, "Ministry would be easy if it weren't for the *people*"? If you're a youth leader, you might *occasionally* be tempted to adjust this adage a bit: "Middle school ministry would be easy if it weren't for the *parents*."

Clearly, neither one of those statements reflects a healthy viewpoint, but let's be honest: Most everyone who's been in middle school ministry for very long has a few stories of challenging interactions with parents. For me (Scott), a few weeks before writing this chapter, I experienced another one. We'd just had our annual "parents weekend," where we invite all the parents to attend our weekend middle school gathering. It's our chance to try to put our best foot forward, to encourage parents, to introduce them to their kids' small group leaders, and to show them how seriously we take this ministry to their sons and daughters. As part of the morning, I get to meet with parents and offer them some encouraging words, as well as some thoughts about issues relevant to raising middle schoolers. Honestly, it was a terrific weekend, and we got lots of good feedback.

But the next weekend at church, I ran into a dad. And this father was *angry* at me. I mean, he was veins-popping-out-of-the-forehead mad. His gripe? Just before I got up to teach the middle school lesson, I'd slipped off my shoes (as I often do). Not because I'm trying to make a point about holy ground or anything. Sock feet are just more comfortable at times, and as long as there's no nasty food odor, middle schoolers never seem to mind. Now, in retrospect, it might have been wise to keep my shoes on when addressing the parents. But this dad couldn't believe how utterly *disrespectful* I'd been to take my shoes off, and he didn't hold back at all in chewing me out. (Let's just say he chose some words that Jesus probably wouldn't have recommended.)

Interestingly, as he "talked" to me, I believe he sorta realized how his words were hitting me like a sucker punch in the stomach. So he tried to equalize it by telling me how excellent my Bible teaching to the students was and how relevant our ministry was for the kids. But at that point, his initial words had already clocked me, and his recovery attempt wasn't very encouraging. In fact, even though I've been doing student ministry for a long time and I knew he was overreacting, I had to find a quiet corner for about five minutes to bring my blood pressure back down. (A few days later, I sought out a conversation with this dad, and he apologized. He's actually a great guy, and he admitted he didn't handle himself well that day.)

I don't know if you've (yet) experienced an interaction with a parent like the one I described, but most likely you will at some point in your ministry. When it happens, it's easy to let our perspective on parents get a bit twisted. Yet, we must remind ourselves that the vast majority of parents aren't adversarial. In fact many parents can be some of the best partners we have in ministry.

In the states where Marko and I live, middle schoolers can't drive cars—so we're really at the parents' mercy when it comes to students being a part of any function.

But most importantly—and with all kidding aside—we need to be absolutely clear on the pivotal significance of the parents' role with the students in our ministries. So the majority of this chapter will explore their position and how we can partner with them to fully impact students.

Parents *Are* the #1 Influence on Kids

Peer pressure pushes its way to the forefront during the middle school years, and the preferences and opinions of same-age friends (as well as rivals) carry much more weight than they did in elementary school. In addition, *media impact* only increases during the middle school era—through TV, online content, movies, and music. (Although similar to adults, students truly believe that the media influences everyone *but* them.[133])

Yet, there is substantial, conclusive evidence that *parents* are clearly the most significant influence on the lives of middle school students. And this isn't just some unsubstantiated notion. Dr. Christian Smith, professor of sociology at the University of Notre Dame and principal investigator of the National Study of Youth and Religion, and his team have done extensive research on teenage spirituality. He says,

> Some observers suggest that American teenagers have outgrown the influence of their parents and other adults, are shaped primarily by their peers, and, in the name of independence, are best set free of adult oversight and support to find their own individual ways. Such views, our observations suggest, are badly misguided.[134]

We've had the privilege of spending some time with Dr. Smith and discussing how this applies to the lives of middle schoolers in particular. (Realistically, we probably did more listening and learning than discussing, since he's way smarter than we are.)

"Spiritually speaking, teenagers are profoundly impacted and shaped by their parents," he told us. "The most important pastor teenagers will ever have is their parents."

In spite of that, though, many middle schoolers *seem* to work hard at convincing their parents they're old, out of touch, and less relevant than ever before. And more than a few exasperated parents are left wondering if they have much sway left at all. (We covered this topic more fully in chapter 7—students are desperate for their independence, but not at all certain about how to handle it.) It's worth the reminder here that despite the fact that parents *know* their kids are developmentally and emotionally changing—parents often *sense* that they're losing influence in their sons' or daughters' lives. And in the midst of that shift, we have the privilege of serving both students and parents during this roller-coaster ride.

Every year I (Scott) meet with the parents of the incoming 6th graders in my ministry, and every year I see the telltale "What in the world is happening to my kid?" look on their faces. See, when there's a newborn in the house, parents often joke that the child didn't come with an instruction manual. And in their elementary school years, lots of problems were vaporized with either a Band-Aid or a Popsicle. The roller coaster of emotions didn't swing quite as low then, or at least it didn't stay there for as long. But once their kids hit middle school, parents' intuitive responses from "the old days" don't work. So these parents, who really do love their kids with a depth they can't describe, are often left shaking their heads in exasperation. They don't *feel* like the most influential people in their kid's lives. In fact, they may feel less influential than ever before. Which is an understandable conclusion, especially when the young-teen voice whines (or growls), "You just don't understand, Mom and Dad!"

Unfortunately, many parents believe they have no better choice than to just back off as their kid may be pleading for them to do. Yet that can prove to be one of the most destructive approaches a parent can take, and it can even add to the frustration. In some ways, it's like sending a young teenager across a minefield and saying, "Good luck!" But this isn't a book on parenting skills, so we won't get into that. Just remember that parents don't choose that approach because they're dumb; it's because sometimes they simply don't know a more constructive approach.

In addition, a parent's spiritual influence can go "both ways." If a parent isn't interested in faith or doesn't take faith very seriously, there's a high probability that it will negatively affect a student's spiritual outlook. While there's no doubt that God can break into anyone's life and radically impact its trajectory independent of any parental views, it's clear that Mom's or Dad's level of spiritual engagement definitively impacts the teenager's perspective—potentially pulling a middle schooler closer to God or pushing her further away. So the argument could be made that the single most powerful thing parents can do to help their kids know the love of Jesus is simply to follow him closely.

Scripture makes it clear that parents are God's Plan A for helping students to know him and follow him: "Impress [these commandments] on your children. Talk about them when you sit at home and when you walk along the road, when you lie down and when you get up" (Deuteronomy 6:7). There's no substitute for that. The family is the original small group and a powerful tool for spiritual formation. Yet we all know that every family doesn't function that way and, unfortunately, not every parent will rise to the occasion and lead as God intended. But in our roles as youth ministers, we can provide information, encouragement, support, partnering opportunities, a voice, and coaching that can help them take the next step in *their* roles. That's when our middle school ministries get to step in as a great Plan B to help point young teens to Jesus. Don't shortchange the way God might use you in this equation.

So if parents really are the number one influence on their kids, it only makes sense that we'd do anything possible to make them our *allies* instead of viewing them as neutral or worse—as our adversaries. After all, we're on the same team. We want what's best for the student. (If, on occasion, there are parents who don't act like this is true, we still need to expand our perspective and always take the high road.)

At times the equation can get even more complex if you're dealing with parents who may be feeling "pushed away" by their young teen. They may be experiencing some resentment (even subconsciously) toward a know-it-all-youth-ministry-type who seems to connect easily with *their* kid. And that leaves us in a place where we may have to do some extra work to be bridge-builders with parents.

When we can properly align with parents, we'll see parents move beyond their "allies status" and become our *advocates* in ministry. And when you have parents as advocates, their voices can be very influential to *other* parents who are still figuring out how to perceive your ministry.

Insights into "Parent World"

Clearly, there's not one type of parent, so it's pointless to come up with a one-size-fits-all strategy. But there are some parental commonalities that we can take into consideration.

PARENTS ARE VITAL, CRUCIAL, AND OF GREAT MAGNITUDE IN THE LIVES OF THEIR KIDS

Hopefully we've already established that point in this chapter, but it's so important that we'll keep it in this list.

PARENTS ARE BUSY

At first glance, that might frustrate us. (And we could have legitimate but dangerously judgmental thoughts like, *How can you be so busy that you're in danger of missing some of the things your kid needs from you?*) But when a kid reaches middle school, their parents are often in "The Crunch Years."

WHY I DO THIS

"Baaaaaaaaaat!"

Decibels rarely heard by human ears broke the late-afternoon stillness. Our leisurely hike was brought to an abrupt halt as I turned to see three terrified girls running toward me. Panting with exhaustion, they doubled over and struggled to get the words out.

"It...was...a bat...you should have seen it...down that hill."

"It looked like this," the last girl raised two fingers on either side of her head in imitation of bat ears. She moved her fingers up and down and bit her lower lip to demonstrate the ferocity of the little critter.

"So, you guys saw a bat?" I asked after the bat imitation and exhausted breathing stopped.

"Yes, it was fuh-reaky!"

"We were afraid for our lives!"

I looked around at their flushed faces and asked if we should head back to the cabins. In unison they uttered a dramatic "Yes!" and we quickly departed for the safety of the main camp. Twenty minutes later the girls were happily diving into their candy stash as they got ready to go waterskiing. I stood outside the cabin and couldn't help secretly smiling to myself.

The "incident of the bat" occurred near the end of my first summer of youth ministry. I spent 10 weeks experiencing the drama of middle school life, and the bat incident was a sort of representation of the summer in miniature. Highs and lows, adventure, laughter, and the joy of relationships—all these characterized my first experience with middle school ministry. Since that summer I've worked with both high school and middle school youth, and the latter group continues to hold a unique place in my heart.

In the midst of their frequently awkward and confusing developmental journey, the middle school youth with whom I've worked often willingly embrace their awkwardness and jump into activities without fear. Watching them play crazy games and enthusiastically sing "Pharaoh, Pharaoh" reminds me why youth ministry is such a fantastic calling. I admit there are times when they're "too cool for school," but middle school youth can often be found stepping out of their comfort zones with gusto. As they go beyond comfortable places, the adults who minister to them are freed to embrace the awkward middle school guy or girl still lurking within. They've allowed me to be dorky, and they've even laughed at some pretty pathetic jokes I've told.

Perhaps what I love most about middle school youth is the way they surprise me with their insights about faith. Unfortunately, some people hold to the misconception that middle school youth don't have the capability to reflect on the ways God is working in their lives. I'm blessed to say I've heard middle school youth talk about the ways God has changed their perceptions through missions, or about how their experience of God's unconditional love in Jesus Christ has allowed them to accept who they are.

Middle school youth aren't just sponges, absorbing what we teach them in Sunday school and at youth group. They're teachers, leaders, and missionaries who teach the church in distinctive ways. The church can respond to middle school youth by reminding them of the truth Paul told his young friend Timothy, "Don't let anyone look down on you because you are young, but set an example for the believers in speech, in life, in love, in faith and in purity" (1 Timothy 4:12).

Jennie Koth is the interim associate director of Youth Mission and Ministry at University Presbyterian Church in Seattle, Washington.

Take a minute and consider the following.

- *Careers* can often be at a seemingly make-or-break point.

- *Finances* can be challenging as parents think about the potential reality of college expenditures being just a few years away, not to mention the ever-increasing expenses of having a middle schooler.

- *Aging (or dying) parents*—and the accompanying issues— are a reality for many parents of middle schoolers.

- *Single parenting* (which affects about half of students' families or more) becomes even more challenging.

- If parents are still together, *marital connection* can be threatened by the busy-ness of life. It can seem like every hour of the day is already accounted for. As a matter of fact, it can be a struggle for parents to find time for any "personal time" when life is moving fast. Parents can feel as though they're always running on empty, despite their best efforts.

The life circumstances of most middle school parents are tougher than they might appear.

PARENTS ARE HUMAN

And because of that human-ness, they're prone to mistakes. Not only is a middle school student navigating a whole bunch of change—but their parents are, too. There are no "exhibition games" in parenting—every at-bat counts. Students are running into new situations; and because of that, parents are running into situations *they've* never encountered either. Even if it's their second (or third or fourth) kid going through middle school, we all know how *differently* siblings can handle similar situations.

PARENTS ARE..."THE PARENTS"

In other words, no matter how "in touch" a parent is with a situation, their kid will still view them as, well, *parental*. So a student will hear their words differently. A mom or dad will often come up and tell me something their kid "learned" in our ministry. "You'll never believe this, Mom! Scott said _____." And the mom looks at me, a little frustrated, and says, "He acts like it's the first time he's ever heard anyone say that—even though I've been telling him that same thing for the last six months."

My (Scott) own son is in 7th grade as I write this. And because of that, I'm deeply indebted to his small group leader, Nick. Because Nick *isn't* my son's dad, Nick's words carry a different kind of weight than mine. (I guess it also helps that Nick is bigger, stronger, and tougher-looking than I am.) I owe you, Nick!

Hi Scott,

Thanks for emailing me back. Thanks for the advice on when God answers you. I think I understand. I also get what you're saying about keeping a pure mind. My Mom told me something similar, but it sounds a lot better coming from a youth paster. (*sic*) —Taylor

PARENTS ARE MARKED BY THE CULTURE, TOO

Here in America, we've developed a consumer mentality when it comes to raising our kids. If you want your kid to be good at playing piano, you drop him off for lessons at the piano teacher's house. If you want her to learn gymnastics, you take her to the experts at the gym. If you believe he's got a future in baseball, you get him on a traveling baseball team and drop him off with a fired-up coach (who gives him lots of opportunities to play in tournaments in far-away states and miss youth ministry connections for weeks on end—a drag). The point is, many parents have the mindset that they're supposed to drop their kids off at church, too—just like they do at other practices, lessons, or classes—so the teens can get their "God training."

So perhaps one of the initial steps in strengthening relationships with parents is actually similar to a key step in building relationships with students—put yourself in their shoes. (Remember what we discussed in chapter 12?) Giving people the benefit of the doubt goes a long way in any relationship—parents included. Being a parent truly is one of the toughest jobs on the planet, complete with pressure, uncertainty, and high stakes. If you haven't raised a middle schooler (we're both in the middle of doing it), well, let's just say it looked a lot simpler a few years back when we were watching *other* people try to do it.

Partnering with Parents

"Partnering with parents" is a phrase that's often used in middle school ministry, and most would agree that it *must* be a high priority. But what in the world does that phrase *mean*? How do you carry it out?

First and foremost, you can't partner with parents if you don't have *relationship* with them. Sure, there are many different levels of parental involvement when it comes to church, including those middle schoolers whose parents aren't even a part of your church (more on that later). But if you don't honor relationship with parents, you'll never even get a chance to begin a partnership.

We need to think about parents *individually* as well as *collectively*. In the same way that every student needs to be known individually, parents can really only be known one at a time. We're all limited in regard to how many students we're able to know personally, and the same is true with parents. It's one more reason why small groups are crucial for the success of a middle school ministry. We could have a fantastic corporate parent strategy in our ministry, but if it doesn't include the opportunity for parents to be known personally, then we've given up the ability to custom-fit our ministry to the needs of each student.

A conversation with a parent can go a long way in trying to discern the needs of middle schoolers. Does a student in your group seem particularly moody? Unusually quiet? Hyperactive in ways that reach beyond their usual state of lunacy? Often there are circumstances that students might not mention, either because they're embarrassed or maybe they're unable to articulate how their current situation is affecting them. Many times we've had conversations with parents that uncover a situation going on behind the scenes. That's when a light bulb goes on, and we smack ourselves on the foreheads and say "Doh! That might explain (*fill in puzzling middle schooler behavior here*)."

Individual conversations are great, but it's already challenging to find time to connect with students one-on-one, much less their parents, right? Even though there's no substitute for knowing a kid's family, there are some things we can do to connect with parents as a group. We want to suggest at least five inputs you can provide for parents. And if you do these well, it just might give you license to offer a sixth (and crucial) input, which we'll share with you at the end.

INPUT #1: INFORMATION

Accurate, helpful, timely information. Okay, so we're starting out simple. But the information we send to parents really does make an impression on them. Dates, times, locations, deadlines, costs—parents know better than to ask their 7th grader for the specifics.

When you send out information, you need to "think like a parent." Better yet, recruit a parent or two to help you preview and assemble what you're sending out, since they obviously think like parents already. When we hastily scribble out incomplete facts and send them home, it doesn't do much to reassure parents that their kids are in good hands. My (Scott) son was recently invited to a retreat at another church, and the registration form looked like they threw it together in about four minutes. It didn't give me any information about where they would be, who the emergency contact person was, or what time I could expect them back. I'm not a detail person, but the lack of specifics made me raise my eyebrows. Sure, my son makes me a little crazy sometimes, but when I send him on a retreat, I like to be confident that I'll get him back.

I messed up this communication area a few years ago when we were doing our much-anticipated "Guy-Girl" series. We wanted to encourage conversations between students and parents about some of the sexually charged topics floating around middle schools. Our only oversight was that we forgot to mention it to the parents. So students were doing as we'd challenged them to—asking Mom and Dad some pretty tough questions—and a bunch of parents felt ambushed. And they let us know about it!

To get some assistance with communication details, consider looking into email templates like Constant Contact that can help you look like you know what you're doing.[135] Blogs, snail-mail, phone calls—whether from a group of volunteers or a "blast" from an automated system—and so on, can all be effective communication tools because many times the printed materials we send home with students get left in their back pockets—and end up in the washing machine.

Another significant area to strengthen your parent communication—and set them up to win—involves informing parents about what happened at the retreat or camp. You know what a life-changing experience these types of events can be for middle schoolers, but how much do you tell the parents about what goes on? Imagine if the conversations that started in a student's small group at camp and any spiritual concepts that were brought up could be further addressed at home? Talk about a win-win!

During the last few years, my (Scott) youth ministry team has taken great strides to debrief our students' parents in regard to what went on at the camp or retreat their students just attended. There are many different avenues you can use to communicate with parents. We've done 30-minute meetings with the parents before their student arrived back at church, online videos and blogs, and handouts with details from the weekend. The key information we communicate is an overview of the event (theme, main session ideas, and small group discussion topics), as well as some questions parents can use to talk further with their student about the weekend. And these questions don't allow for the "fine" or "yep" or "I dunno" answers that students are sometimes famous for. We've gotten overwhelmingly positive feedback from parents on this tool.

INPUT #2: ENCOURAGEMENT

How many people remind parents that their role really is *crucial*? And that they really are the number one influence on their kids' lives, even when they don't feel like it? And that even when they're worn out from all the demands of life and their kids seem to be pushing them away, they must press on? We'll guarantee this: Most parents don't have very many cheerleaders when it comes to the hardest parts of parenting.

Parents *need* our encouragement. Anytime you're speaking with parents—*thank* them for the work they do to allow their kids to be involved in your ministry. But even deeper than that, thank them sincerely for the hard work they're doing as they help their kids grow through middle school. If it feels too awkward to do this in a conversation, write it out and send it to parents. Remind them that every investment they make really *matters*. Remind them that this developmental stage won't last forever. But also remind them that they have only a few more years before their kids will be out of the house and their influence over their kids will be much less than it is now. Remind them that God really is with them and that their hard work can pay big dividends. And let them know you're praying for them.

The biggest encouragement impact though, not surprisingly, comes one parent at a time. When you see a kid welcome a new student in your ministry or take a challenge seriously or offer a really helpful insight on a lesson—leak that story to the teen's parents. There's nothing more encouraging for parents than hearing about how their kids did something honorable or admirable when they weren't around. For bonus points, brag to the parents while the son or daughter is within earshot of your conversation. "I've gotta tell you how cool it was today, when your son _____." The student might act sheepish or even pretend like he's not paying attention, but you know he's drinking in every word. Another cool tactic is to leave a phone message when you know nobody's there. What a blast it is for a kid to walk into his home and hear his parents play a message of someone boasting about how cool he is.

Parents get plenty of warnings, information, and counsel on how to raise their kid. But giving them the gift of encouragement can go a long, long way.

INPUT #3: SUPPORT

Have you ever heard middle schoolers say something negative about their parents, and you felt like shouting back, "Are you *kidding* me? No wonder your parents make you crazy. It's incredible that you've survived this long!" Granted, we do need to take our students' feelings seriously (and, of course, look into any allegations of endangerment or abuse). But frustration between middle schoolers and their parents is a natural part of the process. One huge way we can partner with parents is by trying to help their kids understand them—and value them. We need to help kids understand how tough it is to be a parent—even as we're helping parents remember how tough it is to be in middle school.

This can be tricky, since *empathy* is a key dimension of building relationships with students and your words can be misrepresented when translated from kid to parent. Recently I (Scott) was talking with a few 7th graders, and a girl named Brooke was complaining that her cell phone had broken. She was more exasperated, though, because instead of getting her a new phone, her parents had recycled an older model that one of them used to use. Sure, it was bulkier than her old one, but I was gently making fun of her complaint, saying, "Hey, at least you *have* one. Shouldn't you be grateful for *that*?" But when she handed me the phone, I joked with her and her friends, saying, "It looks a little more like a TV remote control than a phone," and proceeded to pretend to "change channels" with it. We had some good laughs, but a few days later, I happened to see her dad. He said something like, "Brooke told me you can't believe she has a big, clunky remote-control phone." I knew I'd been sold out. Fortunately for me, I know the dad and assured him I'd told her she was lucky to have a phone at all.

Practically speaking, make it a point to *never* undermine parents. Even a casual statement such as, "Why in the world would your mom do *that*?" or "You're right, that wasn't very smart of your dad," can unintentionally hurt the relationship. Don't take sides. For example, don't say something like, "It's crazy that your parents won't let you do that." If you want more information about a situation, then call the parents and gently inquire if you can ask about something their kid said to you. But also, never hesitate to seek some additional counsel from another trusted adult if you believe a student is in real danger.

INPUT #4: PARTNERING OPTIONS

It's simple to be an armchair quarterback, isn't it? Pointing out the flaws and deficiencies of a team (or a ministry) is a lot easier than jumping into the mix and trying to make it better. Inviting critical parents into serving roles in your ministry won't solve every problem. But if we shut these parents out, that can sometimes leave them no choice but to critique from the sidelines.

Not only that, but one great way for parents to understand the world of middle schoolers is to help serve them. Moms and dads can get a window into the lives of other middle schoolers (and possibly realize that their offspring might not be any crazier than any other young teen), and they can also get a front-row seat to the way our ministries engage their kids.

Options is the key word for this one. Not every parent has the relational ability to be a middle school small group leader. (Shocking thought, we know.) Although we're willing to bet that there are *some* parents in your ministry who might be great leaders. But if you're willing to invest some energy into this, you can identify a number of needs that parents can partner with you on—set up and tear down, van driving, administrative needs, hosting gatherings, to name a few.

Another angle to consider is "regular" partnering options versus "one-time" needs. Lots of parents hesitate when asked to commit to a weekly, or even monthly, serving role. But if you have certain events that would benefit from parent help, lean into it. Both of our middle school ministries have annual events that rely heavily on behind-the-scenes parent power. Oftentimes, you can watch parents in one-time service roles and discover that they'd be fantastic as regular volunteers.

Another occasion for parent partnering is to offer father-kid or mother-kid events. It's easy to underestimate how far these experiences can go in catalyzing the relationship between middle schoolers and their parents. If your ministry puts on an event and students know *everybody* there will have a parent along, then it can minimize the embarrassment factor. We've done a "Bowl with your Mom" event for the last few summers and at a place that has not just bowling, but also mini-golf and batting cages. Parents have raved about how cool it was to be able to participate in a middle school ministry event. And to our amazement, the kids loved it, too.

INPUT #5: A VOICE

Parents need to feel as though they have a voice in your ministry—to know it's a place where their opinions can be heard. If parents feel ignored or get the sense that their thoughts, questions, or observations aren't welcome, then you're digging yourself and your ministry into a hole.

There's a key question to ask yourself when a parent is speaking into your ministry: *Does this parent simply need a chance to vent, or is there something we need to revamp?* Because sometimes parents just need to verbalize a frustration or even a point of view. They simply need to vent and feel as though you're willing to listen and *care*. "I really wish you didn't always do the fall retreat on that weekend because that's when we make our annual trip to Jimmy's grandma's house." The parents might not expect you to *change* something, but they do want you to know their opinions. We're betting you've heard some crazy complaints from parents at times—we sure have. But in a world in which people aren't listened to enough, occasionally that's all a parent needs.

However, other times when parents talk, we need to revamp something. When you begin hearing recurring complaints, don't wait too long to do something about it. If we're listening closely, parents' voices can tip us off to changes we need to make in our ministry in order to serve kids more effectively.

We know of many ministries that have some form of "Parent Advisory Council," and that can be a good thing. But I (Scott) have never formed a permanent team like that. Instead, I've sought to gather feedback from as many parents as possible and make decisions based on the whole range of responses.

So what happens if you give your ministry parents information, encouragement, support, partnering opportunities, and a voice? You may have earned yourself the chance to provide Input #6.

INPUT #6: COACHING

Raise your hand if you believe middle school parents could use a little coaching. We're not being arrogant or superior, but we truthfully believe there are times when moms and dads of young teens could use a little counsel, some advice, a few pointers. But if you've neglected to give them the five inputs—if you haven't earned credibility with them—then the odds of parents being open to any parental coaching goes way down. On the other hand, for each one of those inputs that they receive from your ministry, it increases their trust in you and their ability to view you as a partner. As a result, parents will be more interested in receiving any coaching you may offer.

Coaching can come in many forms. It may be as simple as a resource referral or passing along a relevant article for parents to read. It could be bringing in an expert of some type, on parenting a teenager or some other specific area of interest. It might be just you sharing your own insights on student culture and how you see the students in your own group being affected. But if you've built trust with parents, they'll be much more open to hearing whatever you have to say.

A couple of years ago, I (Scott) was concerned about the parents' level of engagement when it came to talking with their middle school kids about sexuality from a biblical perspective. Sure, kids get the obligatory sex ed. at school, but the more I talked to our students, the more I heard reports that many parents were apparently avoiding talking to their kids about Internet porn, relational boundaries, and even sexual concepts that I knew their kids were hearing about from their friends. So I asked the parents to come to a meeting after church, just before we did our annual "Guy-Girl" series, and I boldly offered them some coaching. I challenged them to talk to their kids about specific sexual words, even though it would be awkward. I gave them a few tips. I offered some resources. And I gave more encouragement. I'd built trust with these parents, so I felt I'd earned the right to speak candidly. Yet I was still a little concerned that I might be pushing them too hard. That is, until I received feedback like this voicemail from a mom:

> I wanted to thank you for the talk you provided for the parents this past weekend. It was meaningful, it was relevant, it was encouraging, and it really

continued to fan the flame about our philosophy of making sex education like any other education in our house—an ongoing learning experience for us all. It was just the nudge I needed to talk about some things that I hadn't brought up yet. I had a very funny interaction with my daughter when I brought up (on Sunday) the subject of oral sex and whether or not she knew what it was.

She said, "Well, I know what oral is—it's when you're talking or whatever. So is 'oral sex' talking about sex?" I thought it was a good answer, it was. But at the same time I smiled on the inside thinking, *Oh, those days of being young and naive and all.* But we did straighten her out on that subject; I thank you for giving me the nudge on it. I realized that my oldest daughter didn't learn about that subject until high school, and she learned about it through peers, not through me. I'm just thankful to have the opportunity to straighten out some kinks in the road with my second daughter.

Youth Ministers Who Are Parents... and Those Who Aren't

As you've been reading this chapter, some of you have probably been thinking, *It's easier for you two guys to share with the parents because you are parents of middle school kids.* And the truth is, you're right. There's definitely a kind of advantage when you can look in parents' eyes and say, "Hey, I'm right with you on this one—talking parent to parent." But Marko and I also had plenty of conversations with parents *before* we had middle school kids—or any kids at all. And it *can* be done. You're still an incredibly valuable resource to parents, even if you don't have kids of your own.

Will some parents look at you and think, *You're too young to understand?* Of course. But the same way that Paul told Timothy not to let anyone look down on him because he was young, we believe he'd tell you not to underestimate the impact that a non-parent can have on a parent (1 Timothy 4:12). Do you believe it? We really, truly hope that you do. The love, encouragement, insight, and wisdom that God can provide through another Christ-lover (parent or nonparent) is limitless.

Inside Versus Outside

We've based much of our discussion in this chapter on those parents with whom you have some kind of avenue of communication. But a final dimension in the parent-partnering area that we need to consider is the parent who doesn't attend your church (or any church, for that matter). If your middle school ministry is working like the Acts 2 church did, students are probably inviting their friends to check out the claims of Jesus; or maybe they're just inviting them to your ministry, and *you're* inviting them to think about Jesus. Either way, a parent who's not a Jesus-follower may respond very differently to their kid's involvement than moms and dads inside the church. The key priority in these relationships is *respect*. It should bleed through as you offer these parents—in whatever manner possible—the six inputs we mentioned earlier in this chapter.

There's no blueprint for what nonchurched parents are like—everyone's different. But many, many times we've heard parents say, "I *had* to start attending your church because my kid loved coming to your student ministry so much." God's touched many parents' lives that way—how cool if God reaches more through the ministry *you* serve.

We'll close this chapter with an email I (Scott) received from a parent who served as an elder in our church. (When you see an email from an elder in your inbox, do you ever feel your heart rate increase?) This particular elder had a student in our ministry, so I quickly scrolled through my mind to see if there was anything we could've messed up recently. But it turns out she just wanted to send some encouragement my way:

> Last night Clarence and I were goofing around with Dan [their 7th grader] and playing "one up" and so on. At one point we were laughing and talking, and Dan says to Clarence, "So, what are you going to do for a face when that baboon wants his butt back?" I know it sounds horrible, but we laughed ourselves sick and then Dan got "noogied" within an inch of his life. Later, Clarence and I were talking about how finding the perfect insult is part of the whole developmental process at that age and why that's why most of us are glad not to repeat the experience. But really, it was hilarious and in jest and we had a very funny family moment. Thanks for all you do for the kids when they are half grown, so insecure and so precious. We really appreciate it.
>
> Elizabeth

Maybe it's been a while since you've heard a parent say, "Thanks for all you do." But when you put yourself in those parents' shoes, maybe this chapter can give you a bit more insight into why parents haven't or don't offer their encouragement more readily. Parents are certainly not our adversaries—not at all. Parents really do *treasure* their kids, but not all parents have received the kind of inputs you're in a position to provide.

And the reason we're in youth ministry is because we treasure these students, too—we want them to understand the crazy love God has for them. With some intentionality, we can see parents becoming allies in this mission—and even advocates. Never, never underestimate the role you play in students' lives—and in the lives of their families.

CHAPTER 19

A Few Hard Truths... or Why So Few Stay in Middle School Ministry

First, a sad story.

I (Marko) loved my maternal grandfather. By the time I really knew him, he'd softened into a gentle and generous man (words, I've since gathered, that weren't normally used to describe him earlier in life). For most of his life, Bob Bradley struggled with faith. He wanted to have faith, wanted to believe, but he couldn't seem to muster it up. It was only in his final months of life that he was able to articulate some kind of faith—enough to be an encouragement to him and to us.

Among the many attempts Bob made at finding a workable faith, including multiple seasons of on-and-off church attendance, he once decided that he'd likely acquire faith if he immersed himself in church ministry. And the church, not knowing the whole story, put him in charge of the 7th-grade boys Sunday school class. This was the 1940s or 1950s, long before young teens were considered adolescents. But the squirreliness of his charges was still there, like a bit of foreshadowing to the reality most of us deal with every day. He gave it a try, and then didn't return to church for decades (beyond perfunctory visits).

While middle school ministry might not drive most people away from faith, we find that this unique ministry has a tendency to leave a large wake of burned-out, frustrated, and confused former youth workers.

So here we'll take a quick pass at the common reasons why people get derailed from middle school ministry. Just like a marathon runner must be aware of the potential realities of "hitting the wall" and other run-ending factors, keeping these potential pitfalls on your radar will increase your likelihood of avoiding them.

Middle School Ministry Is (Almost) Thankless

If you teach an adult Sunday school class, you'll likely have people who regularly thank you for your time and effort and maybe even for your insights.

If you work in a nursery, parents who are grateful for the opportunity to have a short break from their children and attend worship without distraction are usually willing to offer a word of thanks as they pick up their kids.

And if you work in middle school ministry? Not so much. We happen to be in the sweet spot for a three-way thanks void. Middle school ministry is the Bermuda Triangle of appreciation.

There are reasons for this:

1. Our churches are often confused about what middle school ministry really is (more about this in a bit).

2. Our churches are only partially concerned with the messiness of what change looks like in real middle schoolers.

3. Our churches are more interested (although they might not admit it) in compliance and keeping the destruction to a minimum.

Parents, bless their hearts, are often so overwhelmed with the challenge of having a young teen in their homes (especially if it's their oldest or only child), they simply don't often have the bandwidth to move beyond their fears and concerns to a place of expressing thanks. Of course, there are wonderful exceptions to this. But let's be honest, you'll get fewer thank yous from parents in middle school ministry than pretty much any other age group.

And the middle schoolers themselves? Well, they just don't have the emotional maturity to think about thanking you. With the massive amount of change going on in their lives, they're understandably self-focused. And they likely have no idea how much time, energy, prayer, thought, resources, and selflessness you put into your ministry with them. When you *do* occasionally receive thanks from a middle schooler, there's often a developmentally conflicting reason for why they're giving it (like, they want you to like them).

So find your fuel in conviction and passion and calling. Receiving thanks and appreciation is never a good impetus or motivator for any kind of ministry. But still, having our efforts acknowledged feels really nice, and it can provide fuel to get beyond many ministry speed bumps. We just can't wait around for the thanks in middle school ministry. The rare bits of appreciation you'll receive are too few and far between to offer any kind of momentum.

That means we have to be extra intentional about looking elsewhere for the necessary fuel. Your conviction, based on the understanding that middle school ministry is critical stuff, will go a long way toward providing this. Identify your passion in working with middle schoolers. (Different middle school youth workers have different areas of passion, by the way.) Nurture that passion by learning more (reading) and by creating a role for yourself that utilizes your particular passion.

Finally, stay deeply connected to God and God's calling on your life for this amazing ministry. Receive your affirmation from the Creator of middle schoolers, the Creator of *you*.

Middle School Ministry Lacks Real Feedback

If you teach a Sunday school class of second graders, you get lots of feedback. They're either engaged or they aren't. They're happy to be there or they aren't. They easily show affection.

If you volunteer in the parking lot ministry of your church, the cars either get parked or they don't. People either easily find their way into church or they're frustrated as they circle the lot.

If you preach sermons in "big church," people let you know what they think, both with their body language and verbal (or written) feedback. It might not all be positive; but you'll get feedback.

Really, almost every other ministry area in the church provides natural feedback loops. But not so with middle school ministry. And we've seen this over and over again—middle school youth workers looking for feedback (a normal and healthy thing to do) in the wrong places. If we hope to get verbal or written feedback from middle schoolers as a barometer of our ministry effectiveness, we'll *always* be wanting more (at best) or be completely misguided (at worst).

What we've observed is this: When middle school youth workers don't get feedback from the kids (or their parents, or the church), they often look to unhelpful measuring sticks to gauge whether or not they're on the right track. And the most frequently used measuring stick, of course, is numbers. We wrongly assume that more kids means we're doing things right, and that—conversely—fewer kids means we're doing things wrong.

Numbers *do* mean something. But they can be misleading. It's entirely possible (we've seen it many times) that your ministry can grow because you're entertaining kids more. Or your numbers can drop because the church down the street is entertaining kids more.[136] If your ministry starts to see an attendance increase or decrease, you should certainly pay attention and do some digging to find out why it might be occurring. But don't assume it's good or bad.

Another measuring stick that middle school youth workers often apply is whether or not kids seem to be quickly "getting it" and radicalizing their lives to the end of being Christlike.[137] Certainly, we *do* want to see middle schoolers move toward Christlikeness; but instant results are often misleading, and an apparent *lack* of movement can be equally misleading.

So use thoughtful measuring sticks. Are we shooting in the dark, then? How are we to know if we're having any impact? What feedback can we look to?

We'd like to suggest a handful of "measuring sticks," but we'd also like to encourage you to look further, pray more, and discern how God might be leading you and your team in the area of considering success, or the lack thereof.

- Are middle schoolers known? Do the kids in your ministry have an adult who knows them by name and is connected with them at a personal level?

- Is our group inclusive or exclusive? Are there kids who can't find belonging? Are new students welcomed and made to feel that their presence is valued?

- Do kids (and leaders) in our group care about the things that God cares about? Does our group notice others, especially those at a disadvantage? Does our group care about worship and justice and serving others? Or do we exist only to make ourselves happy?

WHY I DO THIS

I'd love to offer a pithy spiritual zinger that explains why I'm involved with middle school ministry. Like, that I believe middle schoolers are the church of tomorrow.

Or equally accurate, that they are the church of today.

Or I could use a metaphor about stopping young adolescents from stepping off a cliff so we don't have to hospitalize them at cliff's bottom two years later as mid-adolescents.

All that's true, but I'm involved with middle schoolers for a more simple and selfish reason: I just plain like them.

At the top of the long list of What-I-Like-about-Middle-School-Students is their rawness. Their emotions are raw. They are walking bundles of insecurity, swinging from joy to despair based on their last text message.

Their conversations are raw. They trip and fall over their words, and they pick themselves up verbally—only to stumble again.

Their relationships are raw—with their friends, with their families, and with us.

Their faith is raw. Their pursuit of Jesus is hot one day and lukewarm to icy the next.

Yet middle schoolers are very, very real. I think immediately of an 8th-grade girl whose commitment to helping her friends get a taste of Jesus is indescribable; in fact, it's so hard to describe that I can't find the right words even as I write this. I can say this, though: She tells more people about Jesus almost by accident than I do on purpose.

Or a 7th-grade boy whose recent sacrificial giving to help AIDS orphans in Africa caused me to rethink the stewardship of our family's finances.

Or a 7th-grade girl who stopped me short in a small group prayer time. Toward the end of our gathering, I asked the girls to share their prayer requests. Since time was short and I knew parents would be waiting, once the girls finished sharing, I immediately transitioned, "Let's pray." Christina then spoke up, "What? Don't you need God yourself?"

I like real, raw people, which, by definition, means I like middle school students.

Kara E. Powell, Ph.D., is the executive director of the Fuller Youth Institute at Fuller Theological Seminary, in Pasadena, California.

- Are we actively walking alongside middle schoolers in their physical, emotional, and spiritual development? Are we normalizing their experiences and helping them understand how much God loves them?

- Are we providing opportunities for real belonging, where middle schoolers can know and be known? Are we cultivating genuine communion (community with Christ in the mix)?

- Are we engaged in the mission of God in the world? Are we discerning where God is active and present, bringing restoration and redemption, and are we joining up with that work?

- Are we helping middle schoolers understand Scripture? Are we helping them speculate about how Scripture might implicate their lives? Are we helping them see the scope of God's big story and how their lives connect to what God is doing?

- Are we honoring parents in our ministry? Are we communicating well? Are we working to support parents in the spiritual work of raising their children? Is there anything we're doing that could be counter to this value of supporting and building bridges with parents?

- Are we, as leaders, modeling a life of Christ-connectedness? Are we pursuing God? Are we transparent and real about our pursuit, success, and failure?

- Are we focusing on teens or programs? Which takes priority in our planning, time usage, and resources?

Our suggestion is to do this: Spend time prayerfully discerning, with your middle school leader team, the values and emphases of your ministry. (These might morph and evolve over time, by the way.) Then regularly spend time checking in on this list. Ask—

- How are we doing on each of these?

- What have we allowed to slip?

- What do we need to do to strengthen those areas that are weak?

Ask for input from parents, other church leaders, and middle schoolers themselves.

Middle School Ministry Lacks Immediate Results

Middle schoolers are in such a massive time of transition that they're extremely malleable. They can be easily shaped by so many inputs and influences in their lives. This high level of impressionability is one of the great challenges of middle school ministry. There is great ministry opportunity here, of course, because our lives and our ministries can have a great impact on the direction of middle schoolers' entire lives.

But we have to remember that they're still in sampling or discovery mode. Big, dramatic decisions they make today might not produce the results we believe they'll have. A tear-filled campfire testimony might have a lifelong profound impact, or it might be completely forgotten within 48 hours.

Here's what we've noticed: We can't predict which kids will be walking with God eight years from now. Sure, there are kids whose faith is clearly well developed (for young teens), and they're experiencing the living out of that faith in their daily lives. And we have hope that that faith and that living will continue to grow and become a part of who they are throughout high school and into young adulthood. But we've seen enough deeply engaged leadership kids completely tube out in their later teen or early adult years. And we've continually been pleasantly surprised by those kids who showed no real spiritual interest or commitment in middle school but who grew into men and women of great faith (and who—in a way that makes almost no discernable sense—point back to their middle school ministry experience as a major force in shaping who they've become).

So it's essential that you have a "long view." The reality is that middle school ministry often has a progressive and cumulative effect.

It builds and plants and suggests and points and offers experiences that might show up later in adolescence. Sometimes we see the fruit right away; but just as often, the results of middle school ministry require a long view.

And this means that if you base your "success" (we're not even sure we like that word) on immediate results, you will almost surely be falsely encouraged or falsely discouraged. Middle school youth workers who stay in ministry for a long time are those who, well, plan on staying in middle school ministry for a long time. In other words, be patient and know that God is using your ministry to shape lives, whether you can see it or not.

Middle School Ministry Is Misunderstood

Churches, parents, and even youth workers (especially those new to middle school ministry) regularly misunderstand the point of ministry to young teens. People (and organizations) often see middle school as a holding period at best, an immature period of life when we are doing well just to keep them entertained long enough to get them to their more mature high school years when *real* ministry can commence (or recommence). Or they might perceive the middle school years as the ultimate opportunity to cram kids full of church and Bible information.

Both of these misguided perceptions, along with a general lack of understanding when it comes to young teen developmental realities, can lead to a diminishing or sidelining of middle school ministry. Middle school youth workers are often appreciated only for their willingness to deal with "those kids." ("God bless you, I sure couldn't do it!")

Let's be frank: These perspectives get really old and can easily wear you down like a constant rub that burns off the edge of our calling. Being misunderstood is wearying, often to the core.

So know why you're doing what you're doing. If you don't know, deep down and with conviction, why you're involved in middle school ministry, then you'll most certainly be run off the road by the misunderstandings and misconceptions of others.

We have four recommendations for you on this one:

- Develop community with a group of adults in your ministry who share your calling. You can't do this ministry alone. Share struggles and victories with one another. Doing ministry as a team makes all the difference.

- Be a continual learner. Read books about young teens. Attend seminars and other training events about teenagers. Continue to develop your knowledge about and understanding of early adolescence. This will consistently confirm your calling, as well as increase your effectiveness.

- Get to know other middle school youth workers. Find people from other churches in your area who work with middle schoolers and have coffee or lunch with them on a regular basis. Share ideas. Partner together.

- Stay deeply connected to God. Your calling to middle school ministry comes from God, and God will remind you of why you're doing this great—although sometimes challenging—work.

Middle School Ministry Is Occasionally Frustrating

By this point in the book, we hope you can sense that the two of us absolutely love middle schoolers and almost everything about middle school ministry. But keeping our sanity in this ministry requires us to be honest about the reality that middle schoolers can sometimes be completely infuriating. They can push our buttons like crazy. They can be absurdly irresponsible. They can destroy an otherwise great teaching time or small group discussion in seconds. They can be the squirreliest creatures in all of creation. (Hence the squirrel on the cover of this book.)

And ministry to and with middle schoolers can be downright crazy-making at times. The same realities that we're writing about in this chapter still impact the two of us all the time. Our passion for middle school ministry doesn't make us immune to this stuff. And any person who says she's not occasionally frustrated by middle schoolers is either lying, or she has some deep-seated issues that should keep her out of middle school ministry.

So stay grounded in the "silliness" of God's call. Here's what we mean: If we really believe that the young teen years are as critical to lifelong faith development (and human development in general) as we've written on these pages, then we're forced to see it as an amazing calling that God has chosen for us.

The two of us regularly feel this way: *How is it that God has chosen us, imperfect and faltering as we are, to guide these precious children? How is it that God didn't choose people smarter and nicer and more patient and more creative and more insightful and more fun? It can't just be that we're really, really good looking.* (Although the plain fact that we're really, really good looking must play into this somehow, right?)

The only thing we're left with is that God *has* called us to serve middle schoolers, and God will equip us for this amazing high calling. We're a royal priesthood of middle school youth workers, baby. And as silly as that might seem, that's the beauty and mystery of God's economy. We hope you find yourself in the same humble space.

Middle School Ministry Is Easy to Manipulate

Marko here. Scott might not agree with me on this one, because he's a much nicer person than I am. But I have to confess something that I can't pin on him: I have a natural tendency toward manipulation. I can look back over my life and see it play out from the time I was very young. Many of my girlfriends were manipulated into being so. I was great at manipulating my parents. I found myself manipulating those I worked for in many jobs, including many churches. My wife and children have had to help me with this tendency, as have my current coworkers.

I'm better about it than I used to be, but it's still a natural inclination for me to manipulate my world—and everything in it—to get the results that are best for me in any given moment. It's a deeply dark and broken part of me that God has been steadily working to transform and redeem.

But because I'm so good at manipulation, I spent many years in middle school ministry manipulating kids. I got (and reported) the numbers I longed for. I got the "decisions" that made me feel good and look good. I got kids to say things that sounded right at the time.

I'm happy to report that, as I've uncovered the squiggly things under this rock, I've come a long way in moving away from manipulative ministry. But it's also given me a perspective to quickly see manipulation in other youth workers and youth ministries. And I can sadly report to you that manipulation is alive and well in middle school ministry.

The bottom line of why manipulation is so prevalent in middle school ministry boils down to this: Middle schoolers are really easy to manipulate.

So discipline yourself and go overboard to understand young teens and be thoughtful. We all agree that manipulated "results" are *not* a good thing, right? The ends *do not* justify the means. And if we take a long view of ministry, then it quickly becomes obvious that manipulated "results" either don't last or—worse—morph into the opposite of what we'd hoped for.

This is another place where deeply understanding middle schoolers plays in. When you see a middle schooler responding to a talk or an opportunity for a spiritual decision, when you find your group growing in size, when you begin to see kids "falling in line," it's time to ask yourself a massively hard question: Are they responding to God, or are they responding to me and my manipulation?

That's a tough one, and the answer has to be informed both by prayer and your knowledge of early adolescent development.

Middle School Ministry Is Incredible When You Stick with It

Yes, there are plenty of reasons why middle school youth workers get derailed or don't last. Hopefully, the fact that you're reading this book is one indication that you don't want to be one of those people. And hopefully, this book will arm you with an understanding, a deeper sense of calling, and a renewed passion that will keep you in the game.

After being in middle school ministry for a long time (Scott for more than a dozen years, Marko for more than twice that), we've gone through many cycles of both middle schoolers and youth workers. Scott has spent his middle school ministry years in one church and has seen the beauty of staying put. I (Marko) have worked (either as a paid youth worker or as a volunteer) with middle schoolers in six churches. In each of those, I never felt like I was accomplishing much in my first two years. (I was, but I couldn't see it.) It wasn't until my third year that I started to see things developing that were deeply encouraging.

And we've seen the same thing with volunteers over and over again. When they first start in middle school ministry, they might have a great sense of excitement, or they might have a deep sense of fear (or some combination). As they move into their first year, most volunteers reach a point where they question whether they're having any impact at all, for all the reasons we've unpacked in this chapter. We've found that it's only deep into their second or third year that middle school volunteers start to really hit their stride and catch glimpses of a "return" on their investment of time.

So revel in the call, take joy in the absurdity, and be honored that you're one of the few God knew could handle this ministry.

Did you catch that? God chose *you* to work with middle schoolers. You're one of the few. You're a wonderfully odd and select group of Christ-followers whom God was willing to entrust with this special calling. Take joy in that knowledge; find strength in that understanding; place anchor in that calling.

And don't give up. Stick with it. You'll see what we've seen—that countless young adults will return to tell you what an impact God had on their lives through you.

Mmmm, that's good stuff!

CHAPTER 20

The Very Bestest of the Best Volunteers

(Bonus Chapter by Jim Candy)

Steve could hear his 8th-grade boys laughing while he prayed.[138]

Tim, a "spirited" middle schooler, had left the prayer, wandered over to a trash can in the corner of the room, pulled his pants down, and started urinating. Shocking? Not for this group of guys. This wasn't the first time Steve's patience had been tested. Tim and his friends acted more like frat boys than middle schoolers, but somehow Steve stuck with them.

Thank God he did.

Tim's family history included divorce, drug abuse, and jail time. Steve was the only consistent adult in Tim's life, and Steve's patience slowly drew Tim to Jesus. But it wasn't just Tim that Steve impacted. He influenced many kids over many years by showing patience and love and constantly pointing kids beyond himself and into the arms of Jesus Christ.

Don't you wish there was a limitless supply of leaders like Steve? What makes middle school volunteers like him so effective while others often struggle or quit? Is it giftedness? Personality? Something else? How do we effectively recruit, train, and support more people like Steve? Or if you're a volunteer, what can you learn from someone like Steve?

I decided to ask leaders like Steve what makes them tick. I interviewed Steve and other exceptional volunteers from all over the country—spanning demographics of urban, suburban, ethnicities, big and small churches—to find common traits to help recruit, train, and encourage more leaders like Steve. These aren't just "good" leaders. These volunteers have an *exceptional* history of God using them. The two criteria for leaders in this study were—

1. The lead staff person of the participating ministry described them as *"the most exceptional volunteer leader I've seen work with middle schoolers."*

2. The leader had to have worked with middle schoolers for at least three years to show a long-term history of giftedness.

The results of these interviews will encourage, challenge, and surprise those who work with middle schoolers or want to equip others to do so. I discovered eight common traits among these leaders, and I list the findings here with my observations, as well as practical advice for youth workers who either lead volunteers or are volunteers themselves.

1. Great Volunteers Practice Remarkable Relational Intentionality

It's no secret that meaningful relationships between kids and adults are what God often uses to transform lives. While many youth workers and ministries talk about relationships, these great volunteers *take the art of building relationships to a higher level.*

What are the keys to building great relationships with kids? Here are the top six themes these leaders say volunteers need:

- See into middle school kids' futures and believe in them
- Love middle school kids
- Be patient
- Be flexible
- Be authentic and honest with middle school kids
- Have the ability to put people at ease

As a point of reference, let's contrast this list to the six most important characteristics that Wayne Rice lists in his classic book *Junior High Ministry.*

Our Exceptional Volunteers	**Wayne Rice**
See into kids' futures and believe in them	Understand junior high kids
Love middle school kids	Like junior high kids
Be patient	Be patient
Be flexible	Be a good listener
Be authentic and honest with middle schoolers	Be a positive person
Have the ability to put people at ease	Have time to do it

The first three seem pretty much the same. But great middle school volunteers emphasized flexibility, authenticity, and the ability to "put people at ease" over listening, being positive, and having time.[139]

All this theory is nice, but how do great volunteers actually put this into practice? As one leader said, "It's easy to talk about getting to know kids, but it takes discipline and perseverance to actually do it."

Contrary to what one might believe, these exceptional volunteers don't have lots of extra time on their hands. They're busy people who've discovered how to involve kids in their lives—

including hobbies, meals, and even errands. Some go to even greater lengths.

"We decided the best way to impact kids would be to move into the inner city," said one leader who moved his family into inner-city Kansas City to be near the kids he works with. "We couldn't just live off in the suburbs and have the kind of presence in their lives that God wants us to have."

Moving is an extraordinary example, but all these leaders significantly altered their lives to minister to kids. Here's how they do it:

- *Frequent contact:* They're in contact with kids outside of normal "programmatic time" (usually weekly).

- *They have a strategy:* These leaders can tell you when they spend time with kids and how they've planned to do it in their schedules.

- *They promote many relationships:* They actively promote relationships with other adults as well. (More on this in traits two and six.)

- *Perseverance:* These leaders indicated it took an average of nine months to grow close to their kids—that included going to camps and hanging out beyond "programmed time."

Importantly, these leaders don't view relationships as mere "tools" to influence kids.[140] *They genuinely care.* They're entering the lives of middle schoolers and loving them in the way Jesus Christ enters into ours. These leaders are operating out of more than mere intuition—they realize there's something about God that drives them to love kids the way they do.

PRACTICAL IMPLICATIONS

1. Do volunteers understand the incarnation of Jesus? Just as Jesus enters our world, we must enter the world of middle schoolers in order to know them. Volunteers need to know they walk in the footsteps of Jesus when they selflessly care for kids.

2. Encourage leaders to develop a plan for how they'll make contact with kids outside of programmatic time.

3. Encourage new leaders to be patient—remember the nine-month rule. It takes time.

2. Great Volunteers See Parents as Partners

These volunteers know they cannot fully understand kids *unless they know their students' parents.* As more research surfaces that confirms the foundational role parents play in faith development, great volunteers have mastered the art of seeing kids as part of a family system, not as isolated individuals.[141]

"The parents often tell me stuff about their kids that gives me insight into their worlds," said a volunteer in Michigan. "It helps me have patience."

Connecting with parents is a challenge—in a world of busy schedules, how do these leaders build meaningful relationships with *both* parents and kids? Isn't it hard enough just getting to know the kids?

These volunteers think differently about their time. While spending one-on-one time with a middle schooler is valuable, these leaders use their time to build relationships with both kids and parents. An example is attending a soccer game where both the kids and parents are present. These volunteers support the kids while *intentionally meeting and spending time with their students' parents.* Sounds simple, right? Perhaps, but these leaders practice this type of contact with great intentionality.

It's important to note that this doesn't mean these leaders abandoned one-on-one contact. In fact, just the opposite is true. As they invested in parents, great volunteers find that *parents began creating opportunities for their kids to spend time with the leader.* As one leader said, "Once the parents believed in me, it just took off from there."

This more inclusive view of youth ministry sometimes has surprising results. Tom, an eight-year volunteer at a large church in Los Angeles, recently experienced the result of his care for the whole family. At a family meal sponsored by the middle school ministry, a dad stood up during a whole-group sharing time and looked at Tom.

"I realized this year that I had forgotten how to interact with my son," the dad said fighting back tears. "I have rediscovered my relationship with my own kid by watching him interact with Tom." The gift Tom gave, not only to the kids in his group, but to their families, is one of the things that makes leaders like Tom so great.

PRACTICAL IMPLICATIONS

- Defeat any mindset that would claim that the youth ministry is more important than parents—*both in volunteers and paid staff.*

- Think about time with kids differently so we connect with parents as well. Teach volunteers how to do likewise.

- Ensure your leadership teams have older adults who may grasp family-oriented concepts more deeply.

3. Great Volunteers Have (and Have Not) Been Intentionally Trained

Intentional training by youth ministries is lacking—at least in these volunteers' opinions.

"I know how middle school was for me, and I operate out of that experience," said a volunteer in Cincinnati. "I don't know half of what I should know about kids, their families, and how to reach them."

Here's something that might surprise you: *Every leader interviewed expressed a desire to be trained.* No one said training is unimportant. However, volunteers (even great ones) are fearful training will be too theoretical and time-consuming instead of practical.

"I wish I knew more about kids and ministry," said another leader, "but all we do in our leader meetings is talk business."

Even the best leaders have had to learn intuitively and believe their ministries would be stronger with intentional training. These leaders mentioned two forms of training. I've given them the labels of "organic" and "formalized" training.

ORGANIC TRAINING

Organic training happens when leaders learn "on the job." Volunteers generally figure out how to be a volunteer by watching paid staff and other volunteers. *Organic* doesn't mean "unintentional," but this style of training happens in the course of engaging in ministry, not in a classroom setting or by reading books like this one.

Two major methods of "organic training" continually surfaced—

- Great leaders learned by watching and doing. They watched other youth workers interact with kids and imitated what they saw.

- Interestingly, many leaders said camps and mission trips were *the* single most crucial training factor in becoming great leaders:

  - Camps forced them to be with kids for more than a short period of time. This gave the leader confidence and taught the leader how to relate to kids.

  - Camps were a place where they saw God at work, which encouraged them.

  - Camps taught them perseverance.

Organic training may or may not be intentional. Many youth ministries focus on a system of connecting leaders to one another as a way for leaders to learn and grow. However, very few of the interviews revealed that this kind of training was being done intentionally. Leaders reported that it "just happened."

FORMAL TRAINING

Great leaders, for the most part, have *not* been trained in a formal, informational setting. Very few leaders have ever received any sort of training on youth culture, the nature of adolescence, working with parents, leading a small group, spending time with kids, and so on.

Most leaders indicate the youth pastor or director did a good job of communicating what the leader's role would be when they started. But most add they were never taught how to accomplish that role. Some wondered aloud if the reason they'd never received training was because the youth pastor or director wasn't trained either.

PRACTICAL IMPLICATIONS

- Paid staff needs to seek greater training—both organic and formal. In order to train volunteers, they need to be trained.

- Youth workers should develop plans for both organic and formal training and involve key leaders in the planning process.

- Youth workers should view camping ministry as a training ground for leaders—not merely an important experience for kids.

4. Great Volunteers Exhibit Three Common Personality Traits

Have you ever wondered if personality plays a role in successful volunteers? Are extroverts more effective? Do you have to be a wild risk taker to be a great middle school leader? I decided to see if there were any common traits among these great leaders that might help us identify more people like them.

"I'd be surprised to find commonalities," said one middle school pastor before the results came back. "I believe God uses all kinds of people."

All the volunteers I interviewed took the IPIP-NEO PI-R™ personality test.[142] This exam tests 35 character traits and is a great tool to acquire personality data.

Well, the results came back and—drumroll, please...

The tests confirm conclusively that God uses extroverts, introverts, organized, disorganized, confident, self-conscious, intellects, and otherwise. This is all good news because it means God can even use you. There isn't one type of great leader. Everybody's different, and God isn't limited to the most outrageously funny leaders who have that "kid magnet" label attached to them. Any ministry that limits leadership to a certain personality type is hurting itself and kids as well.

However, there are three similar traits that surfaced in the testing:

> HIGH on "Sympathy"—These leaders all scored high here. This trait is associated with people who "care for those 'weaker' than them" and "value cooperation over competition."

> HIGH on "Agreeableness"—Being high in agreeableness is associated with the relational ability to "put people at ease" and "accept people as they are."

> LOW on "Anger"—These are people who aren't "easily annoyed, seldom lose their cool, and don't complain." The more of this, the better.

Here's a key point: *A score of low anger and high agreeableness might predict patience*—a key trait for anyone working with middle schoolers.

So would you have volunteers take personality tests in order to learn more about them? The youth workers I've put that question to are split evenly on whether or not they'd use personality testing on volunteers. If you choose to use testing, here are some guidelines.

PRACTICAL IMPLICATIONS

- Use testing as a discussion starter. For instance, if a potential volunteer rates high on anger, this might be something worth talking about.

- If a leader shows interest in youth ministry but doesn't know if she should work with middle or high school students, personality testing has the potential to indicate where she may fit best. (In other words, send the angry ones to high school.)

5. The Way Great Volunteers Talk about Jesus Tells You What Kind of Volunteers They Are

Want a question that will help you figure out what kind of volunteer someone will be? Ready? Here it comes...

Who is Jesus Christ?

It may sound obvious, but catch this interesting link: Two of the 30 questions in these interviews were "Who is Jesus?" and "What are the keys to working with middle school kids?" After a number of interviews, a link became apparent between these two questions. *The description of Jesus was often identical to their stated keys to middle school ministry.* How leaders perceive Jesus in their lives may be an indicator of how they'll pursue ministry to middle schoolers.

For example, when I asked a leader named Brittney about Jesus, she responded, "Jesus is someone who is always surprising me in my relationship with him." When I later asked about keys to leading middle schoolers, Brittney said, "Surprise them. Don't always be who they're expecting you to be." Another leader answered, "Jesus pursues me and never gives up." His key to working with middle schoolers? "Pursue them."

Once I noticed this link, I began to predict (with high accuracy) their answers to later questions based on their response to "Who is Jesus?"

PRACTICAL IMPLICATIONS

- It may sound obvious, but encourage volunteers to know, love, and trust Jesus Christ. Grasping Jesus' heart for the lost, broken, and hurting will benefit middle schoolers more than anything else we do.

- Be sure to ask the question, "Who is Jesus?" in recruiting interviews. (You do conduct interviews, right?) *Know that the response to that question may give you practical insight into how this potential volunteer will approach ministry.*

6. Great Volunteers Seek to Build a Caring Network of Adults

Great volunteers not only partner with parents, but they seek out ways to involve other adults as well.

I asked these leaders, "What person has influenced you the most in your faith in Jesus?" The consistent response was, "There were many adults—not just one." A broad range of adults impacted the leaders in their own faith development, and this perspective affects their approach to involving other adults in ministry.

"My friends helped build my faith," said a college student and volunteer, "but looking back, it was a lot of adults that made Jesus real for me."

Great leaders aren't "Lone Rangers." They aren't seeking the "glory" of being idolized by kids. There's no "territoriality" in these leaders—they welcome coleadership and forge bonds between kids and other adults at every opportunity. Traditional youth ministry has seen a 5:1 ratio of kids to an adult volunteer leader. These leaders take seriously the theory that this ratio needs to be reversed—we need five adults for every one kid.[143]

The idea of having multiple adults in the lives of kids hasn't penetrated common youth ministry language. An example is the "life on life" philosophy. "Life on life" means that one "life" (person) cares for another "life." However, a language shift may be in order. These great leaders make it apparent that they're practicing a "*lives* on life" model.

"Life on Life" ⟶ "*Lives* on Life"

This isn't mere semantics. Great leaders include other adults with great intentionality. Perhaps this intentionality could be replicated more broadly if the language of youth ministry were altered to reflect our belief in partnering with parents and other adults.

PRACTICAL IMPLICATIONS

- Youth pastors and volunteers should change their view of youth ministry "leadership." Teachers, coaches, and other adults can be "leaders" without ever showing up at a youth ministry event. More intentional relationships should be built with these people in order to promote a network of caring adults.

- Programming should avoid the "Lone Ranger" model of leadership. Kids should be exposed to and cared for by a broad variety of adults, not just one. For example, encourage small groups to interact with each other both in and outside of youth ministry programming.

- Training is helpful. Leaders need to understand the nature of adolescence and the importance of many adults before they'll actually practice involving other adults.

7. Great Volunteers Discover Roles That Fit Them Perfectly

How nice is it when you're doing something that feels right in the sweet spot of how God made you?

Great volunteers have found a role in the middle school ministry that fits them perfectly. More specifically, they have a supervisor *who allowed or helped them find that role*. These leaders have longevity and passion for ministry because their strengths are being utilized. Take note of this: Great leaders' gifts define their roles—not strict "job descriptions" created by paid staff.

"You need to have a 'plan' that's clear," said a volunteer in Irvine, California, "but not so detailed that it's like a job."

These leaders merge everyday life with ministry. For instance, one volunteer leads a group of kids who attend the school near his work, making it easy for him to bring them lunch. Strategic choices were made (or just "happened") that allowed volunteers to frequently "bump into" kids because their lives overlap.

Practical Implications

- Avoid strict job descriptions for leadership teams. Guidelines are needed, but a customized approach to each leader's gifts and abilities (including time) is helpful.

- Ask potential volunteers, "What are you gifted at? How do you believe God might use you to impact middle schoolers? How much time do you have?" Be open to new possibilities of what leadership could look like.

- Be intentional about how to merge volunteers' everyday lives with the lives of kids. Encourage and structure ministry decisions so leaders are ministering to kids in situations where their lives naturally overlap.

8. Great Leaders Have Received Encouragement from Paid Staff

Last, but not least: Great leaders have been told they are great.

Volunteers consistently mentioned that they've been deeply encouraged by someone on the staff of the church or organization. Whether it was the youth pastor or someone else, *great leaders gained confidence because they were constantly affirmed.*

"When you affirm leaders, it becomes a self-fulfilling prophecy," said one volunteer. "You have to buy into leaders as you expect them to buy into kids."

One leader shared a story about preparing for a final exam in college. The youth pastor called the leader to hear how his exam prep was going. "He didn't call me to check in and make sure I was hanging out with my kids or preparing for Wednesday night's youth group. He was just calling to see how my test was coming along. When he did that, I finally understood what he wanted me to do with my kids."

Practical Implications

- Encourage them. It sounds obvious, but take advantage of opportunities to praise leaders.

- Be a storyteller. Leaders said that hearing stories about kids growing and changing encouraged them. Write them down—share them frequently.

- Invite others to be encouragers. Have a team of parents share stories about how leaders have impacted their kids. Encourage leaders to encourage other leaders. *Create a culture of encouragement.*

With more than a decade in middle school ministry, Jim Candy is a regular speaker at camps and conferences and a frequent contributor to youth ministry publications. He's pastor of Family Life Ministries at Menlo Park Presbyterian Church in the San Francisco Bay Area. Jim also spent seven seasons as a public address announcer for the Denver Nuggets and Colorado Avalanche. He and his wife, Karin, have two boys. You can read more of his thoughts at http://jimcandy.blogspot.com.

Our Prayer for You

We began this book stating that the middle school years are one of the most misunderstood and underappreciated developmental periods of human life.

We hope that after reading these pages that your awareness and appreciation for these unique beings called middle schoolers has grown, and any apprehension about working with them has disappeared. We pray that some experiences and perspectives from our own, sometimes bumbling attempts to serve this classically awkward age group have helped you look at middle schoolers with new eyes.

But we pray for more than that. Much more.

Because somewhere, in a place not far from your own home, lives a middle schooler:

A very *specific* middle schooler.

A middle schooler who desperately wants someone to know his name, his hopes, his story.

A young teen with a head full of particular worries, and insecurities, and wonderings.

A kid who's trying to understand her parents, the opposite sex, and where tears come from.

A person who's discovering new facets in the drama of friend-ship-making. And friendship-losing, too.

A middle schooler frustrated by acne, inclined to frequent goofiness, loved by Jesus.

We don't know that specific middle schooler.

But *you* do! Can you picture a face in your mind right now?

You see, our prayer isn't just that you become smarter or more informed about middle schoolers—or even that you've picked up a few new ideas or strategies.

We pray that you see yourself as even more "use-able" in the life of that one middle school kid.

We pray that you're ready to keep investing, keep listening, keep asking questions, keep praying.

We pray you realize that a moment is never wasted when you're doing middle school ministry—when you're being with them.

Sharing the gospel of Jesus Christ...and sharing life together, too.

> "Because we loved you so much,
> we were delighted to share with you
> not only the gospel of God
> but our lives as well."
>
> 1 Thessalonians 2:8

We'll keep on serving young teens in San Diego and Chicago, as you do the same wherever you are.

With much love from your partners in middle school ministry!

Marko & Scott

APPENDICES

Q&A with Marko and Scott

Q: How do you effectively minister when your children are in the group... does it change your approach, where do you draw the line between parent and middle school minister? I'm about to experience this in the coming years with two of my children. —Larry

A: Great question! And it's one of those questions that should legitimately be answered "It depends!" The great news is that you're *aware* that it will definitely be *different* for your kid with you in the ministry. In some ways it'll be a "good different," in some ways it'll be a "challenging different." We have a responsibility for all the students in our ministry, but clearly we have a very unique responsibility for our own children and their spiritual development. And we must be wise about how our ministry roles affect them.

While you can never completely "turn off" your parenting dimension, you need to be cautious about how you treat your own son or daughter. If your child feels the pressure to be the "youth pastor's perfect kid," it's probably not going to go real well. If your child is goofing around during youth group the way any kid would, but you wouldn't know about it if you were "any other parent" who wasn't in the room—then you need to consider just letting it go. But probably the biggest advice we could give on this one is to *get someone else to help you minister to your kid.* Just as you can say things to other people's kids and they'll hear it differently than if Mom or Dad said it, your kid needs that same experience.

Q: What are the most effective methods of integrating middle schoolers into the church family? —Ed

A: We're going to resist the urge to write, "Great question!" every time, but this is another insightful one. First off, let's realize that the danger of *not* integrating them into the church during their teenage years is that they could end up graduating high school and heading out on their own with a great student ministry experience—but without ever having felt like a part of a church. So it *is* crucial to integrate middle schoolers—but *how*?

This is a conversation that needs more than just student ministry people at the table. The senior leadership of a church has to see the value in the integration and be a part of the strategy. If we throw middle schoolers into "big church" with some regularity, but their presence in the room isn't really valued or maybe even considered, then we run the risk of students assuming that even though middle school ministry is great, church for adults is a snore-fest. Still, it takes more than sitting in a service together for true integration. In your conversation with senior leadership, consider how students and adults can occasionally *serve* together, how *families* can engage in faith-building conversations together, and how Psalm 145:4 can come to life in your church: "One generation commends your works to another; they tell of your mighty acts."

Q: I am a young, female youth director, and one of the biggest challenges I have is relating to my middle school boys. I'm at a loss in how to meet them where they are. —Amanda Mae

How can middle school ministers effectively tap the energy and interests of young adolescent boys while interesting them in the things of faith? —Alaina

A: Well, neither of us have been female youth directors before, but we know many of them, and we've had many conversations about this exact issue. First off, it *is* possible for middle school boys to learn and grow under the leadership of a female youth director. For some women, this will come very easily. For others, "thinking like a boy" will be extremely stretching.

The advantage that we have is that we've both *been* middle school boys—so we have some idea what they're thinking. Because they often behave in such obviously different ways, it can be easy for a woman to think, *They're not listening, they're not learning, nothing is happening...other than the room smells a little worse than if it were just the girls.* Practically speaking, we have to anticipate how boys and girls will experience things differently—even though there's no "typical" middle school guy (or girl). Your perspective needs to include thoughts like: *Boys really do have a need to move around more, they experience the world differently, and they need male role models.*

Finally, do all you can to recruit guy volunteers—at least one. The same way that we guys need women to help us lead middle school girls, female youth leaders need men to help grow up middle school boys.

Q: The typical middle school ministry has students in the 6th through 8th grades. Despite the close proximity in age, the developmental differences in emotional and physical maturity, as well as cognitive and abstract thought processes, are huge. A 6th grader is only two years removed from *Winnie the Pooh*, while an 8th grader is only one or two years away from driver's ed. A typical 6th grader hasn't had sex ed. yet, while an 8th grader is entering the prime sexuality years. In the context of a typically sized church that doesn't have the resources to split up the students by gender or grade, how does a youth leader effectively prepare and teach this age group—with such developmental differences—sitting in the same room? —Rob

A: There's no question that from 6th through 8th grade (or from 11 to 14 years old) is a big developmental span, which is why some churches (and schools) choose to keep 6th graders separate (in a preteen group). Any youth worker with this age span in his group—whether you have 7 or 700 kids—has to be aware of the extremes and take both into consideration.

That said, we'd push back on the notion that the typical church with a smaller group of kids doesn't have the resources to split kids up by gender, at least, if not grade. Even a group of seven kids (assuming there are at least two of any particular gender) would benefit from some "small group" aspect that's gender-specific.

And even a group with seven or eight of each gender can split into four small groups: One younger and one older, for each gender. Yes, this means having at least four leaders (and that can be a challenge in a smaller church). If you really have no way of splitting up along age or grade lines, then the group teaching time has to be a bit more generalized on some subjects, and some of the more significant application discussion (especially for subjects like sexuality) should take place in one-on-one or one-on-two conversations.

Q: How do you "sell" the need for middle school ministry to parents and the church? I've heard things such as, "Kids will burn out if they start in youth group at middle school. You'll lose them by high school." "We need to focus on high school. That's what people want. Those are the kids we need." Or from parents, "If there's a separate group, I have to drive to church an extra time for the middle school kid." Or "One of my kids is in 8th grade and another one is in 9th; they should be together, not separated." How do you address these issues to get the church and parents on board? —Beth

A: This is a tough situation. But this really boils down to a misunderstanding of early adolescence on the part of the church and parents. So our tactic would be to spend time doing some research so you're equipped with facts about the huge importance of building into this age group. Then start seeding ideas about the developmental uniqueness and realities of the young teen years. You can do this in one-on-one conversations, parent meetings, volunteer development, or even church-wide communications. Slowly grow a vision for the value of middle school ministry.

Start doing some middle-school-only activities long before you attempt to start a separate group, just so people get used to the notion that there might be reasons to have age-appropriate stuff for middle schoolers. It would also be extremely important to have conversations with those leading the ministries on either side of middle school (elementary grades, high school) and the senior pastor, so they begin to see you as an expert in the developmental realities of early adolescence. Their support will become absolutely critical before you make the move to start a middle school group.

Q: In the U.K. we don't have "middle school" as such. Do you think that makes any difference? —Ed

A: *Middle school* is just the term we're using for this young teen age group that in the U.K. you call "11 to 14s." It's the same thing, no matter what you call it.

Q: How do you help middle schoolers transition from elementary school to middle school unscathed? From middle school to high school? —Joel

A: There's no doubt that much attention needs to be given to the transitions—on both sides of middle school. And your choice of the word *unscathed* makes us wonder if you've been "scathed" in the past. Transition points are natural exit opportunities from any ministry, so here are some tips:

- *Start early.* A transition isn't a date ("Graduation Sunday") as much as it is a *season*. Get students thinking about where they're headed long before they get there.

- *Team up.* Middle school ministry—being in the middle—needs to reach in both directions, toward kids' ministry and high school ministry. If you don't work together, you can be guaranteed that the students will pay a price.

- *Think selflessly.* Our goal is to get middle schoolers excited about the next season of their journey in following Jesus, which will involve leaving your ministry. Having a freshman tell you, "I miss the middle school group; it was way better than this high school ministry," can make you feel proud for a minute—but it's ultimately a loss for that student.

- *Be about relationship.* If you lead middle school but not high school, your relationship with the high school pastor really matters. Do whatever you can to help him, serve him, pray for him, and set students up for success with him. Your friendship with him *will* make a difference.

Q: What's an effective discipline manner to take with middle schoolers who are misbehaving, without garnering a negative image with them? —Jess

A: Discipline? You mean all your middle schoolers don't behave like little angels? Ha! Ours don't either. There's no doubt that discipline will have to happen at some point, but it really matters more *how* it happens. There's a definite temptation for some leaders to try too hard to "be the students' buddy" and avoid that negative image you're speaking of. But if you take the overly permissive route, middle schoolers won't respect you. They know that in school they're expected to behave in a certain way, so often when they need to be corrected when they're with you, they're not shocked by it. The balance of truth and grace here is key.

Practically speaking, we'll take a page out of our buddy Kurt Johnston's playbook: The three Rs.

- If students are goofing off during your program, the first step is to **Remind** them in a cool but serious way. "Hey, let's cut that out now…"

- The next level is to **Reseat** them or reseat yourself next to them. If they haven't heeded the reminder warning, then often changing where they're sitting can help.

- And the third R is to **Remove** them from the situation. It might mean sending them home or talking to their parents about the problem.

Q: How do we cultivate a "servant's heart" in middle school kids? What are some tangible ways they can serve? —Mookie

A: In middle school life, where self-centeredness seems to be part of the job description, serving is a key developmental opportunity, as well as a chance to "do good." The first thing, though, is to help students understand the biblical vision behind it. A young teen can miss the point of why they should get fired up about helping others. Fortunately, most middle schoolers can catch a vision for serving pretty quickly, and they'll jump in with both feet.

We believe that serving opportunities both *inside* and outside the church are crucial. Middle school students can be a fantastic help assisting elementary school-aged kids, doing work around the church, and even playing key roles in setting up or putting on your middle school ministry. Not only that, but it also increases their sense of ownership when students feel like they helped "make it happen." Serving opportunities outside the church give students a chance to feel like they really can make a difference in a hurting world. But it all comes back to vision—make sure they know *why* it's so important and give them a chance to talk about it, too.

Q: Have you any tips for dealing with bullying? —Ed

A: Without knowing the context of your question, let's differentiate something from the beginning: While we don't have control of bullying activity that takes place outside of our churches, we do have a huge influence on the behaviors we allow in our ministries. Students in our middle school need to have crystal clarity that *no one gets picked on in here.* The tiniest 6th grader needs to feel completely safe around the toughest 8th grader. When students are in our ministries, they need to know "It's different in here!" This value needs to be taught and modeled from up front, as well as in individual interactions throughout your ministry year.

That being said, bullying is a *very* real problem in middle school settings, and it must never be minimized. When a student confides in you that they've been bullied, listening and asking are the key elements. Find out specifics so you can help them strategize on how to deal with the situation and talk to them about getting their parents involved. When bullying happens at school, administrators can be helpful in resolving the problem. Oftentimes, a parent will confide in you that her middle schooler is being bullied, even though the kid would be horrified to know you've been told. When that's the case, carefully asking questions of the student can often give him the safety to confide in you and allow you to talk with him about how to deal with it.

Q: How do you use technology without breaking the rules (for example, MySpace and Facebook have an age restriction of 13 years)? —Mark

A: We all know lots of young students who simply fabricate their age in order to use social networks. And, although these can be fantastic ways to keep in touch with students, this area is one of those "hidden curriculum" issues mentioned in the chapter on teaching. If we teach that deception is wrong but wink at breaking rules, what does that say? Not only that, but when we set up a ministry page using one of those networks and make it a key place of connection for our middle schoolers, we only perpetuate the misuse.

That being said, we definitely do use social networking to communicate with students who are "of age." And the minimum age keeps dropping, so maybe it won't be an issue soon.

Q: How do you effectively minister to or with middle school students when you don't have enough youth to justify a middle school ministry separate from high school? —Mark

Why or when should youth groups separate middle school and high school students? —Eric

A: Obviously, this is another very "situational" question. There are definitely pros and cons to being able to split MS and HS ministry, although not everyone can do it. The biggest pro we can think of is that you get to *focus more clearly on your target.* Most combined ministries seem to either end up aiming too high (leaving 7th graders scratching their heads) or too low (leaving juniors and seniors bored, unchallenged, or feeling underestimated). One of the biggest cons is the amount of *work* it takes. You really need two strategies instead of one, because you don't want to just "dumb down" your high school program and feed it to middle schoolers. And thinking clearly about how to focus separately on middle schoolers *and* high schoolers takes a lot of effort—but the payoff can be huge.

So what happens if resources (for example, people, money, facilities) don't allow you to separate? Do the best you can to not "lump them all together." One strategy for that is to have one "Middle School Minded Point Person" and one "High School Minded Point Person" whose job it is to evaluate and strategize for the separate age groups *within* the larger group. Even if you can't divide the two into separate gatherings, with some intentionality you can still *focus* on each unique age group.

78 Random Ministry Ideas from Marko and Scott

In honor of 7th and 8th graders, we've listed 78 ideas. They're all over the board and not organized in any certain way because, well...they're *random*. We hope some of them are useful to you—or that at least they'll catalyze a different useful thought.

1. The NO WAY Principle. Find ways, once in a while, to do things that result in your kids saying (or thinking), "No way! I can't believe they did that!" (or "I can't believe we're doing this!"). A bit of extra expense, or extra prep, can create a fun and memorable moment.

2. Little Planned Surprises. On a particularly hot day, have someone run to the grocery store and bring back ice cream sandwiches for everyone (bring one to the front and taunt them with yours first, then pass one out to everyone). Plan an event that's all surprises.

3. Big Planned Surprises. Shock your kids with an over-the-top planned surprise every once in a while. Like, after the kids are loaded in the bus or van for camp, gather the parents and tell them you're planning to stop part way through the trip at a water park for a few hours. Then, spring it on the kids when you're in the water park parking lot.

4. Twist It, Baby! Many youth workers don't believe they're creative because they have the wrong idea about creativity. They believe creativity means making stuff up that no one's ever thought of. But we're convinced that often the best "creative" stuff in youth ministry is merely a 10 percent tweak of something you've begged, borrowed, observed, morphed, mutated, modified, or stolen from somewhere else.

5. Create Traditions, Part 1 (serious stuff). The world of young teens is tumultuous and constantly changing. In the midst of that, traditions in your youth group become little safe havens of familiarity, little coat hooks of the known on which to hang out for a moment. Develop meaningful traditions, like a time of communion at the end of a specific retreat every year; or sending letters to oneself from the last day of a mission trip (which you mail a couple months later); or, a particular father-son or mother-daughter rite of passage experience each year, only for the kids in a particular grade.

6. Create Traditions, Part 2 (silly stuff). Goofy traditions can have your kids full of anticipation. In my (Marko) last church, we gave visitors the weirdest canned or bottled foods we could find as a "thanks for visiting" gift. Our kids loved it so much they started bringing more friends just to see what strange stuff we would come up with.

7. Peaks and Plateaus. If we were to graph spiritual growth for middle schoolers (and adults, for that matter), it wouldn't be a straight, steady incline. It'd be a wildly jagged line, with peaks and valleys. And, yes, there are "spiritual highs" that result from a variety of spiritually intense moments. But we've noticed that the plateau on the other side is often a bit higher than it was prior. So, as long as you're not manipulating those "peak" moments, don't be dismissive of the power of those spiritually intense happenings that occur naturally, especially at camps and retreats and on mission trips.

8. Hotels Are Cool! Unless you're in a super-rich church with kids who stay in hotels all the time, you'll discover (probably with some shock) that middle schoolers find hotels cool. Hotel stays DO NOT have to be expensive! Cram six kids in a room. Or take advantage of the many national chains that offer a kids-under-18-stay-free deal. (They sure didn't create those deals with youth ministry in mind, but we'll take it!) If you have to travel with your group and spend the night on the way, don't automatically look for a church floor to sleep on (where no one actually sleeps); consider the fun of a cheap hotel.

9. Hotel Overnighter. Sure, you could have your middle school guys over for an all-nighter of playing video games in your basement. But charge 'em $10 and a bag of chips each, and have the all-nighter in a couple of adjoining hotel rooms. Bring power strips, extension cords, and some extra TVs and gaming systems. You won't need the beds for sleeping; it's just a dude's gaming all-nighter (in an extra-fun location)! Create your own girls variation.

10. Missions and Service Rocks! We really don't want to be prescriptive here, but we've just never experienced anything that brings about the long-lasting, substantive spiritual transformation that mission trips and service projects afford. Getting kids to use their hands and hearts to help others is truly life-changing stuff.

11. Missions and Service (near home). You don't have to go on an overnight trip to emphasize the value of serving to middle schoolers. You could just go clean a gas station's bathroom, rake an old lady's lawn, or ask students what needs they know of that your group could meet. Not to raise money or impress people—just to serve.

12. Space Enhancers, Part 1 (not your room). If you have to share your space with 14 other ministries—as well as the Quilting Circle, Golfers for Christ, and custodial supplies—at least have a big vinyl banner made (they're cheap and easy to create—check online) with a few metal eyelets in the corners. Get permission to put some nondescript hooks in a wall, then hang your banner when your group meets.

13. Space Enhancers, Part 2 (paint, glorious paint). Don't settle for church-approved neutral and blah colors. Come up with a name for your group and have a nifty logo created (be careful that it's not juvenile!). Then project it on a wall where you can trace the outline and paint the whole thing in. There you have it: An almost-instant giant logo, without costly professional painters. Another idea is to have all the kids paint their handprints on a wall (in different colors), then their names underneath them. Over the years this will become a cool collage of all the kids who've passed through your ministry.

14. Space Enhancers, Part 3 (digital photos). Take photos of kids caught in the act of having fun. Not big group shots, but close-ups of individual kids (up to about three kids) laughing, or messy, or in the midst of a crazy game—or all of the latter at once! Print these out as large as you can (8x10 minimum) and laminate them so they can't be easily defaced. Then plaster them all over your walls in a collage format (*not* nice and orderly!). Then keep adding to the collage with every event. The room will become a huge positive memory repository.

15. Change It Up. Do you meet in the same room and use the same format every week? Take a week to just change it up, whether you switch the chairs to face a different direction or switch meeting locations entirely. Even though familiarity can sometimes be helpful, changing it up can help students experience something new.

16. Power Down. Lots of ministries have video games, sound systems, or maybe even fancy lighting. Take one week and eliminate anything that uses electricity. Use candles (carefully) and play music without amplification. Talk about how so many churches point their hearts to God without any of the things we often use.

17. Small Group Covenant. When a small group is beginning a new season together, have *students* set the rules. Ask them what they think would make their small group great, and have someone write down the guidelines they come up with. Watch the ownership increase, and watch students remind each other of the parameters they agreed on together.

18. Small Group Conversation Booster. Lots of us bring something to munch on during small group. Next time you're talking through a small group curriculum, make a rule that no one can speak unless his or her mouth is full.

19. They Say It's Your Birthday. Keep a list of your students' birthdays. Buy some cheap, small boxes of candy. A few days before a birthday, drop the candy in an envelope with a note telling her the reasons you're glad she was born—then mail the package.

20. Just Get Messy. Whether it's at a camp or a retreat or just your regular ministry gathering, do something messy that your kids would never be allowed to do at home. Shaving cream and flour fight, build an ice cream sundae on someone's head, cow heart toss…use your imagination.

21. Name Your Small Group. Challenge each small group to come up with a name for itself. Like a team name, it'll give group members a sense of identity and pull them closer together. The name doesn't have to be serious. In fact, Scott's group's name is "What's That Smell?" No joke.

22. Football = Cup of Coffee. Middle school girls like to "chat." Adults catch up on life while they drink a cup of coffee. For a middle school boy, starting a conversation can be a little tougher. So carry a foam football around your ministry gathering, toss it to a guy (or girl), and see if that helps get any banter going.

23. Steal Games from Jonathan. Jonathan McKee has an excellent resource of games, activities, and advice on his *free* Web site. Check it out at http://www.the-source4ym.com/games.

24. Re-Cover Their Bibles. When you're talking about students taking ownership for reading God's Word, help them personalize their Bibles. Have them tear off the cover (as long as you know their Bible isn't a family heirloom) and have pieces of leather handy. With the help of a glue gun, they can "re-cover" their Bibles.

25. Ask, Ask, Ask. Sometimes we assume *we're* supposed to be the ones with all the answers regarding what'll make a middle school ministry great. Organize a focus group with some handpicked students and come prepared with a list of a dozen specific questions that'll help you discover what *they* think would make the middle school ministry more effective!

26. Ask, Ask, Ask (parents). One more level of discernment is needed to choose the right parents for the focus group. Parents, though, can be extremely helpful translators of what they sense their kids desire from the middle school ministry.

27. Connect the Generations. Is there a senior citizens' ministry at your church? Even if you can't imagine middle schoolers "hanging out" with grandmas and grandpas, consider asking senior adults in your church to adopt-a-middle-schooler-in-prayer. Students could sign up to have someone pray for them, and on a regular basis jot down notes of what challenges they're facing, and you can send them on to the prayer partner.

28. Meet a Middle School Principal. Many public schools are pretty protective of their campuses. But consider calling a middle school principal and telling her about your involvement with students. Ask her if you can come by sometime for 30 minutes and just ask questions about what she's learned about working with young teens. Prepare your questions ahead of time, listen… and be open for relationship.

29. Meet a Middle School Principal, Part 2. Depending how the conversation goes, ask if there's anything you can volunteer to do around the school. Later you might ask if you could come to visit some of your students at a lunch hour sometime. If you've already made an initial contact with the principal, she's more likely to be open to it.

30. S.N.A.P. Team. Invite a few extroverted students to help Show New People Around (we almost got the letters right!). When someone new comes to your ministry gathering, the role of the S.N.A.P. Team is to *stick with the new person the whole time*, not just welcome-and-ditch him.

31. Mini-Golf with Your Mom. Or any activity. Or any excuse for moms and middle schoolers to hang out and build their relationships. Not every student will be up for it, but those who aren't won't feel as strange if *everybody* has a parent (or person acting as a parent) present. If you play mini-golf, post a sign with a question at each hole that parents and kids can ask themselves while they're waiting for their turns.

32. Bowl with Your Dad. After sign-ups, send dads a letter with a challenge to take their kids out for a meal or a snack afterward, just one-on-one. Also include a list of questions that dads can ask their kids—e.g., favorite teacher, hardest class, best family memory, what-would-you-like-to-change-about-our-family, etc.

33. High School Help. Invite carefully screened high schoolers to serve as role models for your middle schoolers. Most young teens aspire to be older and more mature...and high school students can often call them to a higher level more effectively than adults. Whether it's leading a small group or being interviewed during a message, high schoolers can make a difference.

34. Annual Awards. At the end of a ministry season, honor your volunteers with awards specific to the contributions they've made. Give an award to every volunteer, or, create categories and pick an award winner for each. The "Fixture Award" for a long-timer, the "Young Gun Award" for a high school student, the "Spotlight Award" for a behind-the-scenes helper who likes to stay *out* of the spotlight, the "Future Award" for someone who recently started serving in your ministry but has already made a big impact. It's a great tradition and will inspire long-term commitment and community.

35. Prayer Stations. When you gather, give students a focused area and topic they can pray about. Set aside a corner of the room and prep it so students can meet with God there. For more ideas see *Sacred Space* (Dan Kimball & Lilly Lewin, Youth Specialties/Zondervan 2008).

36. 8th-Grade Celebration Day. Before your 8th graders move to high school, set aside one of your regular programs to honor them. Get a team of 8th graders together a month ahead of time and let them choose the topics you'll cover, the games you'll play, etc. Work with a few 8th graders who have communication gifts and help *them* craft a short talk to give to their peers.

37. Serve Little Kids. Find out how your middle schoolers can serve the little kids in your church. Whether it's helping regularly with the 1st and 2nd grade Sunday school class or annually helping with the preschoolers at Christmas, such service gives young teens a vision for "reaching down" to help younger people.

38. Tournament Time. Organize an event that's easy for middle schoolers to invite friends to—even those who don't regularly go to church. Dodge ball tournaments are great; you can use an NCAA "March Madness" bracket format. Teams can pick names and create crazy uniforms; winning team gets a trophy. But also make sure other things are going on so that even those who aren't sports fans (and teams that get eliminated) can keep having a good time. Bring everyone together for "the final game."

39. Act It Out! Have students role-play how they'd engage in a challenging conversation (whether it's disagreeing with a parent, talking with someone who has questions about God, or navigating a tempting situation). Make sure you jot down short descriptions of each person's "role" for reference before the action starts. Afterward talk about what went well, as well as other approaches to take.

40. New Guy Eyes. When your ministry meets next, just before things start, walk outside and then come back in, imagining that you're a first-timer. Pretend you don't know anything about your ministry and see if it's clear where you're supposed to go, and what you're supposed to do. Imagine where a new person would try to connect and think about anything you could do that'd make the experience more welcoming. Even better, consider inviting a couple of students from another ministry in town (who don't know any of your students) to do the same thing and tell you about what they experienced.

41. Dear Dave... Begin "letters" to students when they show up in 6th grade. Every month or two, add a few thoughts to the letters—ways you're seeing them grow, memories you made together, times God was evident in their lives. When they graduate from 8th grade, give them the letters as reminders of how far they've come in their journeys with God.

42. Snail Mail Still Works. Don't underestimate how cool it is for middle schoolers to get paper mail! (They don't get much of it.) Pick a time every week to write at least one card to a student, pointing out something you love about him, a way you see her growing, or celebrating something about him. If you ever go to her house, don't be surprised to see the letter hanging on her bedroom wall months later.

43. Highs and Lows. This is a great tool to get students talking at the beginning of a small group. Most students love to talk about themselves, so ask about their high and low points of the week. Emphasize that there's no wrong answer, and that it doesn't have to be *"the highest"* high or lowest low...just something on that end of the scale.

44. Decorate Yourself. Get an amateur face painter to come to your event. Or order temporary tattoos that your ministry can dole out. They're surprisingly cheap, even for a custom logo of your ministry or event theme.

45. Play Bigger and Better. Give each team (of four to five students each) a penny. With an adult leader, each team goes door-to-door, quickly explaining the game and offering to trade for something bigger or better. When teams return at an agreed-upon time, you can compare who got the biggest and best items—and even discuss whether bigger is always better.

46. Find the Freebies. Lots of companies have money budgeted to respond to requests from nonprofit organizations...and it's there for the asking. It's a great way to get cool prizes for an event, or a raffle, and usually all the companies need is a letter from you with your church's letterhead. A parent can help you make calls to movie theaters, stores, restaurants, etc.

47. Use Your Thumbs. If you're having trouble getting some (or all) students in your small group to answer questions, try some new tactics. You could ask everyone to answer with a thumbs-up or thumbs-down, or have a small object (e.g., pillow, ball) that the question-answerer tosses to another person...who then needs to answer the question. Be creative!

48. Hands On. During small group time, provide clay or paper with fun markers or something else students can have in their hands during your discussion. Sure, such objects have the potential to make things "sillier," but they also might help some students find new ways to express themselves in your group—or just doodle (quietly) while they're thinking about their responses in the conversation.

49. Word of the Day. During your teaching or small group time, choose a "word of the day"—and every time it's used, students have to yell or cheer. Watch how much more attentive everyone is.

50. Cell Phone Craziness. If a bunch of your students have cell phones, get volunteers to choose a random person in the group—then on the count of three, tell the group they have to call or text this person. Whoever gets through first is the contestant for your game. (We hesitated to include this idea because cell phones can also be a crazy distraction...but sometimes you've just gotta embrace the craziness!)

51. Say Cheese! Middle schoolers love to ham it up for the camera, especially if they're with friends. Assign different students to capture the most unique or original photo during your weekly gathering. Have a contest at the end of two months and let your students vote on their favorite photos (after you screen and choose the top 10).

52. The Ceiling. During a small group conversation, have all present lie on their backs and stare at the ceiling during the rest of the group time. When you ask questions, it's fun to try and figure out who's talking...and it might just give someone who doesn't usually speak the courage to share something.

53. Adopt-a-Pet. Consider buying a goldfish (or another "easy to take care of" creature) for your youth group. Have a contest to name the pet, and then keep the pet in the youth room—and then assign different small groups to feed and take care of the pet for the month. (Scott "temporarily" had a tarantula for a ministry pet... probably wouldn't recommend that.)

54. Survey Says... Put together a survey for students in your ministry to complete. It might help you gather information for some upcoming teaching, or maybe it's more to give you a feel for the top issues they're facing. There are some cool Web sites that'll help you set up surveys–although sometimes the old-fashioned paper and pen on-the-spot survey is worth spending five minutes doing when everyone is together, for a higher return rate.

55. Survey Says (small group style). Put together a different kind of survey (a questionnaire) for your small group and have students list details about their likes/

dislikes (e.g., favorite candy, top musical artists, favorite TV shows, etc). When you call your students, keep adding notes to this sheet as you get to know them more. It'll not only help you remember details when you're talking with them, but it'll be fun to see how they change over the years... and they will!

56. Cool or Cheesy? When you're planning future series, events, etc., invite some students to help you. Although not all middle school students can articulate great ideas easily, they'll grow at it with practice. Not only that, having middle schoolers with you in those conversations gives instant feedback on whether some of your ideas are really cool or just cheesy!

57. What's My Job Again? Give your volunteers the gift of job descriptions. Be specific and fun with how you craft what your ministry expects its volunteers to accomplish. Make sure you include estimated hours and specific measurables so your volunteers know they're succeeding.

58. Syrup Chug. Challenge two or three students to see if they can drink a bottle of syrup faster than you. But fill your bottle with ice tea instead. You can admit it later so they don't call you a liar. (Once a student almost drank the whole bottle of syrup as fast as our leader drank the tea!)

59. Mood music. When students are coming into your youth room, always have music playing in the background and use it to your advantage. It really does affect the atmosphere of the room (e.g., if you're trying to start out on a more serious note, you can play slower music, etc.).

60. Dear Me... At the end of each ministry season or school year, have students write notes to themselves about the things they've learned this year. Have the students seal them in envelopes and self-address. Collect the envelopes and mail them out after six months or a year or at the end of their middle school years. They're cool reminders for students of what God has done in their lives.

61. Wave the Middle School Banner. As the point person for the middle school ministry, make sure you're giving positive press to your senior pastor about your students. Tell your boss stories of what students have done, both within and outside the church walls. Too often the only stories that get reported are negative (i.e., something gets broken). And it goes without saying that there's a difference between waving a banner and boasting...you'll know it.

62. Don't Walk Alone. The job of the middle school ministry point leader has the potential to feel lonely. Find peers to connect with at a church in your town that's somewhat like your own or get online to find a youth ministry "network." Share your best ideas and learn from others. (Note: This idea will never hit the top of your list until you decide to put it there!)

63. Keep a List. Develop your arsenal of message illustrations by keeping track of personal happenings that you know you'll be able to use someday—even if it's not soon. Grab a pad of paper, create a computer file, or leave voice mail on your phone—just get 'em down. You'll have food for thought when you're writing your next message.

64. Movie Night. Choose an appropriate movie (maybe one you know most students will watch anyway) and take your whole group. Then meet afterward and talk about not just their favorite parts but lessons learned—and maybe themes students saw that connect with a topic you've been discussing at youth group. Remember: Viewer discretion is advised—consult your senior pastor if you have doubts about content!

65. Middle School Paparazzi. Recruit a few students and loan them the ministry video camera. Ask them to put together an intro clip focused on a topic you'll be discussing in a few weeks or interview 10 students with a question you provide. You'll probably need to do some editing, but what a cool chance to involve students in their own ministry! (Obviously pristine cinematography isn't crucial!)

66. The People's Choice. Give your students the chance to choose the topics for an upcoming series. Gather their input (have them fill out "ballots") and come up with the top three or five topics. You'll increase their ownership and attention—guaranteed.

67. Craft Corner. Not every student in your ministry will want to play video games or jump into the dodge ball game, so have other activity options at the ready. Occasionally set up an easy-to-do, quick craft or creative activity in your youth room. Those who aren't so sports-minded might really love it! (We were doubters until we saw it work so well.) Get a "crafty" parent to head it up, too.

68. Scrolling Photos. Use all those photos from the last gathering or event and put them to good use. Download them into a program such as PowerPoint, iPhoto, etc.—and next time your students walk into the youth room—scroll the photos across whatever screen you have access to. Middle schoolers love to look at photos and say, "That's me!"

69. Don't Miss the Debrief. After every event, big or small, take time to meet with your volunteers to debrief. If it's a weekly program, you might only need a few minutes to discuss what went well and what could be improved. But for those big events you do each year, take notes on the "Must Repeat" and "Need to Adjust" areas—then file away the notes for next year so you don't have to reinvent the wheel...just make the wheel better!

70. Pick and Choose. From all the materials that come your way, choose one occasional resource (article, book, Web site) to recommend to parents. Remember that everyone is bombarded with information, so keep these suggestions regular but not too frequent—and make sure you believe the resource is really good enough to recommend. It can become a big assist to parents.

71. 6th (or 7th) Grade Photo. Take a group photo in the first few weeks that your "new class" or new small group is together…including the leader. Later you can look back and see how they've each changed, and how there are (hopefully) more in the group now.

72. Co-Lead. Think of one of your favorite people to be with (not currently part of your ministry). There's power in the partnership—so invite them to be part of your ministry, in a specific role or roles. It's always more fun to serve when you're standing alongside people you really respect and enjoy. (Here's to you, Kenton!)

73. Wreck Something. Bring something to youth group or small group that you can destroy—then have fun wrecking it. It'll be a fun memory, and maybe nothing beyond that. But it could turn into a cool object lesson…maybe.

74. Out of Season. Organize an event or a theme that makes no sense—like Christmas in July or a luau in January. Shake things up; students don't care about your "reasons" for creating an event…they'll show up if it's fun. Often in adult ministry we spend a lot of time dreaming up themes that "make sense"—but lots of middle schoolers really appreciate great randomness.

75. Practice, Practice. Before going in front of your group, test any game or illustration you're going to use. You don't want to be caught with an illustration or game that just doesn't work. A lot of the things we imagine will work need a little tweaking so you're not standing there saying, "If this had worked like we thought it would…"

76. Pray More Than You Assume You Need To. In those moments when you're not sure what to do next. In those moments when you wonder how effective your middle school ministry actually is. In those moments when life seems too full, too hard, or too confusing. Make space to be with God. Get Quiet. Listen. Remember that you are a treasured child of the All-Powerful God. Breathe deep. (Go ahead! Take a breath now.) And know that there's not one, single moment you spend investing in the life of a middle schooler that's wasted!

77. Volunteer Encouragement. As your ministry season or school year comes to a close, covertly ask parents and students to express their gratitude toward the adult volunteers for the time/energy/prayer they invested all year long. So often parents and students don't realize the power of their encouragement and expressed gratitude; handwritten notes or cards can refuel leaders like nothing else!

78. Volunteer Celebration. As a ministry be sure to express some kind of special recognition toward volunteer leaders of graduating 8th graders. Maybe a party or special awards or gifts…but acknowledge the huge investment they've made in walking with their students to the doorway of high school. (This is especially significant if the leaders have been with the same students during their entire middle school ministry run—that's standing-ovation kind of volunteering!)

ENDNOTES

1. We'll write about this quite a bit more in chapters to come. But for now, be aware that in the early 1970s, puberty began, on average, at about 13 years old; but now puberty begins, on average, at about 11 years old.

2. The first being birth to two years old.

3. Though we certainly hope this book will be helpful in academic settings.

4. Short for *in-between*. Sometimes this age group is referred to as "tweeners" or "tweenagers."

5. These rites of passage still exist in more protected cultures (those without access to the influence of media or a world youth culture, like tribal cultures). And ghosts of them still exist in some cultures, such as the bar mitzvah and bat mitzvah in Jewish culture. In recent years, many people have sounded the call for a return to these practices. Creating "rites of passage" can be wonderfully helpful as a marker in adolescent growth, but they'll never again be what they once were, since they're no longer a cultural norm. And new rites—while wonderful, and something we both highly encourage—should be seen as onramps, not as the adult freeway itself.

6. In 1904, G. Stanley Hall was the first to popularize the word *adolescence* (although he didn't create it) with the publication of his book by the same title (*Adolescence: Its Psychology and Its Relations to Physiology, Anthropology, Sociology, Sex, Crime, and Religion* [New York: Appleton, 1904]). Even then, Hall recognized the upper end of adolescence (then described as about 16 years old) in these terms.

7. Marko unpacks these adolescent tasks in much more detail in his book *Youth Ministry 3.0* (Youth Specialties, 2008).

8. Researchers who study the onset of puberty pretty much always study girls. There are a couple reasons for this. First, while girls officially show signs of puberty with the growth of breast buds and pubic hair, menarche (their first period) is a widely accepted marker. These markers are all visible. And girls—throughout the ages—have been willing to talk about their first period (at least with someone they trust). The start of puberty for boys is less obvious and less agreed upon. Some say it's a boy's first nocturnal emission. Other people have other definitions. Either way, boys don't talk about it. In fact, boys lie about it. So researchers study girls. We do know that boys tend to follow about 12 to 18 months behind girls on puberty and other adolescent development realities.

9. As college students and young adults move into a world where they have less spending power than their parents, it's common for them to experience an ambivalence about fully engaging the world as adults. They often don't have the spending power they'd like to have, and they find it difficult to imagine a life of complete independence from their parents.

10. As youth culture grew to the point of being the dominant pop culture in the Western world, it became more and more acceptable for 20-somethings to be living a life of prolonged adolescence. A 24-year-old living at home in 1968 would have been considered a slacker or to have some sort of significant problem. But a 24-year-old living at home today is rather normal. In our increasingly complex world, we no longer expect high school graduates to have figured out their identity, autonomy, and affinity tasks. Culturally, we've grown to accept that young 20-somethings still "deserve" more years to wrestle with these tasks.

11. With culture change has come a prolonging of many of the physiological aspects assumed to be normal in teen years. For instance, development of abstract thinking has been shown to be slowing, lengthening well into the twenties. New brain research is also showing that parts of the brain aren't fully formed until the mid-twenties, like the prefrontal cortex and the temporal lobes. These parts of the brain are vital to functioning "as an adult." There remains debate as to whether these "not yet ready" brain functions are the chicken or the egg. In other words, it's not clear if this is how brains have always developed (and our understanding of adolescence is just now catching up), or if brain development has slowed because our culture doesn't expect teenagers to use those parts of the brain. Either way, the brain has been shown to be decidedly "teenage" well into the twenties. For more discussion of this—particularly as it pertains to brain development—see Barbara Strauch's excellent book *The Primal Teen* (Anchor, 2004).

12. This number is hotly debated. I (Marko) find it intriguing that people get so passionate about disagreeing with the research on this. Really, the tone of voice when people express their skepticism can

only be described as "threatened." I'm not completely sure what they're threatened by. A generous possibility is that they're hoping to protect the childhood years from being absorbed into adolescence (a trend that—puberty aside—seems to be propelled by marketing to preteens and "tweens"). When I cite these numbers, I'm often asked (sometimes by a skeptic, sometimes by someone who's merely interested and not disagreeing) for references to studies backing this up. While I've included these endnotes, this book is certainly not a truly academic book (duh!), and I'll not fully support my claim other than to say the numbers have been shown over and over again in various studies. I will cite a few of them, if merely to allow us to move on:

> Marcia E. Herman-Giddens, Eric J. Slora, Richard C. Wasserman, Carlos J. Bourdony, Manju V. Bhapkar, Gary G. Koch, and Cynthia M. Hasemeier. "Secondary Sexual Characteristics and Menses in Young Girls Seen in Office Practice: A Study from the Pediatric Research in Office Settings Network," *Pediatrics* 99, (April 1997): 505–512. http://pediatrics.aappublications.org/cgi/content/abstract/99/4/505 (accessed 3/13/09).

> Diana Zuckerman Ph.D., "When Little Girls Become Women: Early Onset of Puberty in Girls," National Research Center for Women and Families—Children's Health, http://www.center4research.org/children11.html (accessed 3/13/09).

> P.B. Kaplowitz, S.E. Oberfield, and the Drug and Therapeutics and Executive Committees of the Lawson Wilkins Pediatric Endocrine Society, "Reexamination of the Age Limit for Defining When Puberty is Precocious in Girls in the United States," *Pediatrics* 104, (October 1999): 936–941. http://pediatrics.aappublications.org/cgi/content/full/104/4/936?ijkey=51a3e30c7ef66356541e2f346991c5cc9300baf7 (accessed 3/13/09).

13. For more on this, see Chap Clark's book *Hurt: Inside the World of Today's Teenagers* (Baker Academic, 2004), as well as Chap and Dee Clark's book *Disconnected: Parenting Teens in a MySpace World* (Baker Books, 2007).

14. The entire text of this open letter can also be found on the Youth Specialties Web site (under the "Advice" link on the Articles page). You're welcome to cut-and-paste it for your use: http://www.youthspecialties.com/freeresources/articles/advice/young_teens.php (accessed 3/13/09).

15. Quote retrieved from Leith Anderson by Heather Flies, 2002.

16. See Barna's article on age of conversion: http://www.barna.org/barna-update/article/5-barna-update/196-evangelism-is-most-effective-among-kids (accessed 4/8/09).

17. For a list of the signers and endorsers of the open letter, see the Web URL in endnote 14.

18. We searched online and in some of Stephen Glenn's books, but we couldn't find this exact description in print anywhere. So we asked Wayne Rice where we could find it. Here's what Wayne emailed to us: "I'm not sure Steve ever wrote it in a book...maybe he did, but I remember it mainly from lectures he gave, first in a seminar called Developing Capable People and then at a "trainer of trainers" seminar that [YS] did with him in San Diego a long time ago. We also had him speak at a couple of conventions...I'm sure I had the little discovery-testing-concluding cycle thing in my notes from his talks. I can still see him drawing PUBERTY in big letters with lightning bolts, sort of like Emeril's 'BAM!' He'd shout, 'PUBERTY!'...when massive doses of progesterone and testosterone come roaring into the body setting off a biophysical disaster of unprecedented proportions!" For a more recent description of these changes, check out Stephen Glenn's foreword for *Positive Discipline for Teenagers* by Jane Nelson and Lynn Lott (Three Rivers Press, 2000).

19. We've adjusted Stephen Glenn's age brackets on this chart, to reflect the shifting age of puberty and the cultural shifts in the length of adolescence. We've also changed his word *discovery* to *sampling*, as we believe it's a more up-to-date descriptor of both the infant stage and of early adolescence.

20. I'm borrowing this metaphor from Brian McLaren, who uses it for a completely different application in some of his writings. (Brian uses it to talk about the current American church, with all its technology and mega-ness, which, he suggests, will continue on for some period of time, even while the new-era-automobile of churches spring up around them.)

21. See the Wikipedia article on puberty: http://en.wikipedia.org/wiki/Puberty (accessed 4/8/09)

22. For more on the technicalities of menstruation, the Wikipedia article is concise and helpful: http://en.wikipedia.org/wiki/Menstruation (accessed 3/13/09).

23. James Dobson, *Preparing for Adolescence* (Regal, 1989), 83-84.

24. For a much more detailed (and helpful!) discussion about masturbation in boys, see pages 66-71 in Steve Gerali's excellent book, *Teenage Guys: Exploring Issues Adolescent Guys Face and Strategies to Help Them* (Zondervan/Youth Specialties, 2006).

25. We've already written about how adolescence has gone from an 18-month window (when it was first identified in 1904), to a six-year window (in the 1970s), to a 15+ year window. But just the other day, we were reading new research that's proposing that adolescence should no longer be bracketed as an age, that the "age limits" of adolescence are going by the wayside, as people in their late twenties and early thirties are living a sort of extended adolescence (referred to in this research as "the golden years of adolescence," which is somewhat humorous). This is fascinating stuff to us, and it will have huge implications for youth ministry in the years to come. Here's the URL to the research we're talking about: http://www.marketingvox.com/youth-no-longer-defined-by-age-consumers-stay-younger-longer-041658/?camp=rssfeed&src=mv&type=textlink (accessed 3/13/09).

26. Read more about Bar Mitzvah and Bat Mitzvah rites of passage on Wikipedia, at: http://en.wikipedia.org/wiki/Bar_Mitzvah (accessed 3/13/09).

27. Read more about the Quinceañera tradition on Wikipedia, at: http://en.wikipedia.org/wiki/Quincea%C3%B1era (accessed 3/13/09).

28. Many teenagers will still say the real rite of passage is an adolescent's first sexual experience, which is usually a much less public "celebration" than the rites we're speaking of!

29. Marko here: I first heard this joke line from Wayne Rice (the grandfather hero of all middle school ministry) and Jim Burns (now host of HomeWord). I don't know who originated it, but I've used it liberally for years.

30. As an example, see Rick Bundschuh's wonderful book about rites of passage for boys, called *Passed Thru Fire: Bringing Boys into Meaningful Manhood* (Tyndale House, 2003).

31. It's rare to see this significant of a change in human physiology over such a short number of years. We're actually quite surprised that we haven't seen scholarly articles connecting this to human evolution and speculating about the future. But, then, we don't read many scholarly articles!

32. See the endnotes from chapter 1 for source stuff on this shifting age. Also, remember that (1) researchers typically study the onset of puberty in girls because the physiological markers (breast buds, menarche) are more easily accessible, and (2) in general, guys tend to follow girls by a year or two.

33. It's interesting to see a resurgence in K-8 approaches to educational models in the United States right now. Many are finding that the shift first to a junior high approach and then to a middle school approach brought good things, as well as a new set of problems. And with the cultural pressure for kids to behave older at younger and younger ages, schools are finding great success in a K-8 approach that allows young teens to live in a world of innocence a bit longer. My (Marko) daughter (and my son, who's a preteen as of this writing) moved from a middle school to a K-8 school at the end of her 6th-grade year (when she was 12), and we found it to be a fantastic experience. Before she changed schools, my daughter was actually speeding—full-throttle—into full-blown adolescence, and the move clearly allowed her to slow down.

34. We've often been surprised by how passionate Christians are about this issue. (Or maybe it would be more accurate to say they're dispassionate and ignore it, or they chalk it up to a purely cultural, nonphysiological shift that's bad and correctible.) Some time ago, Marko posted on his blog a book review of Scot McKnight's *The Real Mary* and merely ruminated about the intersection of God's selection of Mary and the older age of puberty in history. And the responses were shockingly angry! People suggested that since we don't really know when puberty occurred 2,000 years ago that maybe the age of puberty was actually younger than it's been in more recent decades. Well, we don't really know; but all indicators, including rites of passage that were tied to menarche (and occurred in what we would now call mid-adolescence), give us a fairly good indication that puberty was occurring at least at 14.5 years, if not a bit older. Many speculate that it was likely 15 or 16 years old.

35. "Checking for understanding" is a critical component of any teaching with middle schoolers. Because of their in-and-out-of-abstract-thinking minds, what they hear will often be very different than what you're communicating!

36. Piaget first proposed the theory in the early '20s and then published a book that includes the theory in 1957, *Logic and Psychology*.

37. Lots of other developmental theories have been built on Piaget's work. In particular, Lawrence Kohlberg's hotly contested theory of moral development and James Fowler's theory of faith development used the framework and foundation of Piaget's work for lateral implications in related developmental fields.

38. We're going to talk about only the last two stages in this book. But, for reference, the rest of them break down roughly like this:

- Sensorimotor period (years 0–2)

- Preoperational period (years 2–7)

- Concrete operational period (years 7–11)

- Formal operational period (years 11 and up)

For a concise overview of these stages, and the theory as a whole, see the Wikipedia article on "The theory of cognitive development" at http://en.wikipedia.org/wiki/Theory_of_cognitive_development (accessed 3/13/09).

39. I (Marko) remember doing a little firsthand testing for a research paper I wrote while I was in grad school, using some of the instruments Piaget used. I don't remember the whole thing, but I remember setting a few glasses of water in front of children and teens of various ages. In particular, one of the glasses was tall and thin, and another was short and wide. The short and wide glass had more water in it than the tall and thin glass; but the water level in the latter, due to its shape, was higher. When asked which glass had more water in it, the children universally choose the thin glass with the higher water mark.

40. The general thinking regarding the reason for this delayed use of abstract thinking is that our culture doesn't expect teenagers to use abstract thinking, so they don't have much reason to exercise it.

41. Two useless asides here: First, we never found the thumb tip, and I've often morbidly wondered it if ended up as a green olive on someone's pizza. Second, this little skin graft surgery provided one of the most embarrassing moments of my life. I was stripped naked from the waist down and lying on an outpatient table at a teaching hospital. All I had covering my crotch was a little towel. Just as the doctor started his prep work, a nurse walked in with what appeared to be about eight first-day *female* student nurses, all about my age. Just after they arrived, the towel interfered with the doctor's work, and he flicked it. I don't know if a puff of air came through at that moment or what; but I do know that the little towel lifted up like a helicopter and flew away. Now I was lying there, completely naked, in front of eight student nurses who were clearly the same age (about 18 or 19) as me. This would have been bad enough. But what made it horrifically worse was that they started giggling. It was one of those infectious giggles that starts with one person and becomes unavoidable as the others try not to giggle. Once they were all giggling, the nurse assisting in the surgery told the student nurse host to "get them out of here," and I was spared further horror.

42. Recent research has shown that the part of the human brain most responsible for many of these abstract functions—particularly functions such as hypothesizing, speculation, decision making, and all things related to wisdom—is underdeveloped in teenagers and not fully formed (physiologically speaking) until the mid-twenties. There's still a good amount of debate on this, as the findings are so new; but the implications seem to be that teenagers gain this new abstract thinking ability at puberty. They wrestle with putting it into use not only because of inexperience, but also because their brains haven't finished developing yet. In other words, there's a biological explanation for why teenagers are so slow to "get" some of this stuff and why they're so notorious for poor decision making, poor prioritization, and a general lack of wisdom. For more on this, read the excellent book *The Primal Teen: What the New Discoveries about the Teenage Brain Tell Us about Our Kids* by Barbara Strauch (Anchor, 2004). We'll discuss this more in a bit.

43. Psychological literature calls this an "imaginary audience."

44. The best book on this—a must-read for all youth workers—is the fascinating *The Primal Teen: What the New Discoveries about the Teenage Brain Tell Us about Our Kids* by Barbara Strauch (Anchor, 2004). The book covers this brain research in detail and lays out lots of the implications.

45. An excellent overview of all of this brain stuff can be found in this article: http://www.walrusmagazine.com/articles/2006.11-science-the-teenage-brain/1/ (accessed 3/13/09).

46. There has been some pushback on some of this science, particularly from one guy named Robert Epstein (who happens to be the former editor-in-chief of *Psychology Today*). Epstein wrote an important book called *The Case Against Adolescence: Rediscovering the Adult in Every Teen* (Quill Driver Books, 2007), as well as a bunch of scholarly and popular articles. A simple search on his name will quickly locate many of these articles. Epstein's primary contention is a question of the chicken and the egg—which comes first? His argument is that the "new insights" on teenage brain development are an effect, not a cause. He believes teen brains aren't fully developed because, culturally, we don't expect teenagers to use those parts of their brains. He believes that adolescence is a false, only cultural, construct that has no basis in actual science. Interesting stuff, really. Two points bear fleshing out, from our perspective: First, Epstein is in the minority in his position. (This doesn't mean he's wrong, of course—most correct opinions are, at one time, in the minority.) And second, whether underdeveloped teenage brains are a cause or an effect, it's still the reality of the teenagers we're working with, and it has implications for those of us who work with them.

47. Barbara Strauch, *The Primal Teen: What the New Discoveries about the Teenage Brain Tell Us about Our Kids* (Anchor, 2004), 15-18.

48. This is an intentional overstatement, meant to make you think.

49. Here's an article that fleshes this need for sleep out a bit more: http://nymag.com/news/features/38951/ (accessed 3/13/09).

50. Marko wrote a blog post about this, which includes the car insurance ad referenced here: http://www.ysmarko.com/?p=1667 (accessed 3/13/09).

51. I (Marko) have had a 20-ish coleader in my middle school guys' small group for the last four years, and I absolutely love it. Being closer in age to the guys in the group, he's able to bring a "big brother" role, and the guys totally connect with him in ways that are different from how they connect with me. He has more energy—and often, time—than I have. And, in many ways, I get the opportunity to build into him with the (slight) bit of extra wisdom and experience I might have.

52. We're not saying preteens have only four or five emotions at their emotional fingertips. It's a metaphor—stick with us.

53. I feel manlier just typing out this metaphor! Look at me, a guy who talks about tools!

54. If we're really honest with ourselves, we'll admit that this kind of harsh response is often because kids push our buttons with their strong emotions. Our responses become more about us than about them.

55. For an understanding of how emotional development plays out for *Teenage Girls*, we suggest the following two excellent resources: *Odd Girl Out: The Hidden Culture of Aggression in Girls* by Rachel Simmons (Harvest Books, 2003) and *Teenage Girls: Exploring Issues Adolescent Girls Face and Strategies to Help Them* by Ginny Olson (Zondervan/Youth Specialties, 2006).

56. Again, it's not that affinity plays no role in childhood friendships. It's just not the dominant theme. In young adolescence, as affinity becomes a pathway to figuring out one's identity, it begins to play a major role in friendship development—the major role.

57. Much of these gender uniquenesses in friendship formation and culturally informed roles is discussed at length in the excellent books by Ginny Olson, *Teenage Girls* (Zondervan/Youth Specialties, 2006), and Steve Gerali, *Teenage Guys* (Zondervan/Youth Specialties, 2006).

58. There is much that's changing in the world of middle school girls, which is why we asked Kara Powell and Brad Griffin to write a "guest chapter" on new issues facing girls. See chapter 11.

59. Ken Rawson has written a helpful curriculum for middle school guys that addresses this very reality, called *Becoming a Young Man of God* (Zondervan/Youth Specialties, 2008).

60. For more on this, see David Livermore's *Cultural Intelligence: Improving Your CQ to Engage Our Multicultural World* (Baker Academic, 2009), particularly the chapters on "Understanding Our Own Culture" ("The Average American"), and "Cultural Values" ("Why We Do What We Do").

61. One of Youth Specialties' YS One Day team members brought these numbers to us as part of our content development a few years back. Our reference searching seems to indicate that the numbers of 20,000 for females and 7,000 for guys (not the 4,000 we say in the text) comes from *The Female Brain* by Louann Brizendine (Broadway, 2007). This number seems hotly debated and disputed by researchers. But the observable reality is that *girls use more words than boys.*

62. By the way, we'd also worked with the hotel to have all the pay-per-view movies blocked, as well as the hotel's free HBO channel. We encouraged the kids to stay off the phones, and we checked with the front desk to see if any of them were making lots of calls (then went to those rooms and talked to the kids). During our occasional "rounds," we listened for excessive noise (there were other guests in the hotel, of course!) and had a chat with those kids also, reapplying their bit of tape after we opened the door.

63. Zondervan/Youth Specialties, 2008.

64. The other adolescent tasks are identity and affinity. We'll address this more in the chapter on culture (chapter 9).

65. See the Wikipedia article on individuation: http://en.wikipedia.org/wiki/Individuation (accessed 4/8/09).

66. We can add to the problem if we assume parents don't have good motivation in how they address this process. Sure, there are parents who don't have healthy motivations; but the majority are erring because of wrongly applied good motivation.

67. The interesting thing in this case is that this boy's parents actually seem very engaged in his life, and they really want to be good parents. But it seems they must have a slightly skewed view regarding what level of freedom is appropriate for an 11-year-old.

68. Ministry with parents is unique for youth workers in that how you approach it needs to greatly shift with your own age. Your interaction and ministry with parents will look very different if you're a 22-year-old than it will if you're a peer of the parents with teenagers of your own. Marv Penner has developed this concept, along with a bunch of helpful parent ministry ideas, in his book *Youth Worker's Guide to Parent Ministry* (Zondervan/Youth Specialties, 2003).

69. I had to walk back to the movie entrance and call my dad. (Remember the days before cell phones?) He wasn't home, and my older sister agreed to pick us up. When I saw her car enter the parking lot, I decided to add a bit of levity to the awkward situation by jumping around the empty lot like a clown, shouting, "Over here! It's the one with no wheels!" But when the car pulled up, I saw that the driver was my understandably frustrated father. We drove to my girlfriend's house in complete silence. And on the way home, he said one thing: "That's the most expensive date you'll ever go on."

70. The names (junior high, middle school) are somewhat meaningless these days, by the way, as population growth, shrinkage, and growth again have caused school systems to try all kinds of practical solutions, as well as some that are developmentally based.

71. "At that time the disciples came to Jesus and asked, 'Who, then, is the greatest in the kingdom of heaven?' He called a little child, whom he placed among them. And he said: 'Truly I tell you, unless you change and become like little children, you will never enter the kingdom of heaven. Therefore, whoever takes a humble place—becoming like this child—is the greatest in the kingdom of heaven'" (Matthew 18:1-4).

72. This often (although not always) happens at a subconscious, or at least a non-articulated, level.

73. All youth workers need to read *Soul Searching: The Religious and Spiritual Lives of American Teenagers* (Oxford University Press, 2005) by Christian Smith and Melinda Lundquist Denton.

74. This is a modification of "Bloom's Taxonomy," which I (Marko) was first exposed to by Dr. Duane Elmer. I have modified the words, however. See more info on Bloom's Taxonomy here: http://en.wikipedia.org/wiki/Bloom%27s_taxonomy (accessed 3/13/09).

75. Psychologists called this "affect."

76. This even holds true with the trinity of the most interesting middle school subjects: sex, the end times, and "Will there be sex in the end times?"

77. Do you need a better rationale for a middle school ministry rooted in significant relationships than this?

78. Here's where this becomes a cycle, rather than the linear nature of Bloom's Taxonomy. Especially in spiritual growth (but also true in other kinds of learning), that which becomes a part of us in the "doing" phase always informs the next opportunity to take in data for the next pass(es) through the cycle.

79. See the whole story in John 20. We can't help noticing, by the way, that Thomas' response has all that emotional and offensive exaggeration of a middle schooler (not that he was one). It was pretty crass for him to say he'd only believe Jesus was alive if he had the chance to insert his hand in the gory, gaping wound in Jesus' side!

80. The two of us compiled most of this list from our own experience. But we got some additional help from respondents to Marko's blog: http://www.ysmarko.com/?p=4259#comments (accessed 3/13/09).

81. Kara Powell and Brad Griffin wrote an excellent "guest chapter" (chapter 11) in this book, specifically on the subject of what's changed for middle school girls. Make sure you read that chapter!

82. This is the primary premise of Marko's book *Youth Ministry 3.0: A Manifesto of Where We've Been, Where We Are, and Where We Need to Go* (Zondervan/Youth Specialties, 2008). It would be good supplemental reading to this youth culture section.

83. Marko's contention in *Youth Ministry 3.0*, which we won't go into in this book, is that youth ministry did a good job of responding to these shifts in the first and second epochs. Early youth workers, in the '50s and '60s, created approaches to youth ministry that were a response to this new culture and responsive to the identity priority in culture. In the late '60s and early '70s, a new kind of youth ministry sprang up that was responsive to the shift toward autonomy, and the modern "youth group" was formed. The challenge we're facing now is that most of our youth ministries are using models and assumptions and values that are responsive to this second epoch when our kids are part of the third wave of youth culture (with a priority on affinity or belonging).

84. Chap Clark writes about this "going underground" aspect of youth culture extensively in his excellent book, *Hurt: Inside the World of Today's Teenagers* (Baker Academic, 2004).

85. We're not suggesting you throw out all programming, including games and teaching. We simply believe the era of viewing them as youth ministry is over. They are tools we might (or might not) use, and that's all.

86. Dictionary.com Unabridged (v 1.1). Random House, Inc., http://dictionary.reference.com/browse/culture (accessed 3/13/09).

87. M. T. Anderson has written a fascinating piece of young adult fiction called *Feed* (Candlewick, 2004). It tells the futuristic story of teen drama (budding romance, shifting friendships, wrestling with adolescent tasks). But the significant feature of this "brave new world" is the wireless "feed" that's installed in the brains of all teenagers (and most adults), which allows for a constant flow of marketing, video programming, human interaction (think text messaging via brain waves), and other functions. The feed is wired into the brain, so if the characters notice someone's jeans, they start receiving an onslaught of marketing in their minds about sales on jeans. It's nuts. But the most disconcerting thing about the book is that it doesn't seem quite far-fetched enough. Recommended reading.

88. This pressure isn't universal, and these are merely generalizations. But there are certainly adult (parent) subcultural generalizations at play here: White and Asian parents tend to pressure kids more in this academic area, as do suburban parents more than urban or rural parents. Entire books could be written about this, as it's often White and Asian suburban parents who have the most interest in their children "succeeding" in ways that are measured by financial and career success.

89. This sedentary lifestyle (combined with fatty, starch- and sugar-filled diets) is the leading cause in the massive rise of obesity in children and teenagers.

90. Of course, like much of this chapter, this is a generalization. There are lots of kids who spend all of their free time at the skateboard park or living some other physical lifestyle.

91. Incidentally, I (Marko) was with a group of 9th-grade boys recently, standing on the curb of a busy street, waiting to cross. One of them said, "Let's play *Frogger!*" I responded with shock, "What!?" They thought I'd never heard of *Frogger*, which was funny in and of itself since the game was popular before they were even born. When they tried to explain the video game version of *Frogger*, I cut them off, telling them I was very clear what that game was. They went on to explain that they wanted to play a live version, where they run out into traffic, dodging the cars. I looked at them with horror. Were they kidding? No, it was clear they were not. Ah, the judgment skills of young teens. It's a wonder any of them survive. Needless to say, I did not allow the live version of *Frogger* on my watch.

92. I (Marko) asked for help with this metaphor on my blog, and Jose Samuel Merida suggested the color change between adjacent colors in a rainbow. We're not using the rainbow part of his metaphorical suggestion, but the color blend really seemed to work for us.

93. Portions of this chapter were modified from articles titled "New Twists on Not-So-New Issues for Girls," "See Jane Deal With Her Body," and "See Jane Navigate Technology," all authored by Kara Powell and Brad Griffin and available at www.fulleryouthinstitute.org.

94. Harris Interactive, "A Generation Unplugged" Research Report (September 12, 2008), http://www.ctia.org/advocacy/research/index.cfm/AID/11483 (accessed 3/13/09).

95. American Psychological Association (APA), Task Force on the Sexualization of Girls, *Report of the APA Task Force on the Sexualization of Girls* (2007), 3, http://www.apa.org/pi/wpo/sexualizationrep.pdf (accessed 3/13/09).

96. Ibid., 16. For more information, check out the "2005 Age Distribution: Cosmetic Patients (18 or Younger)" PDF available at http://www.plasticsurgery.org/Media/Statistics/2005_Statistics.html (accessed 3/13/09).

97. The Tucker Center for Research on Girls & Women in Sport, University of Minnesota, Minneapolis, MN, "Developing Physically Active Girls: An Evidence-Based Multidisciplinary Approach" (2007), http://cehd.umn.edu/TuckerCenter/projects/TCRR/executive-summary.html (accessed 3/13/09).

98. Lan Nguyen Chaplin and Deborah Roedder John, "Growing up in a Material World: Age Differences in Materialism in Children and Adolescents," *Journal of Consumer Research* 34 (Dec. 2007).

99. Dorothy Espelage, professor of educational psychology at the University of Illinois, Urbana-Champaign, quoted in Vanessa O'Connell, "Fashion Bullies Attack—In Middle School" *Wall Street Journal*, October 25, 2007, D1.

100. *Report of the APA Task Force on the Sexualization of Girls*, 41.

101. The devastating reality is that as many as one in three girls will be sexually abused during their childhood or adolescence, most often by a male family member or someone they know. (Statistics vary, but a very helpful summary sheet, by Emily M. Douglas and David Finkelhor, can be accessed at the Crimes Against Children Research Center Web site, http://www.unh.edu/ccrc/factsheet/pdf/childhoodSexualAbuseFactSheet.pdf.) While we're all aware that—tragically—the youth ministry context is not immune to the possibility of abuse, our response can't be to simply keep all male volunteers and staff away from all girls. Doing so may reinforce for those girls who've been abused that they cannot safely be with men. And for those who haven't been abused, it can prevent them from learning how to communicate with and relate to guys.

102. Kurt Johnston takes a look at the concept of putting yourself in their shoes in his excellent book *Middle School Ministry Made Simple* (Standard Publishing, September 2008.)

103. Karen Kersting, "Driving Teen Egos—and Buying—Through 'Branding,'" *APA Online* 34, no. 6 (June 2004), http://www.apa.org/monitor/jun04/driving.html (accessed 3/13/09).

104. Stanford University, "Research Reveals Brain Has Biological Mechanism To Block Unwanted Memories" *ScienceDaily* (January 9, 2004), http://www.sciencedaily.com/releases/2004/01/040109072004.htm (accessed 3/13/09).

105. Wayne Rice, *Junior High Ministry* (Zondervan/Youth Specialties, 1998), quotes H. Stephen Glenn discussing adult interactions with middle school students and unpacks the concept of being a friend to them while still being an adult (p. 38).

106. Focus on the Family Action, "MTV Survey Reflects Pro-Family Ideals," *CitizenLink.com* (August 21, 2007), http://www.citizenlink.org/content/A000005317.cfm (accessed 3/13/09).

107. You can visit Web sites such as: www.brainyhistory.com/

http://dir.yahoo.com/Arts/Humanities/History/

http://www.historyworld.net/timelines/selectmix.asp

http://www.infoplease.com/yearbyyear.html

(all accessed 3/13/09).

108. Shaunti Feldhahn and Lisa Rice, *For Parents Only: Getting Inside the Head of Your Kid* (Multnomah, 2007), 56.

109. Dale Carnegie, *How to Win Friends and Influence People* (Simon and Schuster, 1982), 77.

110. To expand on this list, try Youth Specialties' line of "Quick Questions" books; titles such as *Choose Your Top 3*, *Gimme Five*, and *Unfinished Sentences* are full of conversation-starting questions and statements for your group.

111. Mark Oestreicher, *Youth Ministry 3.0: A Manifesto of Where We've Been, Where We Are, and Where We Need to Go* (Zondervan/Youth Specialties, 2008), 98.

112. *The Seven Checkpoints for Youth Leaders* by Andy Stanley and Stuart Hall (Howard Books, 2001) is a helpful resource.

113. Check out Youth Specialties' training events at http://youthspecialties.com/events/ or the Willow Creek Association Shift Conference at http://www.shiftexperience.com/ (both accessed 3/13/09).

114. Francis Chan, Youth Specialties National Youth Workers Convention—Nashville, December 2008—General Session #1.

115. Urie Bronfenbrenner, "The Social Ecology of Human Development," in *Brain and Intelligence: The Ecology of Child Development*, ed. Frederick Richardson (National Educational Press, 1973).

116. Mike King, *Presence-Centered Youth Ministry: Guiding Students into Spiritual Formation* (InterVarsity Press, 2006), 68.

117. John Ortberg, *Faith and Doubt* (Zondervan, 2008), 121.

118. Wayne Rice, *Junior High Ministry* (Zondervan/Youth Specialties, 1998), 38.

119. Philip W. Jackson, *Life in Classrooms* (Teachers College Press, 1990).

120. Elliot W. Eisner, *The Educational Imagination: On the Design and Evaluation of School Programs* (Prentice Hall, 2001).

121. "Preaching that Changes Lives," *A Leadership Summit Dialogue with Bill Hybels and John Ortberg*, http://www.preachingtodaysermons.com/prthchli.html (accessed 3/13/09).

122. Kurt Johnston, *Middle School Ministry Made Simple* (Standard Publishing, 2008), 83.

123. Helen Musick and Duffy Robbins, *Everyday Object Lessons for Youth Groups* (Zondervan/Youth Specialties, 1999).

124. A couple of great teaching books are *Speaking to Teenagers* by Doug Fields and Duffy Robbins (Zondervan/Youth Specialties, 2007) and *Communicating for a Change* by Andy Stanley and Lane Jones (Multnomah Books, 2006).

125. These are Web sites from some amazing teachers worth learning from:

John Ortberg (http://www.mppc.org/learn/sermons or http://www.johnortberg.com/), Andy Stanley (http://northpoint.org/podcasts), Mark Batterson (http://theaterchurch.com/), Bill Hybels (http://www.willowcreek.org/MiniSite/), and Frances Chan (http://www.cornerstonesimi.com/getasermon).

126. Bill Hybels, *The Volunteer Revolution: Unleashing the Power of Everybody* (Zondervan, 2004), 105.

127. Bill Hybels, *Axiom: Powerful Leadership Proverbs* (Zondervan, 2008), 78.

128. If you've never flown in one of these bad boys, just so you know: Length = 209' (longer than five school buses), cabin width = 36', weight = 545,000 lbs (272.5 tons), and fuel capacity = 31,000 U.S. gallons. Fun facts: A 777 can fly more than 10,000 miles without stopping. And some 777s can seat more than 370 people. For more information, check out http://www.boeing.com/commercial/777family/pf/pf_facts.html (accessed 3/13/09).

129. These words from Heather are not officially in print anywhere, although Heather has written a great book called *I Want to Talk With My Teen about Girl Stuff* (Standard Publishing, 2006) and coauthored *Help! I'm a Woman in Youth Ministry!* with Kara Powell and Megan Hutchinson (Zondervan/Youth Specialties, 2004). Both books are really worth reading, and Heather is fantastic!

130. Kurt Johnston, *Middle School Ministry Made Simple* (Standard Publishing, 2008), 29.

131. Bill Hybels, *Courageous Leadership* (Zondervan, 2009), 81.

132. Henri Nouwen, "Moving from Solitude to Community to Ministry," *Leadership* XVI, no. 2 (Spring 1995), www.cise.ufl.edu/~nemo/tmp/Article_Moving_from_Solitude_to_Community_to_Ministry.doc (accessed 3/13/09).

133. Victor Strasburger, MD, "'Clueless': Why Do Pediatricians Underestimate the Media's Influence on Children and Adolescents?" *Pediatrics* 117, no. 4 (April 2006): 1427–1431, (doi:10.1542/peds.2005-2336), http://pediatrics.aappublications.org/cgi/content/full/117/4/1427 (accessed 3/13/09).

134. Christian Smith with Melinda Lundquist Denton, *Soul Searching: The Religious and Spiritual Lives of American Teenagers* (Oxford University Press, 2005), 28.

135. The Web site at http://www.constantcontact.com/index.jsp is very helpful.

136. This example of "entertaining kids" is only one of many factors that could result in an increase or decrease of numbers.

137. We've always appreciated Dallas Willard's definition of a disciple: "The disciple is one who, intent upon becoming Christlike…systematically and progressively rearranges his [life] to that end." *The Spirit of the Disciplines: Understanding How God Changes Lives* (Harper Collins, 1990), 261.

138. Portions of this chapter first appeared in the July/August 2008 issue of *YouthWorker Journal* and are used with permission.

139. Wayne Rice, *Junior High Ministry* (Zondervan/Youth Specialties, 1998), 33. This is not to discredit or replace Rice's important characteristics. I'm just using this to draw an interesting comparison.

140. A critical distinction. For more, see Andrew Root's *Revisiting Relational Youth Ministry: From a Strategy of Influence to a Theology of Incarnation* (InterVarsity Press, 2007).

141. Christian Smith with Melinda Lundquist Denton, *Soul Searching: The Religious and Spiritual Lives of American Teenagers* (Oxford Press, 2005). The primary role of parents in faith development is Smith's most significant finding.

142. Check out http://www.personalitytest.net/ipip/ipipneo1.htm if you're interested in learning more about the IPIP-NEO PI-R™ exam. Exams are available to take online as well.

143. Dr. Chap Clark of Fuller Theological Seminary talks a lot about reversing the 5:1 ratio and making sure kids have lots of adults—in different walks of life—who know and care for them.